MW00474071

THE
AMERICAN
PURITANS

THE
AMERICAN PURITANS

Dustin Benge and Nate Pickowicz

Reformation Heritage Books
Grand Rapids, Michigan

The American Puritans
© 2020 by Dustin Benge and Nate Pickowicz

All rights reserved. No part of this book may be used or reproduced in any manner whatsoever without written permission except in the case of brief quotations embodied in critical articles and reviews. Direct your requests to the publisher at the following addresses:

Reformation Heritage Books
3070 29th St. SE
Grand Rapids, MI 49512
616–977–0889
orders@heritagebooks.org
www.heritagebooks.org

Printed in the United States of America
22 23 24 25 26/10 9 8 7 6 5 4 3

Library of Congress Cataloging-in-Publication Data

Names: Benge, Dustin, author. | Pickowicz, Nate, author.
Title: The American Puritans / Dustin Benge and Nate Pickowicz.
Description: Grand Rapids, Michigan : Reformation Heritage Books, 2020. | Includes bibliographical references.
Identifiers: LCCN 2020008336 (print) | LCCN 2020008337 (ebook) | ISBN 9781601787736 (paperback) | ISBN 9781601787743 (epub)
Subjects: LCSH: Puritans—New England—Biography. | Puritans—New England—History—17th century.
Classification: LCC BX9358 .B46 2020 (print) | LCC BX9358 (ebook) | DDC 285/.9092274—dc23
LC record available at https://lccn.loc.gov/2020008336
LC ebook record available at https://lccn.loc.gov/2020008337

For additional Reformed literature, request a free book list from Reformation Heritage Books at the above regular or email address.

*This book is dedicated to
all the families who fled persecution
and braved the perilous journey across the Atlantic Ocean
to seek the freedom to worship the Lord Jesus Christ
with a clear conscience.*

Contents

Foreword

Iain H. Murray has observed that "without New England the history of the United States would have followed a very different pattern." What made New England different from the other British colonies formed in North America was the desire of its settlers to have a distinctive Christian character. Murray reckoned that of "the 102 passengers on the Mayflower it is probable that ninety-eight belonged to the congregation of John Robinson which had been in exile in Holland since 1608." And the majority of the settlers who came to New England in successive waves between 1620 and 1640 were also ardent Christians. The ultimate failure to achieve a "city upon a hill," as John Winthrop once described Puritan New England via his use of Matthew 5:14, should not blind us to these believers' passion, their remarkable achievements, and the way that their lives and thought have shaped the American psyche.

Yet even those who love the Puritans today and have benefited from the current revival of interest in "Puritania" seem to have forgotten many of those who figured large in colonial New England—men such as Thomas Shepard (whom Jonathan Edwards often cited) and John Eliot (not to be confused with the martyr Jim Elliot!). Of course, Baptists remember and love that "subversive" Puritan, Roger Williams, as Mostyn Roberts has recently called him in his marvelous biography, but we who love church history should know many more of these figures. I am therefore deeply grateful to

Dustin Benge and Nate Pickowicz for this prosopographical primer of New England Puritanism, and I hope it gets an extensive reading.

—Michael A. G. Haykin
Chair and Professor of Church History
The Southern Baptist Theological Seminary
September 3, 2019

Acknowledgments

We owe a debt of gratitude to several people for their inspiration, encouragement, and assistance. In addition to writing the foreword, Michael A. G. Haykin gave his wisdom and mentorship when we were getting cold feet during the process. Thank you, Rick Kennedy, for your insight on the Cotton Mather chapter, as well as for your endorsement. Heartfelt thanks go to Steven Lawson, Conrad Mbewe, Michael Reeves, Reiner Smolinski, Derek W. H. Thomas, and Geoff Thomas for endorsing the project. We could not be more overjoyed and thankful for Joel Beeke, Jay Collier, Dave Woollin, and Annette Gysen at Reformation Heritage Books for their tireless labors to make this project happen. We're grateful to Andrew Buss for providing us with a thorough and meticulous edit. Additionally, we want to thank our wives and families for their unending support in this research-intensive project, which required many late nights and early mornings. Finally and foremost, we want to thank our glorious God for graciously allowing us to write this book. Whatever fruit this bears belongs solely to Him!

Time Line

1534   King Henry VIII officially breaks with the Roman
Catholic Church and appoints himself as the official
head of the newly established Church of England,
thus establishing the foundation of the Reformation
in England.

1547   Henry VIII dies, and his son Edward VI becomes
king, furthering the English Reformation under the
advisement of Thomas Cranmer.

1553   Edward VI dies; Mary I ascends the throne and
attempts to reestablish Roman Catholicism in England, thus persecuting Protestants. This leads to the
arrest and execution of leaders such as John Hooper,
Hugh Latimer, Nicholas Ridley, and Thomas Cranmer; many flee England and seek asylum in places
like Geneva.

1558   Mary I dies; Queen Elizabeth ascends the throne
and restores Protestantism to England. She later
establishes the Acts of Uniformity, followed by the
adoption of the Thirty-Nine Articles.

1590   Thomas Cartwright is arrested for his activities in
seeking to further reform the Church of England
beyond the Elizabethan Settlement.

1603   Queen Elizabeth dies; King James I ascends the throne; although sympathetic to the cause of the English Reformation, James opposes all Separatist activities.

1609   The congregation in Scrooby flees England for Holland.

1620   The Scrooby congregation, now residing in Leyden, Holland, joins with Thomas Weston and the Merchant Adventurers to sail to the New World aboard the *Mayflower*.

1625   King James I dies; Charles I ascends the English throne.

1629   The New England Company receives a royal charter for a new settlement in America; the Massachusetts Bay Colony is officially formed.

1630   The Great Migration begins with the sailing of a small fleet, led by the *Arbella*, from England to America. John Winthrop travels with them.

1633   William Laud is appointed the Archbishop of Canterbury and begins arresting nonconformists. John Cotton, Thomas Hooker, and Samuel Stone flee England and arrive in Massachusetts.

1636   Harvard College is founded; the Pequot War begins; the Antinomian Controversy commences; Roger Williams, having been convicted of sedition by the General Court in October 1635, sets out for Rhode Island. The following year, along with Ezekiel Holliman, Williams establishes the first Baptist church in America at Providence.

1637–1638 Anne Hutchinson and John Wheelwright are banished from Massachusetts.

1640	Charles I is forced to call the "Long Parliament"; petitions for reforms are introduced; Archbishop Laud is imprisoned; with turmoil in England increasing, the Great Migration effectively comes to an end.
1642	With tensions mounting between Charles and the English Parliament, the English Civil War begins.
1643	The Westminster Assembly of Divines is established in order to make recommendations for religious reforms; Thomas Hooker, John Davenport, and John Cotton decline an invitation to appear at the assembly.
1648	Having surrendered two years earlier, Charles I regroups and launches an unsuccessful attack against the New Model Army. He is tried and executed the following year.
1658	The Congregational ministers in England gather for the Savoy Conference, adopting the Savoy Declaration of Faith and Order. Oliver Cromwell dies in England.
1662	Parliament passes the Act of Uniformity. More than two thousand English ministers refuse to sign and are banished from their pulpits. In America the Synod of 1662 adopts the Half-Way Covenant.
1675	The Indian chief Metacom (King Philip) attacks the English residents in New England. King Philip's War ensues and lasts for nearly three years.
1679	The New England Reforming Synod adopts the Savoy Declaration.
1684	The Massachusetts charter is revoked by King Charles II, who later dies in 1685.

1686   Sir Edmund Andros arrives in Massachusetts,
         appointed as the royal governor of New England. A
         rebellion begins to mount, led by the Mathers.

1689   New England citizens stage a revolt against Andros;
         he is arrested and deposed. Andros is eventually
         deported back to England. William and Mary are
         crowned as England's monarchs.

1690   John Eliot, "the apostle to the Indians," dies.

1692   Witch Trials begin in Salem; Increase Mather returns
         from England with a revised charter.

1702   Cotton Mather publishes *Magnalia Christi Ameri-
         cana*, the most important work of early American
         church history.

1703   Jonathan Edwards is born in East Windsor,
         Connecticut.

1723   Increase Mather dies at age eighty-four.

1728   Cotton Mather dies in Boston.

WHO ARE THE AMERICAN PURITANS?

"There is no such thing as an *American Puritan*" is a sentiment we have often heard. By all rights, Puritanism as we know it was "a movement for church reform, pastoral renewal and evangelism, and spiritual revival" that took place in England from around 1560 to 1660.[1] However, over the course of the seventeenth century, it is estimated that nearly a hundred Puritan ministers migrated to America, along with tens of thousands of English believers, all to pursue lives of faithfulness to the gospel of Jesus Christ.[2] The earliest settlers in New England were cut from the same cloth as many of the Puritans in England. But to understand who they were and why they came, we first need to go back a hundred years to the birth of the English Reformation.

The English Reformation

When most people think of the Protestant Reformation, their minds often latch on to the image of Martin Luther nailing his Ninety-Five Theses to the door of the castle at Wittenberg on October 31, 1517. However, the movement that began in Germany quickly spread like wildfire throughout all of Europe. It arrived in England by way of

---

1. J. I. Packer, *A Quest for Godliness: The Puritan Vision of the Christian Life* (Wheaton, Ill.: Crossway, 1990), 28.

2. John Brown, *The English Puritans: The Rise and Fall of the Puritan Movement* (1910; repr., Fearn, Ross-shire: Christian Focus, 1998), 126–27.

an unlikely champion, King Henry VIII (1491–1547). When Pope Clement VII failed to grant Henry a divorce from his first wife, Catherine of Aragon, he responded by severing ties with the Roman Catholic Church and attached himself to the fast-growing Reformation movement. In 1534, he influenced Parliament to pass the Act of Supremacy, effectively decreeing the English monarch as the head of the Church of England. Thus, the English Reformation was born.

With the advent of the Church of England came a wave of ecclesiastical reforms. Henry appointed Thomas Cranmer (1489–1556) to the highest ministerial office—the archbishop of Canterbury. As the first Protestant to hold the coveted position, Cranmer ushered in sweeping changes, removing icons and images from the church buildings and replacing the Roman Catholic Missal (service book) with the Book of Common Prayer.[3] Upon King Henry's death in 1547, his young son, Edward VI (1537–1553), ascended the throne with Cranmer by his side to guide him in the ways of Reformation.

In 1549 Parliament passed the Act of Uniformity, which effectively institutionalized Protestantism into the Church of England. All vestiges of Roman Catholic imagery were officially removed from the churches, the clergy were no longer required to be celibate, and the Book of Common Prayer was required to be used in worship services. Whatever progress was made toward Reformation under King Edward VI came to an abrupt halt upon his death on July 6, 1553, at age fifteen. His replacement would not be a sympathetic Protestant but an embittered Roman Catholic monarch named Mary.

After her father, Henry VIII, divorced her mother, Catherine, Mary I (1516–1558) vowed to remain faithful to Roman Catholicism and oppose her father's apostasy. When her stepbrother, Edward, had attempted to bypass Mary from the line of succession by appointing his cousin, Lady Jane Grey (1537–1554), to the

---

3. S. M. Houghton, *Sketches from Church History* (Edinburgh: Banner of Truth, 1980), 113.

throne following his imminent death, Mary promptly deposed her and had her beheaded only nine days into her reign. For the next three years, "Bloody Mary" systematically reversed every Protestant element from England, lashing out vehemently. When she had 283 Christians martyred in 1555, many Protestants went into hiding. Several hundred leading Protestant leaders fled to Geneva, Switzerland, where they were warmly received by the Reformed pastor and theologian John Calvin (1509–1564). This short stint in Calvin's Geneva would set the course in England for the next hundred years.

The Emergence of Puritanism
By November 1558, Mary I was dead and Queen Elizabeth I (1533–1603) had ascended the throne. This change of power signaled the safe return of many Protestant exiles from hiding. However, Elizabeth had a difficult challenge on her hands. Sympathetic to their causes, she worked to provide toleration for the dissenting Protestants. At this time, she established the Elizabethan Settlement, which would draw together "Reformed or Calvinistic *doctrine*, the continuation of a liturgical and…Catholic *form of worship*, and an episcopal *church government*."[4] Essentially, this move was designed to keep all parties happy by incorporating key elements from each major group, but many of the English Reformers would have nothing of it. Having spent time in Geneva, many of the Protestants had seen an example of a fully Reformed city and purposed to bring about its fruits in their homeland.

While the term *Puritan* was initially used as a derogatory term in the 1560s, it came to refer to a large contingent of Protestants who were seeking to purify and further reform the Church of England. However, not all Protestants who bore the name of Puritan believed and practiced the same way. According to Everett Emerson

---

4. Leland Ryken, *Worldly Saints: The Puritans as They Really Were* (Grand Rapids: Zondervan, 1986), 7, emphasis original.

in his book *Puritanism in America*, four groups emerged within the Church of England in response to the Elizabethan Settlement.[5]

The first group sought only mild reforms (the elimination of vestments, more emphasis on preaching, etc.) within the church and largely conformed to Elizabethan standards. Adherents to this position included John Foxe, Edmund Spenser, and Edmund Grindal.

The second group sought to reform the episcopal structure and diminish the hierarchy of church power; their efforts were focused on parliamentary changes, which proved unsuccessful. This movement included strong leaders such as Thomas Cartwright and John Field.

The third group also opposed the Church of England's hierarchy but sought more passive, grassroots reform that they would practice in their local churches. Further, they were committed to nonconformity—dissension and opposition to the Elizabethan standards spelled out in the Act of Uniformity (1559). A large group of Puritans rejected many of the practices listed in the Book of Common Prayer (owing to their similarity to Roman Catholic dogma) and adhered to their convictions, citing the offense of their own consciences. Key leaders in this movement were men such as Laurence Chaderton, Richard Greenham, and William Perkins, along with the leaders of the Massachusetts Bay Colony.

The fourth group grew frustrated with the lack of reformation within the Church of England and withdrew from it completely. They sought to form their own congregations and were maligned as "Separatists" and persecuted vigorously by church officials. Key leaders in this movement included men such as Richard Clyfton, John Smyth, William Brewster, and William Bradford.

Of the four main groups, the latter two practiced various degrees of nonconformity, and many of their adherents fled persecution to America.

---

5. Everett Emerson, *Puritanism in America, 1620–1750* (Boston: G. K. Hall, 1977), 18–19.

Nonconformity

When the "Marian exiles" returned to England, they had hoped they would be able to pick up where Edward VI had left off and further reform the Church of England. However, Queen Elizabeth was quite content to demand strict observance to the Book of Common Prayer and the Articles of Religion, which many Puritans believe left the church only "half reformed." Believing many of the Elizabethan standards to be eerily similar to Roman Catholicism, many Puritans vowed not to conform.

Furthermore, having experienced the feast of biblical preaching and sound doctrine in Geneva, the Puritans were appalled at the quality of ministry that was being streamlined. Some English preachers were so unskilled and ignorant, and others so puffed up and pretentious, that they could barely lead the congregation in any sort of way of godliness. Historian Edmund S. Morgan notes, "In England, they said, too many ministers substituted an affected eloquence for sound knowledge and indulged themselves 'in [fond] fables to make their hearers [laugh], or in ostentation of learning of their Latin, their [Greek], their [Hebrew] tongue, and of their great reading of antiquities.' Worse than these dilettante preachers were the ignorant and evil ministers, incapable of preaching at all."[6]

Not only were the ministers awful but corruption in the church was prevalent. Church membership was not reserved for those who maintained a credible profession of faith but was freely granted to many unregenerate persons. And since all disciplinary power was maintained solely by the bishops, there was no way for a church to rid itself of sinning members, making the task of purification nearly impossible.

The reigns of James I (1566–1625) and Charles I (1600–1649) brought increased opposition against nonconformity. While King James focused much of his energy on weeding out the Separatists, King Charles very quickly took to uprooting the nonconformist

---

6. Edmund S. Morgan, *Visible Saints: The History of the Puritan Idea* (New York: New York University Press, 1963), 7.

movement. In 1633, Charles appointed William Laud (1573–1645) as the archbishop of Canterbury and tasked him with enforcing the standards of the Church of England. For the next decade, Laud systematically investigated, pursued, arrested, and prosecuted every nonconformist minister he could lay his hands on. While many Puritans were imprisoned, others fled to Holland and America.

Separatism

The most radical of all the English Puritans were the Separatists. They believed that the Church of England had become apostate and that their only course of action was to remove themselves and begin their own independent churches. When King James I came to power in 1603, he set out to uproot all opposition to his rule as head of the Church of England. No group angered King James more than the Separatists. He famously vowed to "make them conform or harry them out of the land!"[7] He not only drove out the Separatists but threw them into prisons whenever he could. In 1609, a group of Puritan Separatists in Scrooby, England, decided to flee to Holland. Very quickly they realized that life was not much better there, and their children were still being exposed to the same revelry they found in England. Finally, they decided to set sail for the New World.

The New England Way

Strictly speaking, the first arrivals to New England were not regarded as Puritans but as Separatists. However, their devotion to Scripture, sound preaching, Reformed doctrine, and visible piety places them within the sanctified realm of Puritanism. The Separatists in Plymouth fled from England "in order to establish churches of their own in which the membership would more closely approximate that of the invisible church."[8] The Church of England, they

---

7. B. K. Kuiper, *The Church in History* (Grand Rapids: Eerdmans, 1951), 327.
8. Morgan, *Visible Saints*, 33.

believed, though technically Protestant in designation, still did not value faithfulness, righteousness, and individual soul liberty. Much of English religion was politicized. They observed that the fires of English Reformation had simmered down to lukewarm coals. All told, while many migrated to America in the early 1600s for various reasons, many residents writing back to England argued that "the only valid reason for migrating to Massachusetts was religion."[9] In short, the Puritans' primary focus was to establish "pure" churches.

When the Massachusetts Bay Colony became populated with ten thousand people in the 1630s, the leaders sought to perfect what had begun in England. Unlike the Plymouth Separatists, they still regarded the Church of England as their "dear sister" but desired to purify what remained in America.

The New England Puritans believed they were in covenant with God and needed to honor the terms of that covenant through their faithfulness. "It is evident," declared John Cotton, "by the light of nature that all civil relations are founded on covenant."[10] Further, they recognized that there needed to be a way to govern themselves civilly as well as religiously. With the help of leaders such as John Cotton, they established "The New England Way." At its core, the "Way" was an expression of Congregationalism that sought to impact all areas of public life. American church historian Mark Noll writes, "New England was, thus, no theocracy, where ministers exercised direct control of public life. It was, however, a place where magistrates frequently called upon the reverend fathers for advice, including how best they might promote the religious life of the colonies. The churches were also nonseparating. Local congregations had responsibilities for the good of the whole, not just for themselves."[11]

While steering themselves away from the Presbyterian form of government found in the Church of England, the American

9. Emerson, *Puritanism in America*, 32.
10. Cited in Emerson, *Puritanism in America*, 49.
11. Mark A. Noll, *A History of Christianity in the United States and Canada* (Grand Rapids: Eerdmans, 1992), 42.

Puritans sought to implement the best of what they knew of Calvin's Geneva as well as the Protestantism of their beloved homeland. For a short season, the New England Puritans attained what they were striving for. While they failed to create "New Jerusalem" on the New England shores, they succeeded in embedding Christianity into the fabric of American society.

Introducing the American Puritans

While the English Puritans were not the only peoples to migrate to America, they were some of the most influential in establishing American society. Furthermore, there are countless magistrates, ministers, artisans, and influencers who deserve to be memorialized, such as William Brewster, Edward Winslow, John Endecott, John Wilson, John Norton, Samuel Stone, John Davenport, Peter Bulkeley, Richard Mather, Increase Mather, Samuel Sewall, Simon Bradstreet, Edward Taylor, Michael Wigglesworth, and Theophilus Eaton. However, for the purposes of this book, we have chosen to tell the story of the first hundred years of Puritanism in America through the lives of nine key figures.

It is our conviction that the American Puritans have a great deal to offer the church of today. And while every Christian in history is clay-footed and inherently sinful, God works through their lives to advance the kingdom of Jesus Christ. Our aim is threefold. First, we hope to clarify and correct many of the myths and half-truths associated with the American Puritans. Second, we hope to showcase their story—without hiding their faults—in order to inspire and edify this generation of Christian believers. Lastly, we hope to encourage further study into their lives, beliefs, struggles, and accomplishments so that we might have a fair and accurate view of our spiritual fathers.

May the Lord be glorified!

WILLIAM BRADFORD

Tears streamed down Pastor John Robinson's cheeks as he preached his farewell sermon. Heading for the New World via Southampton, Dartmouth, and Plymouth, England, the people later known as Pilgrims would part ways with most of their church family at a town called Delftshaven, Holland. Although they were hopeful the rest of their congregation that remained in Leyden would follow them shortly, for some it would be their final farewell this side of heaven. The scene was filled with such heartache, a large number of Dutch strangers gathered around them, unable to hold back their own tears. Finally aboard, these brave men and women hoisted sail into "a prosperous wind" that would carry them down to Southampton. While history doesn't record all that was said during this historic departure, one thing we know is that William Bradford left half his heart that day on the dock at Delftshaven.

Early Life in Austerfield

Halfway between London, England, and the Scottish border, just off the Great North Road, sits the rural town of Austerfield, the home of the Bradford family. While there is no official record of his birth, William Bradford was baptized as an infant on March 29, 1590.[1] When he was sixteen months old, his father, William Sr.,

---

1. In 1752, the American colonies changed from the Julian to the Gregorian

died, leaving young William in the care of his mother, Alice. When he was four, William's mother remarried and sent him to live with his grandfather, who died a mere two years later. Alice died shortly after her son was returned to her, and, now orphaned, he went to live with his two uncles.

Having no siblings, William spent his childhood alone. At first, his uncles determined to instruct him in the family trade of husbandry,[2] but "a soon and long sickness" prevented William from doing much in his uncles' fields. However, Bradford seized the opportunity of convalescence to immerse himself in his books. Since no school existed in Austerfield, William likely received his education from a local minister.[3] No doubt he would have been immersed in the popular books of the day such as Erasmus's *In Praise of Folly* (1511) and John Foxe's *Book of Martyrs* (1563). It was not long before William became absorbed with the Bible.

Eight miles from his home in Austerfield, a Separatist preacher named Richard Clyfton (d. 1616) was ministering in Babworth at All Saints' Church, which Bradford began attending when he was twelve years old. At this time, Bradford became acquainted with a Scrooby postmaster named William Brewster (1566–1644). Later on, Bradford remembered Brewster as "wise and discreet and well spoken, having a grave and deliberate utterance, of a very cheerful spirit, very sociable and pleasant amongst his friends, of an humble and modest mind, of a peaceable disposition, undervaluing himself and his own abilities and sometime overvaluing others. Inoffensive and innocent in his life and conversation, which gained him the love of those without as well as those within."[4] The two developed a

---

calendar (New Style). At that time, the change effectively shifted the start of the year from March 1 to January 1. According to the Old Style, his baptism date is March 19, 1589.

2. Farming, agriculture.

3. Gary Schmidt, *William Bradford: Plymouth's Faithful Pilgrim* (Grand Rapids: Eerdmans, 1999), 7.

4. William Bradford, *Of Plymouth Plantation, 1620–1647*, ed. Samuel Eliot Morison (New York: Modern Library, 1952), 327.

lasting friendship, and Brewster became a lifelong father figure and mentor to Bradford.

At Babworth, Richard Clyfton believed that the Church of England retained too many Roman Catholic practices and had wandered away from the biblical model of the church as described in the New Testament. In an effort to purge their own congregation of the vestiges of Rome, the Babworth congregation effectively separated from the Church of England. Babworth was not the first church to proclaim separation from the officially sanctioned church; another pastored by Mr. John Smyth (1570–1612) in Gainsborough seceded from the Church of England in 1605. When King James I (1566–1625) ascended the throne in 1603, he immediately saw Separatism as a threat to his authority as the self-proclaimed "head of the church." Therefore, he launched a vehement opposition against the Separatists, famously vowing to "make them conform, or harry them out of the land!" Under the weight of the king's threats, the Babworth church decided to split, with forty or fifty of them meeting in William Brewster's home in Scrooby.

When Bradford's uncles received word that he was aligning with the Separatist movement, they were furious and forbade him from attending any of their gatherings. Regardless, Bradford was resolute in his determination to attend church services. In his biographical account of Bradford, Cotton Mather notes, "Some lamented him, some derided him, *all* dissuaded him: nevertheless, the more they did it, the more fixed he was in his purpose to seek the ordinances of the gospel."[5] Bradford was convinced that Clyfton was faithful in his teaching, and at Scrooby he found what he had longed for— a family.

For the first time in his life, he did not feel alone.

---

5. Cotton Mather, *Magnalia Christi Americana* (1702; repr., Edinburgh: Banner of Truth, 1979), 1:110.

Seeking a Better Life in Holland

When the king dispatched officers of the Church of England to force the Separatists into conformity, the Scrooby church "would not submit to their ceremonies and become slaves to them and their popish trash," Bradford wrote, "which have no ground in the Word of God, but are relics of that man of sin."[6] In the face of growing opposition, the Scrooby church decided to escape England for Holland in the fall of 1607. The thought of leaving everything behind was daunting, but, Bradford wrote, "these things did not dismay them, though they did sometimes trouble them; for their desires were set on the ways of God and to enjoy His ordinances; but they rested on His providence, and knew Whom they had believed."[7] They secretly hired a ship to sneak them into Holland, but after all their goods were aboard, they were ambushed by the king's officers. They knew immediately that the ship's captain had betrayed them, and several of the men were jailed for a month, including Clyfton, Brewster, and seventeen-year-old Bradford.

Their brief stay in a Boston, Lincolnshire, prison did nothing to quell their ardent desire to flee the country so they might freely worship. After selling nearly everything else they owned, and forsaking family and countrymen, they made a second attempt at escape. This time they hired a Dutch captain to ferry them across. With their wives and children still ashore, half of the men were aboard the ship, preparing for departure. Suddenly, a large group of armed pursuivants[8] arrived to arrest the group. Fearing capture, the captain weighed anchor and set sail. "The poor men which were got aboard were in great distress for their wives and children which they saw to be taken," wrote Bradford. "It drew tears from their eyes, and anything they had they would have given to have been ashore again."[9] Of the men left behind, both Bradford and Brewster assisted the families in their trouble, seeing "these poor women in this distress...

6. Bradford, *Of Plymouth Plantation*, 7.
7. Bradford, *Of Plymouth Plantation*, 11.
8. Officers of the Church of England.
9. Bradford, *Of Plymouth Plantation*, 13.

their poor little ones hanging about them, crying for fear and quak-
ing with cold."[10] When news of the heart-wrenching ordeal became
public, the magistrates were unsure of how to proceed. After several
examinations, the families were finally released to return to their
homes. They took on a new strategy, escaping in smaller numbers,
all finally arriving in Amsterdam in August of 1608.

They had chosen exile in Holland because of its religious toleration, which came at a high cost. Added to the cultural shock of
living in Amsterdam, the Scrooby congregation was forced to take
unskilled jobs to survive.[11] After struggling for nine months, the
group decided to move twenty-two miles away, to the city of Leyden. According to Bradford, Leyden was "a fair and beautiful city,"[12]
and despite the uncomfortable cultural differences, the Separatists
were able to make a home for themselves. When Richard Clyfton
stepped down from his pastorate in 1608, his assistant, John Robinson (1575–1625), was called to fill his shoes as the pastor of the
Scrooby assembly. Cambridge-trained and fully competent, Robinson remained the church's pastor until his death. The church loved
Robinson and sat joyfully under his teaching. Bradford wrote, "His
love was great towards them, and his care was always bent for their
best good, both for soul and body."[13] Historian Williston Walker
notes, "No nobler figure stands forth in the story of early Congregationalism than that of this moderate, earnest, patient, learned,
kindly man, who was for the next sixteen years to be Bradford's
friend and guide."[14]

The whole congregation lived in close proximity to one another,
many of them on the same parcel of land. When Bradford reached

---

10. Bradford, *Of Plymouth Plantation*, 14.
11. Many of them worked "hard and continual labour," with textiles, metal, and
leather, the lowest-paying jobs.
12. Bradford, *Of Plymouth Plantation*, 17.
13. Bradford, *Of Plymouth Plantation*, 18.
14. Williston Walker, *Ten New England Leaders* (New York: Silver, Burdett, and
Co., 1901), 17.

the legal age of twenty-one, he received "a comfortable inheritance"[15] from his family's estate, which he sold, using a large portion of it to help purchase a building for the church. Despite his youth, Bradford quickly established himself as a vital member of both the congregation and the local community. In 1612, he became a citizen of Leyden and established himself up as silk weaver. On November 30, 1613, he married Dorothy May, who would later give birth to their only son.

After living ten years in Holland, the assembly at Leyden once again began considering options for departure. While many of them made enough money to sustain their families, others struggled to survive and were even forced to send their children to work. Additionally, they noticed an increased temptation to be "drawn away by evil examples into extravagant and dangerous courses, getting the reins off their necks and departing from their parents."[16] Beyond this, their religious freedom was being threatened by the end of the Spanish truce, due to expire in 1621.[17] Further exciting their desire to leave was the fact that William Brewster was a fugitive from King James, and after Dutch agents raided his home, Brewster was destined to remain on the run for as long as he stayed in Holland. After entertaining several options, the Leyden church decided on departing for America.

Journey to the New World

Among the numerous reasons for leaving Leyden, Bradford noted yet another purpose for traveling to the New World. He wrote that they had "a great hope and inward zeal…for the propagating and advancing the gospel of the kingdom of Christ in those remote parts of the world."[18] As children of the Protestant Reformation, their

---

15. Mather, *Magnalia*, 1:109.

16. Bradford, *Of Plymouth Plantation*, 25.

17. In 1609, Holland and Spain signed a truce that was set to last twelve years. If war resumed in 1621, and Spain were to be victorious, the Roman Catholic Church would become the state church. The Inquisition would oppress and persecute all non-Catholics, and the Separatists would no doubt be persecuted the greatest.

18. Bradford, *Of Plymouth Plantation*, 25.

earnest desire was to see the gospel of Jesus Christ advance to the far reaches of the known world. Before leaving, however, the group had to secure a patent—that is, permission from the king to settle in the new land. After two years of lobbying and pleading with the king, they eventually changed their approach, signing instead with Thomas Weston, a London businessman who had assembled a team of seventy investors called the "Merchant Adventurers."[19] These investors would fund the excursion in exchange for the first fruits of the settlers' labors. America was rumored to be bountiful with natural resources, and this was the Adventurers' chance to capitalize on the untapped land. For the Leyden congregation, it seemed an acceptable arrangement in exchange for the freedom to worship God in the way He desired.

The church members sold whatever they still had in Holland and prepared for their new life in America. However, at the last minute, Weston began demanding more money and a larger share of their claim. After a series of bitter disputes, the group sold off a large amount of supplies to satisfy Weston's requests, and they were soon on their way. They had purchased a sixty-ton ship called the *Speedwell* that would also serve as a fishing and scouting vessel in the New World. In addition, they would also charter a larger vessel called the *Mayflower*, which they would rendezvous with in London before their departure across the Atlantic.

At the Dutch port of Delftshaven, the Leyden congregation gathered for departure on July 21, 1620. Of the nearly three hundred congregants, only 120 would depart aboard the *Speedwell*; the rest were scheduled to follow in the coming few years. Along

---

19. The Merchant Adventurers were essentially an investment group assembled by Thomas Weston. In exchange for financing the voyage and their supplies, the Pilgrims would pay the Adventurers back over seven years. However, at the last minute, Weston attempted to change the arrangement, insisting the Pilgrims spend seven days a week working to pay their debts. The Pilgrims countered, offering to work five days a week; Weston reluctantly accepted. Strained from the beginning, the relationship between the Pilgrims and the Adventurers would end up being a miserable arrangement until, in 1627, the Pilgrims were in a position to buy out their entire interest, thus freeing themselves from their financial obligation.

with several key leaders, their pastor, John Robinson, chose to stay behind and guide the church until the rest could make the transatlantic journey. On the deck of the *Speedwell*, Robinson preached an impassioned sermon from Ezra 8:21, "And there at the river, by Ahava, I proclaimed a fast, that we might humble ourselves before our God, and seek of him a right way for us, and for our children, and for all our substance."[20] He fell to his knees "with watery cheeks" and "commended them with most fervent prayers to the Lord."[21] However, the sobs of William and Dorothy Bradford must have carried in the breeze as they said goodbye to their three-year-old son, John, whom they were leaving behind.

This small, faithful band fixed their hope on the Lord, entrusting their lives to His providential hand. Remembering this departure, Bradford wrote, "So they left that goodly and pleasant city which had been their resting place for near twelve years; but *they knew they were pilgrims*, and looked not much on those things, but lift up their eyes to the heavens, their dearest country, and quieted their spirits."[22]

Trouble started immediately as the *Speedwell* began taking on water.[23] After two attempts to keep her seaworthy, the ship was abandoned due to "general weakness,"[24] and half the Pilgrims hesitantly returned to Holland. Weston insisted on equipping the remaining ship with his own complement of men, which the Pilgrims pejoratively referred to as Strangers. With the loss of the *Speedwell*, compounded by the presence of an unseemly crew, only half of the 102 passengers aboard were from the Leyden church.

---

20. Quoted in the 1599 Geneva Bible.

21. Bradford, *Of Plymouth Plantation*, 48.

22. Bradford, *Of Plymouth Plantation*, 47, emphasis added. This is the first reference of the group being referred to as pilgrims, a title given to them here by Bradford himself.

23. It is believed that when the *Speedwell* was refit for the voyage, it was overmasted, meaning that the crew installed a mast too big for the ship. Once at sea, the added stress forced open the seams in the hull, causing leaks to spring. According to Bradford, this was done intentionally and deceptively by the ship's captain to sabotage the voyage, thus freeing themselves from their obligation to stay in New England for the next year.

24. Bradford, *Of Plymouth Plantation*, 53.

After months of delays, they set sail for the New World. After sixty-five tumultuous days at sea, the *Mayflower* finally arrived at Provincetown Harbor on November 11, 1620. However, they spent nearly a month searching for a suitable location to settle. A small contingent of men loaded up the shallop[25] and undertook shorter trips to land in hopes of reporting back with a spot to build their settlement. After braving rough surfs that "froze so hard as the spray of the sea lighting on their coats, they were as if they had been glazed,"[26] they returned to the *Mayflower* with a report that Plymouth Harbor would be as fit a place as any, and they weighed anchor there on December 15. Upon his return from an expedition, Bradford was given the dreadful news that his wife, Dorothy, had fallen overboard and drowned only a few days prior on December 7. The specific details surrounding her death are still a mystery. One historian notes, "If Dorothy took her own life, she would not be the last of those facing the desolation of the frontier to do so."[27] With Dorothy gone, and his young son an ocean away, Bradford was once again alone.

The Mayflower Compact

The Pilgrims' initial plan was to establish a society where they could order all religious and civil life and practice according to the Bible. However, they were not the only travelers aboard the *Mayflower*. The Merchant Adventurers, or Strangers, occupied half of their number, many of whom were irreligious, uncouth, and uncommitted to the Separatist religious ideal. The two-month voyage did nothing but exacerbate their differences.

Having drifted from their original course in arriving at Cape Cod, the patent secured by Weston for Virginia would be rendered null and void. They were therefore settling illegally, in a governmental no-man's-land. According to Bradford, the Strangers were "discontented

---

25. A small sailboat.
26. Bradford, *Of Plymouth Plantation*, 68.
27. George D. Langdon Jr., *Pilgrim Colony: A History of New Plymouth, 1620–1691* (New Haven, Conn.: Yale University Press, 1966), 12.

and mutinous," vowing that they would "use their own liberty" once they came ashore.[28] Knowing that such hostility and division would jeopardize everything they had worked so hard for, the two groups agreed together and drafted the Mayflower Compact.

Prior to their departure, Pastor John Robinson had sent his farewell letter, urging his congregation abroad to "become a body politic" of "civil government" that elected their own leaders who would "promote the common good."[29] Both groups knew that it was a radical idea, untested and untried by anyone before in England. Yet with the king three thousand miles away, they covenanted together aboard the ship, drafting the following:

> Having undertaken, for the Glory of God and advancement of the Christian Faith and Honour of our King and Country, a Voyage to plant the First Colony in the Northern Parts of Virginia, do by these presents solemnly and mutually in the presence of God and one of another, Covenant and Combine ourselves together into a Civil Body Politic, for our better ordering and preservation and furtherance of the ends aforesaid; and by virtue hereof to enact, constitute and frame such just and equal Laws, Ordinances, Acts, Constitutions and Offices, from time to time, as shall be thought most meet and convenient for the general good of the Colony, unto which we promise all due submission and obedience.[30]

Representative of all the people, forty-one men from both groups signed the compact and jointly confirmed John Carver (1576–1621) as their governor for the first year.

The significance of the Mayflower Compact cannot be overstated. In 1802, John Quincy Adams noted that it was "the first example in modern times of a social compact or system of government instituted by voluntary agreement, conformably to the laws of nature, by men of equal rights, and about to establish their

---

28. Bradford, *Of Plymouth Plantation*, 75.
29. Cited in Bradford, *Of Plymouth Plantation*, 370.
30. Bradford, *Of Plymouth Plantation*, 76.

community in a new country."[31] While it was designed to protect the interest of all residents present and future, in the end it was a "creation of a political union by common consent, and a settlement devoted to God's glory."[32]

The Early Years of the Colony

The first New England winter was severe and killed nearly half of the early settlement. Those who survived were "infected with scurvy and other diseases" to the point that only six or seven people were healthy enough at a time to work on building their homes.[33] On March 16, a tall, scantily clad Indian man named Samoset (c. 1590–c. 1653) walked out of the woods and into the settlement. In broken English, he told them of the land's native inhabitants and their recent dealings with other European settlers. While in Holland, the Pilgrims heard stories of "savage people, who are cruel, barbarous and most treacherous." Not merely content to kill, the Indians were rumored to torture and cannibalize their victims "in the most bloody manner."[34] Soon after his arrival, Samoset brought with him a man named Squanto,[35] who befriended the settlers and helped them learn to survive for the next few years.

For months the Pilgrims had seen only traces of the Indians, with a few brief encounters, but soon after meeting Samoset and Squanto, sixty armed warriors accompanied their chief, Massasoit (c. 1581–1661), to Plymouth colony. A young Edward Winslow (1595–1655)

---

31. Cited in Bradford Smith, *Bradford of Plymouth* (Philadelphia: J. B. Lippincott, 1951), 133.

32. Thomas S. Kidd, *American Colonial History: Clashing Cultures and Faiths* (New Haven, Conn.: Yale University Press, 2016), 85–86.

33. Bradford, *Of Plymouth Plantation*, 77.

34. Bradford, *Of Plymouth Plantation*, 26.

35. Squanto (c. 1585–1622) was the last surviving member of the Patuxet tribe, which previously lived on the land the Pilgrims were seeking refuge. Squanto himself had been abducted by a merchant named Thomas Hunt, who sold him into slavery in Spain. With the help of English explorer Thomas Dermer (c. 1590–1620), he was able to escape and return to America, only to find his entire tribe wiped out by a plague. With none of his own people left, Squanto made a home with the Wampanoag.

functioned as their diplomat, ushering the chief to the home of Governor John Carver. After an exchange of pleasantries and gifts, the two leaders spoke of peace; both men were seeking allies in one another. They established a treaty founded on the principles of trust, friendship, and justice. Both parties promised not to "injure or do hurt to any of their people." They agreed that if any trespass occurred, the offender would be tried and punished by the laws of the other party. Further, both parties were agreed to come to the aid of the other in war, and when they came together, "they should leave their bows and arrows [i.e., all weapons] behind them."[36] The Pilgrims found nothing but friendship with Massasoit and the Wampanoag tribe. For years it was not uncommon to find several Indians living in Plymouth— Squanto himself became a constant companion of William Bradford. While history records the joyful details of their first thanksgiving celebration, in truth they often feasted together. As more ships arrived from Holland and England, the colony slowly began to expand, and the lives of both peoples became increasingly intertwined.

In April 1621, Governor Carver, having returned from working in the fields, complained of a severe headache and was dead within a few days. In seeking to appoint a new governor, the colony unanimously chose William Bradford. At age thirty-two, Bradford stepped in to bear the responsibility not only of leading the struggling colony but also of maintaining peace with the Indians. In the end, Bradford and Massasoit remained friends for the rest of their lives, and the peace treaty between the Pilgrims and the Wampanoag lasted more than forty years.

In the winter of 1623, word traveled to Plymouth that Massasoit was gravely ill and on the verge of death. A concerned Bradford sent Edward Winslow to provide what aid he could. Upon his arrival, he saw the chief surrounded by several women "who chafed his arms, legs, and thighs, to keep heat in him,"[37] but they were

---

36. Bradford, *Of Plymouth Plantation*, 80–81.
37. Edward Winslow, *Good News from New England*, ed. Kelly Wisecup (1624; repr., Amherst: University of Massachusetts Press, 2014), 81.

not hopeful of his condition. Seeing that Massasoit was likely suffering from typhus, Winslow wasted no time in prying the chief's jaws open with the point of his knife to feed him some medicine. Winslow refused to leave his side during the several days he nursed the sachem back to health. Upon his recovery, Massasoit declared, "Now I see the English are my friends and love me, and whilst I live I will never forget this kindness they have shewed me."[38] It was then that he recounted a conspiracy plot against the English by a number of hostile Indians, led by a chief named Wituwamat. When the report came back to Bradford, he had a difficult decision to make.

While Bradford had no desire to lead his people into war, Massasoit had already proven himself to be a trustworthy friend, even helping defend them from earlier threats. He knew he would do well to heed the sachem's warning. Wituwamat was determined to "kill all the English people in one day."[39] Their only option was to launch a preemptive attack. Bradford dispatched his military officer, Captain Myles Standish (c. 1584–1656), along with eight men, to stop the threat. When it was all done, several Indians were dead, including their leader, Wituwamat. While Standish's actions effectively spared Plymouth from certain demise, Bradford did not receive the news with joy. Even more stinging than his own conscience was a letter he received from Pastor John Robinson, lamenting the attack:

> Concerning the killing of those poor Indians, of which we heard at first by report, and since by more certain relation. Oh, how happy a thing had it been, if you had converted some before you had killed any!… It is also a thing more glorious, in men's eyes, than pleasing in God's or convenient for Christians, to be a terrour to poor barbarous people. And indeed I am afraid lest, by these occasions, others should be drawn to affect a kind of ruffling course in the world.[40]

---

38. Winslow, *"Good News from New England,"* 84.

39. From the account given by Phineas Pratt, cited in Nathaniel Philbrick, *Mayflower: A Story of Courage, Community, and War* (New York: Viking, 2006), 147.

40. Bradford, *Of Plymouth Plantation*, 374–75.

Despite later confirmation that an Indian attack had, in fact, been imminent, Bradford shouldered the moral responsibility in sanctioning the action. After suffering loss and sacrificing all, the Pilgrims had come too far to be wiped out. With his hope in God, Bradford continued to lead the settlers in their fight for survival.

Challenges in Leadership

Bradford's leadership was put to the test in the colony's early years, and such challenges would be incessant during his three decades as governor. When exposure and starvation nearly wiped out the colony the first winter, the Pilgrims set all their attention on building homes and planting gardens, with the help of the Indians. For the first three years, everyone in the colony worked together for the common interest. However, the increased number of travelers heavily taxed the already struggling colony, and many of the new arrivals were not as eager to contribute to the community effort. In 1623, Bradford oversaw the allotment of private property to each family and found that private ownership incentivized the Pilgrims to work harder. According to Bradford, "This had very good success, for it made all hands very industrious, so as much more corn was planted than otherwise would have been by any means the Governor or any other could use, and saved him a great deal of trouble, and gave far better content."[41] The notion of communal living was romantic, but the human condition would surely hinder its success. Writing about the difficulty of their trials and the folly of communal living, Bradford noted, "The experience that was had in this common course and condition, tried sundry years and that amongst godly and sober men, may well evince the vanity of that conceit of Plato's and other ancients applauded by some of later times; that the taking away of private property and bringing in community into a commonwealth would make them happy and flourishing; as if they were wiser than God."[42] Bradford believed that hard work and personal

---

41. Bradford, *Of Plymouth Plantation*, 120.
42. Bradford, *Of Plymouth Plantation*, 120–21.

responsibility were pleasing to the Lord. His actions had saved the colony, ushering in a long pattern of flourishing for years to come.

Despite the temporary success, Bradford soon had to face the threat of rival colonies. From the very beginning, Thomas Weston had proved to be a nuisance, as he was prone to change agreements and burden the colony. When word arrived in Plymouth that Weston had established a rival colony forty miles north called Wessagusset, the Pilgrims were both shocked and relieved, hoping it to be the end of their engagement with Weston and his troublesome men. However, Wessagusset soon became nothing but a regional liability. Those at the new outpost not only struggled to feed themselves but lacked the wherewithal to maintain peace with the surrounding Indians. Bradford knew that their antagonism of the Indians would surely plunge the region into war, so he decided to act. He sent Myles Standish to persuade the new colony to dissolve, which it quickly did. Many of the men either returned to Plymouth or traveled back to England.

Not every new settler was committed to the separatist ideals of the Pilgrims, but the majority of arrivals were Christians who were eager to submit to the colony's statutes. One colony's beginning was particularly problematic. A man named Captain Richard Wollaston (d. 1626) led a small team of men to establish an illegal trading post just north of Plymouth. In 1626, he quarreled over the site with one of his leaders, Thomas Morton (c. 1579–c. 1647). Wollaston lost out and Morton seized control, renaming it Merrymount. Immediately trouble began to ensue. Morton's actions posed a twofold threat.

First, Morton himself was godless and atheistic, becoming, as Bradford notes, "Lord of Misrule." Committed to debauchery, Morton and his followers engaged in drunken orgies and feasts to pagan gods. Whereas the Pilgrims had established Plymouth for the glory of God, they feared that the idolatry emanating from Merrymount would elicit God's judgment.

Second, Morton was selling firearms and alcohol to the Indians indiscriminately. Along with other allied Indian tribes, Bradford's concern was that the weapons would end up falling into the hands of certain tribes who would use them to attack the English.[43] In this way, Morton was a traitor, and Bradford knew he had to be stopped. Standish was dispatched to Merrymount to force them to shut down. Upon his arrival, Morton's men scurried to attack the small army but were too drunk to aim their weapons. Morton was so intoxicated that Standish was able to walk up and grab his gun out of his hand. So ended the Merrymount trading post.

In March 1624, John Lyford (c. 1580–1634), an ordained Anglican minister, arrived in Plymouth. His mere presence was a cause for alarm, as the Pilgrims were committed to utter separation from the Church of England. They had hoped their pastor, John Robinson, would be sent to them, but the Merchant Adventurers sent Lyford instead. However, he immediately disavowed his allegiance to the Church of England. While his arrival seemed promising at first, none in Plymouth wanted to call Lyford as their pastor, since they were still waiting for John Robinson.[44] Embittered by this, Lyford led a quiet rebellion against the colony's leadership. Sensing the growing disenfranchisement, Bradford intercepted a batch of letters written by Lyford headed for England. Although the letters were filled with slanderous accusations, Bradford chose not to play his hand until a short time later, when he summoned Lyford and his co-conspirators to court and questioned them about their efforts to stir up turmoil in the colony. When Lyford's associate, John Oldham, flew into a rage at the charges, Bradford produced the letters and read them aloud. The townspeople were appalled, and as a result Lyford and Oldham were banished. Bradford's stealthy actions were further vindicated when it came to light that Lyford had previously deceived his own wife, fathering a child out of wedlock, and had also been banished from Ireland for "satisf[ying] his lust on" a young woman engaged to one of his parishioners.[45] With Lyford's character in ruins, the threat was neutralized. The Lyford ordeal affirmed Bradford's belief that the

43. Bradford, *Of Plymouth Plantation*, 205–8.

44. John Robison never made the journey; he died in Holland in 1625.

45. Smith, *Bradford of Plymouth*, 208.

Merchant Adventurers would continue to meddle in their religious affairs. Something had to be done.

By 1627, Plymouth Colony was positioned to establish itself as its own entity. A year earlier they had severed ties with the Merchant Adventurers, effectively buying out their interest for £1,800, which was payable over nine yearly installments. Along with eleven other men, Bradford assumed financial responsibility for making the payments, even signing the new patent in his own name. However, questions began to arise about the land interest of the original settlers. Prior to 1639, Bradford and seven assistants had exercised control over all land distribution and business transactions. Now being free from their obligation to the Adventurers, the members of the colony sought to retain a measure of control over the assets. By March the tensions were mounting as residents began making demands of Bradford and his associates. In an unexpected move, Bradford graciously handed over the patent, signifying the surrender of the colony into their hands, "whereupon the freemen promptly handed the patent back to him for safekeeping."[46] While this event functioned as the end of his dominant interest, Bradford continued to be retained as governor more than thirty times until the year before his death in 1657.

The Church and the State
The founding of the Massachusetts Bay Colony in 1629 was both a blessing and a curse. While not a Separatist colony, Massachusetts Bay soon became sympathetic to the Plymouth ideal. When Governor Bradford got word that John Endecott (c. 1588–1665), governor of the Massachusetts Bay Colony, and his associates were sick with disease, he quickly dispatched physician Samuel Fuller (1580–1633) to tend to their needs. During his stay, Fuller spent time speaking to Endecott about Separatism, and the two became well-acquainted. No doubt influenced by their time with Fuller, the Puritans in Massachusetts were soon conducting their church services similarly to

---

46. Langdon, *Pilgrim Colony*, 41.

the Pilgrims, even electing their own ministers—an unthinkable act within the Church of England.[47] While Separatism had been despised in England, those in Massachusetts came to see that they had much more in common with their Plymouth neighbors than they had originally thought. In a letter written to Bradford, John Endecott professed,

> God's people are all marked with one and the same marke, and sealed with one and the same seale, and have for the mayne one & the same hart, guided by one & the same spirite of truth; and where this is, there can be no discorde; nay, here must needs be sweete harmonie. I acknowledge myself much bound to you for your kind love and care in sending Mr. Fuller among us, and rejoyce much that I am by him satisfied touching your judgements of the outward forme of God's worshipe.[48]

By 1630, the last members of the Leyden congregation arrived from Holland. In the same year, thirteen ships brought more than one thousand colonists to Massachusetts Bay. In June, John Winthrop (1588–1649) arrived on the *Arbella*, along with four other ships. Having taken office as governor, he was eager to meet the already famous governor of Plymouth colony. When Winthrop finally met Bradford in 1632, he described him as "a very discreet and grave man."[49] The two felt an instant connection and remained in frequent contact through correspondence for the rest of their lives. However, their relationship would suffer duress as both colonies jockeyed for financial advancement. In the end, Massachusetts Bay would outpace Plymouth at every turn, even drawing many of their own people away to settle in the Bay Area. More than thirty thousand colonists would brave the Atlantic over the next ten years,

---

47. Schmidt, *William Bradford*, 165–66.
48. Cited in Schmidt, *William Bradford*, 165.
49. John Winthrop, *Winthrop's Journal, "History of New England," 1630–1649*, ed. James Kendall Hosmer (New York: Charles Scribner's Sons, 1908), 1:93.

and nearly all of them would settle near Massachusetts Bay, with Plymouth growing at a noticeably slower pace.

Perhaps the greatest benefit of having the burgeoning new Bay colony nearby was the solidarity and support in the face of opposition. In 1648 the colonies of Plymouth and Massachusetts, along with Connecticut and New Haven, joined together to form the New England Confederation. The colonies had previously banded together when the Pequot Indians attacked in 1637, defeating them with the help of the Narragansetts. But now they would be unified in protecting their common interests, both economic and spiritual.

Unlike Massachusetts Bay, Plymouth was not attempting to be a theocracy. Yet as one historian has noted, "The Pilgrims had come to Plymouth resolved to build a society structured and governed according to the will of God: to achieve this goal and to sustain their society they knew that their civil government must support and nourish religion."[50] With no strong ministerial influence, Bradford instituted and enforced laws to restrain evil and encourage flourishing. In 1636, Plymouth enacted a new legal code designed to be "a brief, sensible, understandable rendering of the law by which it governed itself."[51] The code regulated land deeds, civil litigation, and criminal offenses. Taking cues from the Bible, capital punishment was decreed for treason, murder, witchcraft, sodomy, rape, and buggery.[52] To Bradford's dismay, the occurrences of rank debauchery and wickedness seemed to escalate within the colony. In his journal, Bradford records some of the instances, lamenting that "even sodomy and buggery (things fearful to name) have broke forth in this land oftener than once."[53] He attributed the rampant sinfulness to several factors, including satanic attacks against New England, the exacerbating effects of moral law, and the increased visibility due to the small size of the colony. One thing soon became abundantly

50. Langdon, *Pilgrim Colony*, 58.
51. Smith, *Bradford of Plymouth*, 224.
52. Smith, *Bradford of Plymouth*, 222.
53. Bradford, *Of Plymouth Plantation*, 316.

clear: the colony was changing, and there was nothing William Bradford could do about it.

Fading Hope

As the original Pilgrim Fathers began to die, so did the founding vision for Plymouth. For Bradford, the most difficult loss came in 1644 with the death of his friend and mentor, William Brewster. Devoting several pages to Brewster in his journal, Bradford memorialized "a man that had done and suffered much for the Lord Jesus and the gospel's sake, and had borne his part in weal and woe with this poor persecuted church above 36 years in England, Holland and in this wilderness, and done the Lord and them faithful service in his place and calling."[54] By 1656 Edward Winslow and Myles Standish were also gone, and Bradford was "growne aged." He had become increasingly frustrated with the moral laxity and greediness of Plymouth residents. It was clear that hope was all but gone, and "the community of Saints he had hoped to create in New England had never come to be."[55] After a long winter of sickness, William Bradford died on May 9, 1657.

Bradford's successor as governor was a stern and tactless man named Thomas Prence (1600–1673). Exploiting the full measure of Plymouth's law code, Prence tirelessly pursued and persecuted dissenters and religious zealots with a heavy hand. Under the guise of subduing heresy, Prence mercilessly attacked the Quakers,[56] earning

---

54. Bradford, *Of Plymouth Plantation*, 324.

55. Philbrick, *Mayflower*, 189.

56. Quakerism was founded by George Fox in the mid-1650s in England. The basic premise was that a relationship with Jesus Christ came through religious experiences divorced from Scripture, even through sexual encounters. The Quakers tended to deemphasize the Scriptures, leaning more on their own subjective "inner light" to guide them. In response to their lewd and defiant behavior, the government of the New England colonies began to arrest Quakers in 1656. When fines and banishment failed to deter their extremism, many Quakers were imprisoned and executed. Over time, the Quakers modified their practices, becoming less radical and more restrained in their behavior. For a helpful overview, see Francis J. Bremer, *The Puritan Experiment: New*

himself the title "a Terrour to evill doers."[57] Beyond the tensions with fellow Englishmen, hostility toward the Indians began to mount as well. When Massasoit died in 1661, the forty-year truce forged on that spring day in 1621 died with him. Within fifteen years his own son, Metacom, would wage war on New England. To be sure, the latter days of Plymouth were darker than its earlier ones. Finally, after years of failing to obtain its own patent, Plymouth was swallowed up into the Massachusetts Bay Colony in 1691.

Bradford's Legacy

The greatest Christians are seldom aware of their own greatness. They simply rise to meet their unique challenges and endure by the grace of God. Called "the first American" by one of his biographers,[58] William Bradford typified the American spirit: courageous, adventurous, tireless, and free. While the eighteenth-century Founding Fathers have their rightful place of honor, Bradford stands preeminent: "To Bradford belongs the singular honor of being the first ruler to demonstrate, with his associates, true Christian democracy, not exaggerated into communism, as a successful principle of government."[59] While he was certainly a Christian first and a governor second, Bradford labored tirelessly for a society that was ordered around the freedom to worship God.

As for Bradford's role as governor of Plymouth, Cotton Mather writes, "The leader of a people in a wilderness had need be a Moses; and if a Moses had not led the people of Plymouth Colony, when this worthy person was their governour, the people had never with so much unanimity and importunity still called him to lead them."[60] Despite numerous challenges, the colonists insisted on Bradford's

---

England Society from Bradford to Edwards, rev. ed. (Hanover, N.H.: University Press of New England, 1995), 154–58.

57. Langdon, *Pilgrim Colony*, 72.

58. Smith, *Bradford of Plymouth*, 12.

59. Albert Hale Plumb, *William Bradford of Plymouth* (Boston: Richard G. Badger, 1920), 106.

60. Mather, *Magnalia*, 1:113.

hand at the helm. He would have governed every year of his life had he not requested five intermittent years of rest. On the nature of his governance, it has been written, "His administration exhibited a happy blending of his constitutional mildness and moderation, combined with a firmness that could not be shaken, a patience that would not wear out, and an optimistic hope that was based upon his Christian faith."[61] Further, "It was not power or wealth he wanted, but a way of life—a community of dedicated men and women, bound together as close and warm as a family is bound, by covenants sacred and inviolable."[62] When he died, all of New England mourned the great loss.

In his later years, with the colony's survival a distant thought, Bradford began to occupy himself with reading, studying, and writing. With the founding generation passing on, he quickly saw the need to instruct the next generation on the nature and necessity of Separatism. Framed in a question-and-answer format, the didactic piece came to be known as the "Dialogue" and showcased Bradford's own apt theological acumen. A few years later, in 1652, Bradford took up his pen again and retold the fateful beginnings of Plymouth Colony from 1620 to 1647. What was first referred to as his journal, or history, was published two hundred years later as *Of Plymouth Plantation*. Historian Williston Walker notes, "His writings are marked throughout by courage and cheer. They give us the best picture of the man himself; the modest, kindly, grateful, generous, honorable leader in a great enterprise. Shrewd and sober of judgment, profoundly religious with a religion that masters his actions rather than seeks expression in words, self-forgetful, without cant, and with far less superstition than many of his associates, it is a sweet, strong, noble character that has unconsciously written itself in the pages of his *History*."[63] One is hard pressed to find its equal in early American literature.

---

61. Plumb, *William Bradford of Plymouth*, 42.
62. Smith, *Bradford of Plymouth*, 282.
63. Walker, *Ten New England Leaders*, 41.

While many have sought to psychoanalyze Bradford as a political figure, it must be noted that "we cannot understand William Bradford without attempting to enter into his feeling of a close walk with God."[64] Orphaned by the world, he was adopted by God at age twelve. Even when he perceived himself to be the only Christian in Austerfield, William held fast to his faith in Jesus Christ. After losing his wife to the sea, Bradford remarried the widow Alice Southworth, "a woman of devout mind and great force of character."[65] Bradford saw to it that they would not only care for their own blended family but also take many orphaned children into their home, thus extending the godly kindness of adoption. All his life, Bradford never stopped seeking the Lord. Even in his old age, he taught himself Hebrew so he would see with his own eyes "the ancient oracles of God in their native beauty."[66] And when he grew weak, teetering on the brink of eternity, he at last said, "The good Spirit of God has given me a pledge of my happiness in another world, and the first-fruits of eternal glory."[67] In his passing, William Bradford joined his heavenly Father, the One in whom he had hoped all his life.

---

64. Smith, *Bradford of Plymouth*, 135–36.
65. Plumb, *William Bradford of Plymouth*, 59.
66. Mather, *Magnalia*, 1:113.
67. Plumb, *William Bradford of Plymouth*, 106.

2

JOHN WINTHROP

The *Arbella*, the flagship vessel of the Winthrop fleet, was spotted from the Massachusetts coast in June 1630. Its tired, cold, hungry, and worn passengers had been at sea for more than two months. Yet despite the struggle of the voyage, a flicker of joy resided in the heart of governor John Winthrop, who, with many others, had been planning this moment for months. They had essentially been driven from their homeland by a king who wanted to control how they worshiped the God they so ardently served. They would have nothing of it and set their vision on what they dreamed would become a "city on a hill." Sailing into port, Winthrop recorded in his diary, "Monday, June 14, 1630. In the morning early we weighed anchor and, the wind being against us and the channel so narrow as we could not well turn in,…we came to anchor in the inward harbor. In the afternoon we went with most of our company on shore, and our captain gave us 5 pieces (salute)."[1] In July, many of the other ships began to arrive. Winthrop wrote with excitement:

> July 1, Thursday. The *Mayflower* and the *Whale* arrived safe.
> July 2, Friday. The *Talbot* arrived. She had lost 14 passengers.
> July 3, Saturday. The *Hopewell* and *William and Francis* arrived.

1. John Winthrop, *The Journal of John Winthrop 1630–1649*, ed. Richard S. Dunn and Laetitia Yeandle (Cambridge, Mass.: Belknap Press, 1996), 29.

July 5, Monday. The *Trial* arrived at Charlestown, and the *Charles* at Salem.

July 6, Tuesday. The *Success* arrived. Many of her passengers near starved.

July 8, Thursday. We kept a day of thanksgiving.[2]

Ship after ship dropped anchor off the coast of Massachusetts seeking freedom to worship God, representation in government, fairness in policies, and a new and prosperous life. Although they would meet with difficulties and hardships that are unimaginable today, they were driven by an indomitable spirit, and John Winthrop was their governor.

Boyhood

John Winthrop was born in the rural village of Edwardstone in Suffolk, England, on January 12, 1588. The Stour Valley, as it was known, would be the setting for much of John's boyhood before he migrated to the New World. The Winthrop family belonged to what would today be called the upper middle class. In his youth, John's grandfather Adam had traveled from the Suffolk town of Lavenham to London to apprentice as a clothworker.[3] From these humble beginnings, Adam became quite successful and ascended to be the head of the Clothworkers Guild in London. Adam's success dealing in English cloths afforded him the opportunity to purchase a stately home called Groton Manor, where he settled with his family in the 1550s. John's father, also named Adam, being the youngest son in the family, inherited only a small portion of the clothworker's wealth and land. Studying for a short time at Cambridge University and the Inns of Court, Adam later became manager of Groton Manor for his older brother and moved his family from Edwardstone to Groton.

Groton Manor was a quintessential English estate surrounded by crops of rye, barley, peas, and all manner of farm animals,

2. Winthrop, *Journal*, 30.

3. Francis J. Bremer, *John Winthrop: America's Forgotten Founding Father* (New York: Oxford University Press, 2003), 13.

including sheep, cattle, and pigs. Much of John's boyhood was spent exploring the fields, eating honey from the beehives, and fishing in the estate ponds.[4] He also became an avid hunter, stalking the neighboring forests for hares with his bow and arrow, and eventually a gun. John and his sisters were taught to read and write by their parents, but after the basics were mastered, their father hired a tutor to prepare John for further instruction in a grammar school, where he learned the Greek and Latin skills necessary to enter university. John received the compulsory education of one who would eventually attend Oxford or Cambridge University.

Like most Englishmen, the Winthrop family were not strangers to the religious turmoil of the period. John's uncle, William, had played an important role in the underground Protestant network during the harsh persecutions of "Bloody" Mary. In addition, William had passed along to John Foxe (1516–1587) several accounts of Protestant martyrs during this period, which were later published in Foxe's *The Book of Martyrs* (1563). Young John Winthrop was well acquainted with the faithful Protestant martyrs, hearing numerous stories of how his uncle William had aided the Reformed effort in London and abroad. Outside of Hadley, John often passed the field where Rowland Taylor (1510–1555), the Protestant reformer, was burned at the stake during the reign of Mary Tudor. The Stour Valley in which John was reared became a centralized stronghold of Puritan reform, with many of the religious leaders dining at Groton Manor with the Winthrop family.

Faithful Puritan families like the Winthrops spent part of their day reading and discussing Scripture and sermons they had heard. John was accustomed to psalm singing, daily prayers, religious counsel with others, and discussing doctrinal issues. He developed strict disciplines of study, meditation on Scripture, prayer, and other habits that would lead to a life of piety and holiness. John was reared to recognize that he was born corrupted by original sin,

---

4. Bremer, *John Winthrop: America's Forgotten Founding Father*, 73.

completely unable to earn his way to heaven, for salvation was a gift from a sovereign God.

Discovering His Path

Toward the end of grammar school, students would decide the course of their life—what type of life would support their family, where one should study to be most prepared for a successful career. What John eventually inherited from his father would not be an adequate amount to give him a leadership role in the community. At best he could only continue in his father's footsteps in a meager legal practice or as a land manager. With an ardent devotion to his faith, John entered Cambridge University with the desire to become a minister of the gospel.

In December 1602, at the age of fourteen, John entered one of the most Puritan colleges at Cambridge University, Trinity College. His typical day would begin at 5:00 a.m. when he woke up in a chamber occupied by three or four other students under the guidance of a faculty tutor.[5] He began his day praying in the chapel, and after breakfast he would spend much of his day discussing readings with his tutor and debating with his fellow students, sharpening his skills in logic and rhetoric. Outside the halls of debate, John may have enjoyed soccer, playing chess, or other seventeenth-century extracurricular activities.

In November 1604, while visiting with the family of a close friend, John met his future wife, Mary Forth (1583–1615). After a rapid courtship the two were wed in March 1605 when John was only sixteen years old. The new couple divided their time between John's parents at Groton and the land of Mary's father in Great Stambridge, Essex. However, it was not long until the couple saw they were unsuited for one another. Mary possessed very little education, which became a source of frustration for John, who had been raised in a household that valued education next to godliness. Regarding religious conversation, John recorded that he could "not

---

5. Bremer, *John Winthrop: America's Forgotten Founding Father*, 81.

prevail, not so much as to make her answer me, or talk with me about any goodness."[6] Southeast Essex also proved to be a difficult place to live for John, who was so accustomed to the acceptance of Puritanism.[7] Mary's family home proved to be merely tolerant of the Puritan cause, and the truly devoted were forced to huddle together in a small group. The godly disciplines and practices of which John had been so familiar since boyhood were now the subject of stark criticism by his new neighbors.

By the age of twenty, when things should have been settled regarding his future, John was very uncertain of what was in store for his life. Up to this point, no one would have predicted that John would have been a stalwart leader in his community, much less play a key role in the founding of a new nation. With few other viable career options, John made the difficult decision to withdraw his plans to enter pastoral ministry. He had two sons and a wife in his care and an estate that was significantly smaller than his successful grandfather's. All indications pointed to John Winthrop as a failure, but it was during this time that he sought to depend on the faith of his youth and his present trust in God. He had learned, again and again, that regardless of the seemingly impossible circumstances surrounding him, God was faithful and could be trusted to direct his path.

English Magistrate

The difficult circumstances in which John found himself began to change when his father was able to purchase Groton Manor from his uncle, who had abandoned his wife and migrated to Ireland. John immediately returned to the home of his childhood in the Stour Valley and became quite respectable as a land owner, which provided opportunities for government service. In 1609 his new position was acknowledged when he chaired the manorial court, which dealt with minor disputes that took place on the estate.

---

6. John Winthrop, "Experiencia," in *Winthrop Papers* (Boston: Massachusetts Historical Society, 1929–1947), 1:163.

7. Bremer, *John Winthrop: America's Forgotten Founding Father*, 89–90.

Recognizing the necessity of legal knowledge, John enrolled at Gray's Inn, one of the Inns of Court, where men were trained in the law. Although John did not remain long enough to pass the bar, the familiarity with the law he acquired at Gray's Inn proved vital in the coming years.

The early years of the seventeenth century saw many changes for the Winthrop family as John and Mary welcomed John Winthrop Jr. in 1606, followed by Henry in 1608, Forth in 1609, and Mary in 1612. In 1614 John grieved the loss of his daughter Anne, who died shortly after birth. The following year John's wife died in childbirth along with another daughter, who died without being named. With such a sizable family and grieving the loss of Mary, John married Thomasine Clopton (1583–1616) of Groton. John and Thomasine had known each other since their early years of exploring the Groton fields. He was also drawn to her ardent piety and obvious godliness. She demonstrated such godliness very quietly, John recalled, in her "loving and tender regard" for her stepchildren.[8] Heartbreakingly, only one year after marriage, Thomasine experienced a difficult childbirth in which the baby died and she also, after experiencing weeks of difficulty, died from complications. John remained at her bedside, reading to her from Scripture and comforting her with prayers.

John had little time to grieve the loss of his second wife; he immediately set out to find a woman who would be a mother for his children and act as a manager of his domestic household. In late 1617, he entered into a courtship with Margaret Tyndal (1591–1647) of Great Maplestead, a town in Essex about half a day's ride to the south of Groton. Margaret's family, headed by a distinguished judge of the national Court of Chancery, possessed a higher social status than the Winthrops. Regardless of their social differences, John and Margaret found within each other true companionship and affectionate love. The two were married before God and friends in April 1618.[9] Following their marriage, Margaret gave birth to Stephen

---

8. Winthrop, "Experiencia," 182–90.
9. Bremer, *John Winthrop: America's Forgotten Founding Father*, 115.

in 1619, Adam in 1620, Deane in 1623, and Samuel in 1627. Four
other children died shortly or within a year of birth. While John was
away studying law at Gray's Inn, Margaret assumed responsibility
and oversight of the Manor. While separated on numerous occasions, John and Margaret maintained a faithful correspondence that
testifies to their love for one another, which stands in stark contrast
to the contemporary view of the cold austerity of the Puritans. He
always addressed her with words of endearment such as "mine own,
mine only, my best beloved" and "my love, my joy, my faithful one."
In London one February, he wrote teasingly to Margaret, "Thou
must be my valentine."[10]

It would have been easy for John and Margaret to spend the rest
of their lives managing the manor lands, harvesting honey, tending their crops, and watching their children grow. However, John
believed that someone who wished "surer peace and joy in Christianity must not aim at a condition retired from the world and
free from temptation, but rather engage in public affairs."[11] In 1615
such an opportunity of engagement presented itself, and John was
appointed to the Suffolk Commission of Peace. Once applauded
by Puritans as a stronghold of godly magistrates, the Suffolk Commission of Peace was changing when John joined its ranks. By
the reign of James I, Puritan representation within the court had
declined significantly, and many were beginning to view Puritanism
as a roadblock to meaningful advancement. In 1618 Samuel Ward
(1577–1640), a Puritan clergyman from Ipswich, preached before
the Suffolk justices and warned that too few residing on the bench
were there "by God's door and not the Devil's window." He sol-
emnly appraised the "mercenary lawyers who sell both their tongues

10. Bremer, *John Winthrop: America's Forgotten Founding Father*, 116. See also Lawrence Shaw Mayo, *The Winthrop Family in America* (Boston: Massachusetts Historical
Society, 1948); and Robert C. Winthrop, *Life and Letters of John Winthrop: Governor
of the Massachusetts-Bay Company at Their Emigration to New England, 1630*, 2 vols.
(Boston: Little, Brown, 1869).

11. Winthrop, "Experiencia," 209.

and their silence, their clients' causes and their own consciences."[12] John listened closely to Ward's instruction on what characteristics established a godly magistrate. Such a man must "have strength of mind to govern and manage passion and unruly affections" as well as "courage and spirit."[13] Taking in the counsel of fellow godly magistrates and other godly ministers, John learned to temper justice with mercy and to use his God-appointed influence to advance the common good among the people.

During his time as an English magistrate, John became widely lauded as a compassionate and fair judge. In 1627, he was appointed as an attorney at the Court of Wards, which designated managers over large tracts of land inherited by those who were too young to assume the responsibility of oversight. As one might imagine, such a system was often an open sewer of corruption and mismanagement, often making wealthy men out of those who accepted bribes from people seeking license to do as they wished. After living in London for long periods of time, John soon realized he would be unable to fulfill his duties and maintain his integrity. This, along with other circumstances during the 1620s, clearly demonstrated to John that to lead as he wished, according to the rule of God, he would not be able to remain in England. His attention increasingly turned to the New World.

Into the Wilderness
When Charles I ascended to the English throne in 1625, he named Bishop William Laud to help him enforce conformity to the ceremonies of the church. His marriage to a French Catholic princess caused many to worry that Charles was retreating from the Protestant reforms of his forebears. Puritans in the Stour Valley, where they had significant influence, began to find their power destabilized. More and more Puritan pastors were removed from their pulpits by the English bishops who demanded conformity to the state church.

---

12. Samuel Ward, *Jethro's Justice of the Peace* (London: Edwards Griffin, 1618).

13. Ward, *Jethro's Justice.*

When Charles declared that he would rule without Parliament, the Puritans lost their only possibility of appeal for the atrocities taking place. During this tumultuous period of religious unrest, Hugh Peter (1598–1660) and Thomas Hooker (1586–1647) sailed for the Netherlands. However, it appeared that no outpost, however far, was free from the immediate influence of the English Crown, except America.

In July 1628, John made the journey to the estate of the Earl of Lincoln in Lincolnshire, where a series of meetings were being held to discuss the possibility of an American Puritan colony. As John began to contemplate immigration to America, he surveyed the providence of God and weighed his difficult circumstances in the balance, viewing them as God's manner of severing his ties to the country of his birth. During his journey to Lincolnshire, John's horse stumbled, throwing him into the deep marshes. He found himself immersed in water, but thankfully he came out alive. He later recalled the event and wrote, "The lord preserved me from further danger. Blessed be his name."[14] John viewed this near-death experience as the providence of God and as a sign that he should proceed with plans to sail to the New World. Many of his friends and acquaintances attempted to dissuade now forty-year-old John from traveling, as such a journey was more suited for younger and more adventurous men. Yet because his wife and children fully supported him, none of the arguments leveled against him stood.

The Charter

England's first colony was established in Virginia in 1607, although it had been ravaged by high mortality. A band of English Separatists—those who shared many Puritan views but had ultimately separated from the established church—had migrated to the Netherlands from Scrooby, England, and then to America in 1620, settling in Plymouth. During this same period many English men and women attempted to establish a colony in the West Indies. Henry Winthrop (1608–1630), John's son, was part of a contingency that attempted

---

14. Winthrop, "Experiencia," 103.

such a settlement in Barbados. Another group from Dorchester, England, had founded a fishing outpost on the coast of New England. However, when these enterprises failed, some of their financial investors decided to reorganize their settlement as a religious refuge. The idea garnered support from London and also Boston in Lincolnshire. These various Puritan groups assembled, and in 1629 King Charles I granted them a royal charter, incorporating them as the Massachusetts Bay Colony. The charter authorized those of the company to meet in a General Court or legislature to choose a governor and deputy governor and to appoint assistants, seven of whom could function as the General Court. The charter vested power in these Puritans to govern Massachusetts Bay in every respect and guaranteed that all inhabitants "shall have and enjoy all liberties and immunities of free and natural subjects…as if they…were born within the real of England."[15] The Massachusetts Bay Colony became the first English-chartered colony whose board of governors did not reside in England. The Puritans, being granted royal permission through the charter to govern themselves, saw this as a providential act of God.

Some colonies were the sole property of an individual, such as William Penn (1644–1718), who owned Pennsylvania, while others were owned by chartered corporations under the direction of a board of directors, like the Massachusetts Bay Colony. If the individuals or chartered corporations directed their affairs in keeping with the objectives of their charter, all was well, but if they violated the charter, the colony was in danger of being taken over by the king, who made it a "royal colony."

A month after receiving the royal charter, the Bay Company contracted with Francis Higginson (1588–1630), Samuel Skelton (c. 1592–1634), and Francis Bright (b. c. 1602) to journey to New England to "do their true endeavor in their places of the ministry as well as preaching, catechizing… [and] teaching, or causing to be taught, the Company's servants and their children, as also

---

15. William T. Davis, "Charter of the Province of the Massachusetts Bay," in *History of the Judiciary of Massachusetts* (Boston: Boston Book Company, 1900), 401.

the savages and their children."[16] At the end of the month John
Endecott, already in the Bay, was granted the title of governor of
the settlement.[17] However, Winthrop (who had become a financial
investor in the Bay Company) and other stockholders of the Massachusetts Bay did not trust their investment in the hands of those
who were three thousand miles away. As a result a meeting was convened at Cambridge to decide the fate of the colony. It was decided
that the headquarters would be moved to Massachusetts only if they
could bring the charter with them. Winthrop had continually demonstrated himself to be a man of fair-mindedness, godly demeanor,
and complete wisdom; thus, he was truly fit to be involved in the
establishment of a new Puritan colony. In October 1629, the plan
was approved by the investors, and those present elected Winthrop
to be their first governor. Upon his arrival in America, he would also
continue as the governor of the new colony. Together these men at
Cambridge, who never envisaged being thrust into colonial leadership, signed an agreement whereby,

> For the better encouragement of ourselves and others that shall
> join with us in this action, and to the end that every man may
> without scruple dispose of his estate and affairs as may best fit
> his preparation for this voyage...[each] doth hereby freely and
> sincerely promise and bind himself, in the word of a Christian,
> and in the presence of God, who is the searcher of all hearts,
> that we will so really endeavour the prosecution of this work,
> as by God's assistance we will be ready in our persons, and with
> such of our several families as are to go with us, and such provi-
> sions as we are able conveniently to furnish ourselves withal, to
> embark for the said Plantation by the first of March next,...to
> inhabit and continue in New England.[18]

16. *Records of the Governor and Company of the Massachusetts Bay*, ed. Nathaniel B.
Shurtleff (Boston: W. White, 1851), 1:37e–37f (hereafter *RMB*).

17. *RMB*, 1:37j.

18. Thomas Hutchinson, "The Agreement at Cambridge," in *Collection of Original
Papers* (Boston: Massachusetts Historical Society, 1769), 25–26.

The winter of 1629–1630 proved to be a time of enthusiastic preparation for the long journey. Supplies had to be gathered and purchased while Winthrop traveled to encourage others to join in their efforts. John's beloved Groton Manor had to be sold, although the sale would be completed by Margaret before she joined John in America. By the final days of March 1630, the fleet had amassed at the port of Southampton. John Cotton (1585–1652), a Puritan pastor, assembled with those preparing to depart their homeland to preach and assure them that God was on their side and would bless their efforts. Following Cotton, Winthrop entered the pulpit and eloquently explained what they were called to accomplish in their efforts. This lay sermon, referred to as the "Model of Christian Charity," was a key document in properly understanding the New England Puritan experiment. From views on how ardently reform was to be enacted to how they should interact and love their neighbor, Winthrop called on these men and women to live in a community that would properly exemplify true Christian charity. He implored the people to use their skills and talents on behalf of their neighbors—for the carpenter, farmer, and merchant to all depend on one another and willingly give themselves to the advance of their mutual well-being.

Winthrop employed Scripture as a source of inspiration for his fellow colonists to be "a company" bound together by "mutual consent" and seeking a "place of cohabitation and consort-ship."[19] Describing them as ligaments of Christian love, he employed the analogy of a human body to describe how all individuals must do their part for the mutual benefit of the whole. They had one goal—to live godly lives in binding themselves to the covenant of God in forming a marriage between Massachusetts and the Lord. Those who chose to join this company were to "love brotherly without dissimulation...love one another with a pure heart, fervently...[and] bear one another's burdens." He implored them all to be "knit together in his work as one man" and treat each other with "meekness, gentleness, patience, and liberality." They were to "delight in each other,

---

19. John Winthrop, "A Model of Christian Charity," in *Winthrop Papers*, 2:293.

make others' conditions our own; rejoice together, mourn together, labor and suffer together—always having before our eyes our commission and community in the work, our community as members of the same body."[20]

Winthrop proclaimed, "The eyes of all people are upon us," and if they lived by these principles set forth, the colony would be "as a City upon a Hill."[21] Drawing from the Gospel of Matthew, the Puritans often employed the phrase "city upon a hill" in describing an exemplary community of godly people. Without any hesitation to the contrary, they were to live godly lives; if they succeeded, God would bless them, and others would be drawn to imitate them. Contrary to the polemic nature of Winthrop's message, it was not a clear blueprint for the new colony. However, he indicated that the colonists were to go beyond what they had first attempted in England: "That which most in their churches maintain as a truth in profession only, we must bring into familiar and constant practice, as in this duty of love," resulting in seeing "much more of his wisdom, power, goodness and truth than we have formerly been acquainted with."[22]

Voyage

In early April, with more than seven hundred passengers, the fleet embarked on an arduous journey across the Atlantic led by Winthrop's flagship, the *Arbella*. Although the sailing was relatively smooth, the passengers were hardly ready for what they had to endure aboard these wooden vessels—cold, damp, and cramped quarters; tossing to and fro on waves of twenty feet or higher; and hardly any hot meals. The prayer of everyone was that no disease would begin aboard, for it would spread rapidly among the enclosed environment. One particular day aboard, John observed, "The sun did not give so much heat as in England."[23]

---

20. Winthrop, "Model of Christian Charity," 282–95.
21. Winthrop, "Model of Christian Charity," 295.
22. Winthrop, "Model of Christianity Charity," 294.
23. Winthrop, *Journal*, 19.

On June 6, land was sighted. The panorama observed from the deck of the *Arbella* was studded with tall oak trees, rolling hills, and seas of green forests. The coastal estuaries were full of shellfish and large waterfowl, while the small islands that dotted the coastline would produce fruitful orchards and crops free from the rabbits and deer so plentiful to the area. Unseen to those aboard were the multitudes of Native Americans who had inhabited these lands long before the arrival of the Europeans. The area that would later become known as Rhode Island was occupied by the Narragansetts. To the west lived the Pequots and the Mohegans. On the eastern shores of the Narragansett Bay were the Pokanoket Wampanoags, and farther east along Cape Cod, the Nauset.[24]

The *Arbella*, along with other ships in the English contingency, anchored off Salem on June 12. In the afternoon, John Endecott and the Reverend Samuel Skelton came aboard to invite Winthrop and others to dine on shore. They supped on "a good venison pasty and good beer," which was a feast to those accustomed to the scant meals on board ship.[25] Those who disembarked in the New World were physically weakened by the journey and automatically faced overwhelming challenges upon their arrival. No homes or shelter and no stores for supplies—just unending wilderness. In addition to cutting down trees for protection from the elements, the colonists had to immediately plant crops to survive the much hotter summer and harsh, quickly approaching winter. There were no cows, sheep, oxen, pigs, chickens, or other familiar English livestock in this new wilderness. Any livestock must also be imported. Life proved to be immediately different and very challenging.

Many of the colonists faced not only physical trials in leaving their homes but also the emotional struggle of leaving behind dear family and friends for an unknown world. Pastors left behind congregations, fathers left behind children, and everyone left behind godly friends on whom they depended for spiritual encouragement.

---

24. Bremer, *John Winthrop: America's Forgotten Founding Father*, 191.
25. Bremer, *John Winthrop: America's Forgotten Founding Father*, 191.

Despite the seemingly insurmountable challenges facing the new colony, Winthrop never lost hope. He labored incessantly to convince anyone who would listen that the colony would survive to become an example to all.[26]

The Foundations

If Massachusetts was to be a "city on a hill" it was essential to quickly begin establishing forms of government and churches. Winthrop was convinced that for the colony to survive, it must be organized in stark contrast to the previous attempts of colonization. "Christian Charity" had been an attempt to cement the commitment of the colonists to the principles of order and brotherhood.[27] In Charlestown, on August 23, 1630, Winthrop convened the first Court of Assistants in the colony. Very few of the men convened had previous experience in governmental affairs or knowledge of how law should be implemented for the good of the people and betterment of society. Standing head and shoulders above his fellow colonists in terms of experience and background was John Winthrop.[28]

Winthrop believed that those who occupied the colony should be the ones shaping its legal and political future. He persuaded his fellow leaders to begin by duplicating some of the more popular elements of English government, and he used his influence to transform the Court of Assistance (meetings of colony leaders) to resemble that of an English county's Commission of the Peace. This court, with new authority, began by adopting English procedures for criminal, civil, and legal proceedings; licensing alehouses and ferry operators; appointing local constables and militia leaders; levying taxes to support the needs of the colony as a whole; and dispensing land for the settlement of new towns.[29] In this new

---

26. Bremer, *John Winthrop: America's Forgotten Founding Father*, 195.
27. Bremer, *John Winthrop: America's Forgotten Founding Father*, 196.
28. Bremer, *John Winthrop: America's Forgotten Founding Father*, 196.
29. Francis J. Bremer, *John Winthrop* (New York: Continuum International, 2009), 29.

government, Winthrop, although presiding as governor over their meetings, possessed no greater power than other magistrates. In his skills as a leader, Winthrop was quickly recognized as a man of fairness, though criticized by some for his leniency in certain cases. He desired to promote a godly culture and sought to lead by example. In order to properly encourage such a culture, churches had to be established as models of reform.

Church

Following the arrival of Roger Williams (c. 1603–1683) in the Bay Colony in February 1631, it became clear that he was there to promote a complete separation from the Church of England and had intentions of founding a church that was institutionally as well as physically separate. This path of separatism from their "dear Mother," for Winthrop and his company, was rejected.[30] In response to Williams, Winthrop defended his and the company's position against complete separation in writing, "Reasons to prove a necessity of reformation from the corruptions of Antichrist which hath defiled the Christian Churches, & yet without an absolute separation from them."[31] Winthrop criticized those "censurers [of the Church of England who] will not give them leave to distinguish between corrupt Churches and false Churches, as they do term the Congregations. Neither will they put any difference between the Churches as they are technically appointed by man, and as they are particular congregations, and appointed by Christ; for so they are, as they remain particular Congregations, even Churches of Christ's own appointing, although now they be corrupted."[32]

Despite Winthrop's arguments to the contrary, Salem invited Williams to be the teacher of their congregation, leading the Court

---

30. John Winthrop, *Humble Request*, in *Winthrop Papers*, 2:232.

31. John Winthrop, "Reformation without Separation," in *Winthrop Papers* (Boston: Massachusetts Historical Society, 1929–1947), 3:10–14.

32. Winthrop, "Reformation without Separation," 10–14.

of Assistants to question the choice. As a result, Williams moved to the more "congenial atmosphere" of Plymouth Plantation.[33]

While in England, Puritans had experienced a blurred boundary between church and state; in Massachusetts they desired to found churches separate from the governing political bodies. As a result, it was decided that no clergyman or lay person holding a church office would be allowed to hold public office. Marriage, a sacrament of the church performed by the clergy in England, was transformed to be a civil ceremony performed by a magistrate in Massachusetts.[34] The colonists built simple meetinghouses and rejected the designation of certain places as "holy" both for worship and burial.

In the late spring and summer of 1630, Winthrop and other members of the community assembled under a large tree in Charlestown to hear the preaching of John Wilson (c. 1588–1667). Wilson had sailed to New England with the Winthrop fleet and served as the first minister of the settlers who established themselves in Charlestown before crossing the Charles River into Boston. As the minister of the First Church of Boston until his death in 1667, Wilson became embroiled in several controversies in the colonies, specifically with Anne Hutchinson during the Antinomian Controversy from 1636 to 1638.

In late July of 1630, a day of prayer and fasting was called for the task of organizing the colonial church. Winthrop and several other leaders wrote and signed a covenant pledging themselves to "walk in all our ways according to the rule of [the] Gospel, and in all sincere conformity to His holy ordinances, and in mutual love and respect each to other, so near God shall give us grace."[35] The church immediately elected John Wilson to serve as their first pastor. This church was founded on the idea of Congregationalism, meaning a church formed and controlled by the believers who made up the

33. Bremer, *John Winthrop: America's Forgotten Founding Father*, 199.

34. Bremer, *John Winthrop*, 33.

35. Richard D. Pierce, ed., *The Records of the First Church in Boson, 1630–1868*, Publications of the Colonial Society of Massachusetts (Boston: Colonial Society of Massachusetts, 1961), 39:xviii.

congregation and not subject to any higher church or national authority.[36] Although not a pastor, Winthrop held a firm belief, like most Puritans, that it was the duty of the civil government to safeguard and nurture the Puritan churches formed in New England.

Domestic

By the end of 1631, the foundations of the Massachusetts colony had been established. The Court of Assistances was functioning properly and individual justices of the peace were supervising the growth of the towns. Churches had been formed and pastors were called to instruct them in all manner of godliness and piety. But the next three years were not as smooth as one might have anticipated. Winthrop was intimately involved in the refining of policies, town administration, and the practice of the churches.[37] In a letter sent to an English friend in 1633, Winthrop indicated that the colonists "cannot profess a perfection in either political or ecclesiastical government" and acknowledged that such perfection "is not to be looked for in this world."[38] Although perfection was something Puritans ardently strived for, they knew it was impossible to attain in this life. Therefore, the challenges they faced were met with an equal amount of tolerance and submission to the providence of God. In the ten short years since the *Arbella* had touched the sandy shores of Massachusetts, the colony had grown to fourteen thousand. With such significant growth of the colony, Winthrop and his associates were forced to give attention to all aspects of the body politic.

Not only was Winthrop shouldering an enormous responsibility in the forming of Massachusetts, he was no doubt grieving the long separation from his beloved wife, Margaret, who had remained behind in England for the sale of Groton Manor. John longed to be in her company again and wrote regularly, assuring her of his health and that of the children who had accompanied him on the initial

---

36. Bremer, *John Winthrop*, 32.
37. Bremer, *John Winthrop: America's Forgotten Founding Father*, 205.
38. John Winthrop to Sir Simonds D'Ewes, September 26, 1633, in *Winthrop Papers*, 3:139.

voyage. In 1631, Margaret and John were reunited when she joined him in his "city on a hill."

Winthrop brought to his numerous tasks and responsibilities a true sense of humility and recognition of his own sinfulness.[39] Like his father who cared for the poor and destitute, John never let his judgment of an individual overshadow his care for the same individual. The one contemporary reference to his service as an English justice recalled his kindness and respect for others.[40] Winthrop's call for the colonists to love one another with true Christian affection came quite natural for him.

In 1634, things dramatically changed for Winthrop. In May the colony's leaders were elected for the coming year, and Winthrop received barely enough votes to be retained as an assistant; Thomas Dudley (1576–1653) had been elected governor and Roger Ludlow (1590–1664) as deputy governor. It was quite a different sensation for Winthrop to find a seat among the other magistrates on the lower bench as he watched another man assume the governor's chair in the meetinghouse. When the day was finally over, Winthrop recorded his defeat in his journal and noted that he had in fact entertained his fellow magistrates for dinner.[41] With fewer responsibilities, Winthrop became involved in the affairs of his own town, as he was the most prominent magistrate in Boston. Additionally, because of his reduced governmental duties, John was able to spend more time with his wife and family. John and Margaret likely spent some of their summers at Ten Hills, the Winthrop farm on the Mystic River. He oversaw his grazing cattle, planted fruit trees, and meandered through the nearby forests, losing himself in the wind as it wafted through the oaks and maples.

39. Bremer, *John Winthrop: America's Forgotten Founding Father*, 205.
40. Edward Revell to John Winthrop, April 20, 1635, in *Winthrop Papers*, 2:251–53.
41. Bremer, *John Winthrop: America's Forgotten Founding Father*, 241.

Controversy

The election of May 1637 thrust Winthrop back into the rushing torrent of colonial government when he was reelected governor, with Thomas Dudley chosen as deputy governor. By this time, Winthrop had many opponents who made it difficult for him to govern as freely as he had before, and a significant controversy was on the horizon, perhaps the largest he had encountered. After the 1634 migration of William and Anne Hutchinson (1591–1643) to the Massachusetts Bay Colony, Anne began to organize weekly meetings among the women of Boston to discuss the sermons of John Cotton. As other ministers and magistrates started to join in the meetings, she soon stressed the individual's intuition as a means of reaching God and salvation rather than the observance of the church's institutionalized beliefs. Her opponents accused her of antinomianism.[42] Anne began to garner support for her views among those in Boston as she challenged the authority of the clergy. After Winthrop was reelected as governor of the colony, she lost much of her support as he immediately began to oppose her efforts. Anne was tried by the General Court chiefly for "traducing the ministers," convicted in 1637, and sentenced to banishment. Refusing to recant her views, she was tried before the Boston church and formally excommunicated. After the death of her husband in 1642, she settled on Long Island Sound. In 1643, she and all of her servants and children except one were killed by Indians.

Final Days

By the early 1640s the colony had swollen to a population of more than twelve thousand residents who lived in more than twenty towns. These growing numbers presented new challenges and revived old questions as to how the colony was best governed, such as defining boundaries and jurisdictions, and, after the Pequot War (a war with a neighboring Native American tribe), the necessity

---

42. Antinomianism is the view that God's grace has freed the Christian from the need to observe established moral precepts.

of maintaining a common and united front against the Indians. Therefore, the colony once again called on Winthrop to assume the presiding chair of leadership. However, after much disapproval of his handling of certain colonial decisions, Winthrop was kept out of the governorship in 1644 and 1645.[43]

In 1647, an epidemic of yellow fever spread from Barbados through New England and claimed the lives of Thomas Hooker and John's beloved wife, Margaret. John remembered her as "a woman of singular virtue, prudence, modesty, and piety, and especially honored of all the country."[44] Perhaps as a result of the same epidemic, John fell very ill during the summer of 1647. When he regained his health, before the end of 1647, John married the widowed Martha Rainsborough Cotymore, who became his fourth wife. A year after their marriage, Martha gave birth to a son who was baptized in the Boston church. Not long after the baptism of his son, John became ill but continued his public obligations despite a continual fever for six weeks. Through the winter, John's health worsened. In March 1649, his longtime friend John Endecott (c. 1588–1665) wrote to him inquiring of his health. He urged Winthrop that they "labor to love one another and harbor the best thoughts one of another." He continued, "We have not long to live in this life, yet we here remain as long as our appointed times are set."[45] A few weeks later, John's son Adam wrote to his brother, John Jr., who was in Connecticut, reporting that their father had been bedridden for a month with a severe fever and cough. John Cotton asked the Boston church to pray for the governor, referring to him as one who had "been to us a friend… [and] a governor, who had been unto us a brother."[46] Along with others, Cotton prayed at his bedside, and on March 26 John Winthrop passed from this life into the next. His burial was delayed as they awaited the arrival of his son John from Connecticut, and on

43. Bremer, *John Winthrop: America's Forgotten Founding Father*, 346.

44. Winthrop, *Journal*, 711–12.

45. John Endecott to John Winthrop, March 1, 1649, in *Winthrop Papers*, 5:316–17.

46. Cotton Mather, *Magnalia Christi Americana* (1702; repr., Edinburgh: Banner of Truth, 1979), 1:131.

April 3 he was laid beside Margaret in the town burial ground. One of his contemporaries wrote that Winthrop had a "sweet temper and disposition sweated in a heart of bounty and goodness."[47] A fellow New Englander wrote to him that he was known as one of "worth and inward candor," whom neither "frowns nor flattery could ever force from its true goodness for the general good." All this meant that Winthrop's "constant zeal for the things of God and man may truly entitle you to be the father and first founder of this flourishing colony."[48] Reflecting on his services to the colony, John Cotton said that Winthrop had "been unto us a mother, parent-like distributing his goods to brethren and neighbors at his first coming, and gently bearing our infirmities without taking notice of them."[49]

Deputy Governor John Endecott became the new governor of Massachusetts following Winthrop's death. Finally, in 1684, the Massachusetts Bay Company had their charter revoked by the English courts, and New England was subjected to rule by an English general. However, by this time the values within the hearts of the colonists of Massachusetts had been forever ingrained by John Winthrop—the value of education, participatory government, and a moral approach to politics. These foundational characteristics were now too well established to be uprooted by any tyrannical king.

Conclusion

In July 1645, John Winthrop stood before the Massachusetts General Court and delivered an eloquent speech on the subject of liberty. He divided liberty into two categories. There was a type in which people could do as they wished, and there was a civil liberty that obliged people to do good. Throughout Winthrop's time as governor and leader in the Bay Colony he sought to promote and spread his zeal for civil liberty. He desired to see a land freely governed by selfless

---

47. Thomas James to John Winthrop, c. 1639, in *Winthrop Papers*, 4:89–90.

48. Francis Williams to John Winthrop, May 9, 1643, in *Winthrop Papers*, 4:375–76.

49. Mather, *Magnalia*, 1:131.

people for the good of prompting justice and the general welfare. One such selfless act performed under his leadership was the passing of laws that required the education of all children and advocated support for teachers from public funds. Although it was not easy, Winthrop promoted his views of government and society for the purpose of creating a shining beacon for all the world to follow and imitate. Would Winthrop say that this has been achieved? Probably not to the degree he desired, but nonetheless his dream lives on in the hearts of all those who promote and fight for the cause of liberty.

JOHN COTTON

While the *Griffin* weighed anchor at the Downs, two shadowy figures boarded the ship headed for Boston, Massachusetts. The ship had previously been searched from bow to stern by Archbishop Laud's men while at the Isle of Wight, but they did not find whom they were looking for. However, just prior to setting sail across the Atlantic, the captain agreed to make one more stop to pick up a few stray passengers. With their families safely aboard, John Cotton and Thomas Hooker kept themselves hidden until the voyage was under way. They would later be regarded by some as "the Luther and Melanchthon of New-England,"[1] but at that moment, they were merely tired men being led by the Lord to a new harvest field.

Early Life and Training

John Cotton was born in Derby, England, on December 4, 1585, to Rowland Cotton, "a lawyer of strenuous religious life," and Mary Hurlbert, "a devotedly Christian mother."[2] After receiving his early education at Derby School under the tutelage of Richard Johnson, a minister of the Church of England, Cotton was enrolled at Trinity

---

1. Quote taken from the biographical sketch by Thomas Prince in Thomas Hooker, *The Poor Doubting Christian Drawn to Christ* (1629; repr., Grand Rapids: Baker, 1981), 17.

2. Williston Walker, *Ten New England Leaders* (New York: Silver, Burdett, and Co., 1901), 54–55.

College, Cambridge, in 1598. Despite being a hard-working lawyer, Rowland Cotton did not earn a substantial income from his practice, often taking on pro bono cases for those who could ill afford legal services. Due to the family's financial situation, young Cotton performed menial tasks of service to help pay his way, even sharing a bed with another student in the dormitory.[3]

However, Cotton worked hard and soon matriculated to Emmanuel College in 1605. Largely through the influence of William Perkins (1558–1602), Cambridge had become a distinctly Puritan institution.[4] A diligent student, Cotton received a robust education that included logic, rhetoric, theology, history, and the Latin, Greek, and Hebrew languages. At Emmanuel College, he became head lecturer, dean, and catechist, tutoring many younger students.[5] Unexpectedly, Rowland Cotton's law practice began to pick up and he was better able to pay the college tuition. Later on, John Cotton reflected on the blessed providence of the Lord, rejoicing to declare, "God kept me at the University!"[6]

Conversion to Christ

During his studies at Cambridge, Cotton was also confronted with the timeless truths of the gospel through the greatest Puritan preachers of the day.[7] However, it was the preaching of William Perkins that stirred in Cotton a sense of discontent and despair. In fact, he was so averse to God that when Cotton heard the bell

---

3. Larzer Ziff, *The Career of John Cotton* (Princeton, N.J.: Princeton University Press, 1962), 17.

4. Glenda Faye Mathes and Joel R. Beeke, *Puritan Heroes* (Grand Rapids: Reformation Heritage Books, 2018), 22.

5. Alexander Young, "Samuel Whiting's Life of John Cotton," in *Chronicles of the First Planters of the Colony of Massachusetts Bay, from 1623 to 1636* (1846; repr., Boston: New England Historic Genealogical Society, 2016), 421.

6. Young, "Life of John Cotton," 420.

7. The following two sections are adapted from an article by Nate Pickowicz, "The Two Conversions of John Cotton," *TableTalk*, September 2, 2019.

toll for Perkins's funeral, he was "secretly glad in his heart, that he would now be rid of him who had…laid siege to and beleaguer'd his heart."[8]

However, the Lord would not allow young Cotton to evade His sovereign grasp. He soon sat under the tutelage of a preacher named Richard Sibbes (1577–1635). For three years, he was plagued with spiritual depression, and "the arrows of these convictions did stick so fast upon him."[9] With constant care and admonition, Sibbes gently ministered to Cotton, although in a different way than that of the powerful Perkins. Known as a "physician of the soul,"[10] the good doctor pleaded with his pupil to respond to the gospel call. And then, in 1612, Cotton heard Sibbes preach on the doctrine of regeneration. Suddenly, "all his false hopes and grounds now failed him" as he "look[ed] unto Christ for healing" and was saved.[11]

Cotton Adopts the "Plain Style" of Preaching
Popular English preaching was known for its erudition and dramatic flair. Sermons were characteristically loaded with abstract philosophical quotes, clever rhetoric, and flashy delivery. The goal was to astound and entertain the audience rather than convict or edify them. While at Cambridge, Cotton had risen to fame after preaching the funeral sermon of Dr. Robert Some (1542–1609). In vogue with other Cambridge students, his sermons were routinely "pompous harangues, stuffed with a huge mass of learning and soaring conceits."[12] The funeral sermon was no exception. John Norton records that it was "so accurately performed, in respect of invention, elegancy, purity of style, ornaments of rhetoric, elocution, and oratorious beauty of the whole, as that he was thenceforth looked at as

---

8. John Norton, *Memoir of John Cotton* (Boston: Perkins & Marvin, 1834), 29.

9. Cotton Mather, *Magnalia Christi Americana* (1702; repr., Edinburgh: Banner of Truth, 1979), 1:255.

10. Ziff, *Career of John Cotton*, 31.

11. Norton, *Memoir*, 30.

12. A. W. M'Clure, *The Life of John Cotton* (Boston: Massachusetts Sabbath School Society, 1846), 16–17.

another *Xenophon*, or *Musa Attica*, throughout the University."[13] By contrast, however, both Perkins and Sibbes were not flashy preachers yet wielded significant power through their exposition of the Scriptures. Having been converted through such preaching, Cotton quickly became convinced of the necessity of the "plain style."

While biblical preaching is as old as the Old Testament prophets, the "plain style" was popularized in England by men like William Perkins. In his influential book *The Art of Prophesying*, Perkins notes that, contrary to the popular views of Cotton's day, "Scripture is the exclusive subject of preaching, the only field in which the preacher is to labour."[14] In short, the task of the preacher is to clearly communicate the truths of Scripture. As a primary discipline, he adds, "Interpretation is the opening up of the words and statements of Scripture in order to bring out its single, full and natural sense."[15] The preacher is not the star of the show; he is merely a mouthpiece used of God to communicate to His people.

The true test of Cotton's resolve came in his last year at Emmanuel College. His biographer, Larzer Ziff, records, "He was now convinced that the plain style was the saving style, and he realized that he must abandon his elegant oratory."[16] He was scheduled to preach at St. Marie's Church in Cambridge to a full house of students and professors, all eager to hear the gifted young preacher. However, to their dismay, Cotton stood up and delivered a sermon on the doctrine of repentance in the "plain style," full of doctrines, reasons, and uses. The room filled with loud groans as listeners pulled their caps over their ears in disapproval. Cotton finished his sermon and quietly returned to his room. After a few minutes, he heard a knock on the door. To his surprise, the already eminent Puritan John Preston (1587–1628), fellow at Queen's College, had arrived secretly and confessed his utter despair and need for salvation. So powerfully had

---

13. Norton, *Memoir*, 30.
14. William Perkins, *The Art of Prophesying* (1606; repr., Edinburgh: Banner of Truth, 1996), 9.
15. Perkins, *Art of Prophesying*, 26.
16. Ziff, *Career of John Cotton*, 32.

God spoken "effectually unto his heart by that sermon,"[17] that he was "pierced to the heart" and converted.

Ministry in Boston, Lincolnshire

After leaving Emmanuel College, Cotton was called to his first pastorate at the beautiful St. Botolph's Church in Boston, Lincolnshire, on June 24, 1612. He briefly returned to Cambridge to receive his much desired bachelor of divinity degree—an eminently prestigious Puritan accomplishment. However, his greatest acquisition his first year was his lovely wife, Elizabeth Horrocks. In marrying Elizabeth, he later wrote that he "received that assurance of God's love unto his own soul," and expressing his thankfulness to God, he joyfully declared, "God made that day, a day of double marriage to me!"[18]

His ministry at St. Botolph's was a vibrant one, full of preaching, writing, and training. The city of Boston was coming to be well known for its "feast of preaching," and Cotton quickly rose to fame for his gifted exposition.[19] Of his training efforts, his friend Samuel Whiting noted, "He took much pains in private, and read to sundry young scholars that were in his house, and some that came out of Germany, and he his house full of auditors."[20] Additionally, Cotton sustained a friendship with John Preston, whereby Preston would often send his students to live with Cotton as interns. In time, there arose a proverb of sorts: "That Mr. Cotton was Dr. Preston's seasoning vessel."[21]

With the English Reformation still in full swing, it did not take long before theological controversy arose. When the students of Jacobus Arminius (1560–1609) sought to refute the core doctrines of the Reformation as systematized by John Calvin (1509–1564) and Theodore Beza (1519–1605), Arminian factions began sprouting up

17. Norton, *Memoir*, 32.
18. Mather, *Magnalia*, 1:258.
19. Ziff, *Career of John Cotton*, 41.
20. As cited in Young, "Samuel Whiting's Life of John Cotton," 424–25.
21. Mather, *Magnalia*, 1:260.

all over Europe, even in Cotton's Boston harvest field. Cotton listened intently until he learned all of their arguments, then set out to systematically dismantle the Arminian position. He later wrote, "I began publicly to preach, and in private meetings to defend, the doctrine of God's eternal election before all foresight of good or evil in the creature; and the redemption (ex gratia) only of the elect; the effectual vocation of the sinner by irresistible grace, without respect of the preparations of free will; and the impossibility of the fall of a sincere believer either totally or finally from a state of grace."[22] Due to his efforts, not only did the local party of Arminianism in Lincolnshire diminish, but for the rest of his ministry, Cotton was an ardent champion of Calvinism.

By 1615, Cotton became fully convinced of the necessity of nonconformity. He observed a number of nonreformed practices in the Church of England and could not square them with the truth of Scripture. Of all his concerns, two things stood out. He notes, "First, that in *England* I fell off but from some of the Ceremonies…. The significancy and efficacy put upon them in the Preface to the Book of Common-Prayer… The second was the limitation of Church-power, (even of the highest Apostolical Commission) to the observation of the Commandments of Christ."[23]

Through examining the Scriptures, Cotton understood that there was more to Christianity than a mere outward identification with a visible church. The true church of Jesus Christ comprised the elect of God, those with a credible profession of faith who lived a life of visible godliness. As a nonconformist, Cotton refused to wear vestments, make the sign of the cross, or pray strictly from the Book of Common Prayer.[24] Before long, however, Cotton took radical

---

22. Norton, *Memoir*, 97.

23. John Cotton, "The Way of Congregational Churches Cleared," in *John Cotton on the Churches of New England*, ed. Larzer Ziff (Cambridge, Mass.: Belknap Press, 1968), 196–97.

24. Charles E. Hambrick-Stowe, "Christ the Fountain of Life by John Cotton (1584–1652)," in *The Devoted Life: An Invitation to the Puritan Classics*, ed. Kelly M. Kapic and Randall C. Gleason (Downers Grove, Ill.: InterVarsity Press, 2004), 70.

and decisive action within his own church, effectively dividing the congregation into two groups: the "lilies" and the "thorns"—imagery taken from the Song of Solomon. This created "a congregation within a congregation."[25] Cotton later wrote, "We entered into a covenant with the Lord, and one with another, to follow after the Lord in the purity of his worship."[26] While he was opposed to strict separation as "schismatic," Cotton was emphatic in his belief that true Christians could not in good conscience conform to the standards set by the Church of England.

With the increasing pressure to conform coming from the leaders of the Church of England, nonconformist ministers were either being arrested and jailed or fleeing to places like Holland. However, Cotton was able to escape censure, living and ministering with relative freedom for nearly two decades. In that time, both he and his wife, Elizabeth, fell sick with malaria. She would eventually succumb to the illness. On April 6, 1632, Cotton married the widow Sarah Hawkridge Story, who would eventually give him the children he never had in eighteen years with Elizabeth.

When he was summoned by Archbishop William Laud to appear in High Commission Court in 1632, Cotton resigned from his pastorate and went into hiding with his new wife, Sarah, and her daughter. After John escaped to London, two of his friends, Thomas Goodwin and John Davenport, met him privately to convince him to conform to the Church of England's religious standards. In the course of their conversation, however, it was Cotton who persuaded Goodwin and Davenport to embrace nonconformity. With Archbishop Laud's men on the hunt, Cotton weighed his options. At that time, Thomas Hooker, who had recently returned from exile in Holland, met up with Cotton in London to discuss the possibility of fleeing to New England. It soon became clear that their options were to either leave or be arrested; Cotton noted that "we could offer a much clearer and fuller witness in another land than in the

---

25. Ziff, *Career of John Cotton*, 49.
26. Cotton, "Way of Congregational Churches Cleared," 198.

wretched and loathsome prisons of London."[27] On May 7, 1633, John Cotton resigned his pastorate at St. Botolph's in Boston, Lincolnshire, and secretly boarded a ship headed for another Boston.

Migration to Boston, Massachusetts, and Pastoral Calling

When the *Griffin* finally docked in Boston Harbor on September 4, 1633, the passengers had been at sea for eight weeks. On their voyage, they had been blessed by the preaching labors of three ministers aboard: Thomas Hooker, Samuel Stone, and John Cotton. Unknown to the men at the time, the residents of Massachusetts Bay had been fervently praying for the Lord to send them faithful ministers. At the arrival of the *Griffin*, the people joyfully declared that "the God of heaven had supplied them, with what would in some sort answer their three great necessities, *Cotton* for their *clothing, Hooker* for their *fishing*, and *Stone* for their *building*."[28]

Four days after arriving, John and Sarah Cotton were admitted to membership at the First Church of Boston, where they promptly baptized their son who had been born at sea. Cotton himself named the child Seaborn, a token of thanksgiving to God for giving them safe passage to New England. Once settled, several churches expressed interest in calling them as their pastor, but the town council met in Boston and, on October 10, voted to call John Cotton as the teacher of the First Church, along with John Wilson (c. 1588–1667) as minister. Of his second Boston pastorate, historian Williston Walker notes, "Here his ministry had much the same quality as in the home land. The same indefatigable labor in preaching and in the exposition of Scripture, the same affectionate reverence from his congregation, the same capacity to mold strong

---

27. Cited in Francis J. Bremer, *The Puritan Experiment: New England Society from Bradford to Edwards*, rev. ed. (Hanover, N.H.: University Press of New England, 1995), 38.

28. Mather, *Magnalia*, 1:265.

men to his way of thinking, that had marked his career in old Boston, were his in added degree."[29]

Preaching Ministry

While still in Lincolnshire, Cotton committed himself to the exposition of the Scriptures, preaching thousands of sermons. According to John Norton, he preached on Thursday and Friday mornings and Saturday afternoons in addition to the Lord's Day.[30] Once in Massachusetts, he preached systematically through much of the Old Testament and one and a half times through the New Testament. Because of their popularity overseas, he also retained the Thursday lectures in which he worked back through several New Testament books as well as the whole "body of divinity in a cathechistical way."[31]

However, Cotton was not a dry or stoic teacher. From his earliest days at Cambridge, he had made a name for himself as a powerful preacher. Some have even called him "one of the greatest, if not the greatest Puritan preacher in England"[32] and, certainly, "the greatest preacher in New England."[33] One of his contemporaries, John Wilson, testified, "Mr. Cotton preaches with such authority, demonstration, and life that, methinks, when he preaches out of any prophet or apostle I hear not him; I hear that very prophet and apostle. Yea, I hear the Lord Jesus Christ speaking in my heart."[34]

As a preacher, Cotton was plain and perspicuous, not given to showiness or erudition. On his simplicity, he would say, "If I preach more scholastically, then only the learned, and not the unlearned, can so understand as to profit by me; but if I preach plainly, then both the learned and unlearned will understand me, and so I shall

29. Walker, *Ten New England Leaders*, 70.
30. Norton, *Memoir*, 37–38.
31. The Puritans referred to their systematic studies of theology as "body of divinity." Norton records that while in England, Cotton instructed his church through the "body of divinity" three times. *Memoir*, 37.
32. Ziff, *Career of John Cotton*, 105.
33. Everett Emerson, *John Cotton*, rev. ed. (Boston: Twayne, 1990), 1.
34. Cited in Mather, *Magnalia*, 1:275.

profit all."[35] Yet through Cotton's preaching, people by the thousands came to hear Jesus Christ expounded clearly and powerfully. John Winthrop even noted that "more were converted and added to that church [Cotton's] than to all the other churches in the Bay."[36] However, his true power did not rest in his personality or abilities, but in his faithful exposition of Scripture and the doctrines of grace.

Trials and Controversies

Despite the vast fruitfulness of his labors in New England, Cotton found himself embroiled in several controversies. The first major controversy in his ministry pertained to the events surrounding the Antinomian Controversy. After he departed from England in 1633, Cotton was followed to New England by several church families, including William and Anne Hutchinson. As soon as they settled in Boston, Anne began to serve the town as a midwife. Beyond her caring capacities, she was also highly intelligent and theologically astute, no doubt due to years of sitting under John Cotton's teaching. Soon she began to host Bible studies in her home, herself leading upward of sixty men and women. Word began to travel that Anne had been making disparaging remarks about all the New England ministers, claiming they were preaching a works-based gospel—with the exception of her own pastor, John Cotton, and her brother-in-law, John Wheelwright, who was also a minister.

In October 1636 the General Court began to inquire about Hutchinson's teachings, identifying nearly eighty instances of questionable doctrines. However, the most damning of her views pertained to "an extreme assertion of personal indwelling of the Holy Spirit in the believer, that divine Person becoming so one with him as to render all other proof of sanctification than a consciousness of this indwelling not merely unnecessary but vain."[37] Following this line of thinking, the believer would not need to manifest any outward

---

35. M'Clure, *Life of John Cotton*, 273–74.
36. Cited in Emerson, *John Cotton*, 79.
37. Walker, *Ten New England Leaders*, 76.

fruit of sanctification or practical obedience to Christ. Before too long, the charge of antinomianism[38] began flying around. Upon further examination, Cotton was questioned vigorously about his own teaching and whether he himself had taught antinomianism. At first, Cotton defended Hutchinson, but it quickly became apparent that she was teaching doctrines divergent from orthodoxy. In a plea for temperance, Cotton was nearly able to persuade the court to soften their stance on Hutchinson, when suddenly she spoke out and claimed to be receiving direct revelation from God in the midst of the proceedings. With that, the court had all they needed to convict her of heresy. She was eventually banished from the colony in 1637 and was killed in an Indian massacre in 1642.

John Cotton was deeply affected by the Hutchinson trial. He had cared for the Hutchinson family and desired to believe the best about Anne. Yet once he realized that he had been abused and "made [her] *stalking horse*,"[39] he spent a great deal of time in introspection, rehearsing the errors in order to better understand how someone so devout could go so wrong. The Antinomian Controversy, while not destroying Cotton, tarnished his reputation for a time.

A second major challenge surrounded the person of Roger Williams (c. 1603–1683). Arriving in the New World in February 1631, Williams and his wife, Mary, first settled in Boston. Already a respected Puritan minister, he was temporarily offered John Wilson's pastorate while he traveled to England to fetch his wife, but Williams declined. As a strict Separatist, he believed the Boston church to be compromised because they did not withhold fellowship with members of the Church of England, which he believed had become corrupt. He soon left Boston for Salem, followed by Plymouth, where he ministered for two years. However, Williams grew increasingly intolerant of the New England churches' lack of separation from unregenerate persons.

---

38. Essentially, anti-law, rebellion, disobedience to the commands of God.
39. Norton, *Memoir*, 105.

Believing the church was not pure enough, Williams soon left Plymouth to return to Salem. By this time, many in the colonies believed him to be sowing seeds of discord. In October 1635 he was summoned before the General Court of Massachusetts to defend his charge that the churches of New England were violating the first four of the Ten Commandments by not separating from perceived nonbelievers. In the end, he was convicted of sedition and set to be banished the following spring. However, Williams fled to what is now Rhode Island in January 1636. At that point, John Cotton entered the debate, effectively functioning as spiritual spokesman for the New England churches. For the next several years, Cotton and Williams began a protracted exchange of correspondence over the issue of separation of the church from state affairs. After a series of letters between the two men, Williams published a reply to Cotton titled *The Bloudy Tenent of Persecution, for Cause of Conscience, Discussed* (1644). Cotton replied with *The Bloudy Tenent, Washed and Made White in the Bloud of the Lambe* (1647). Finally, in 1652, Williams published an extensive response titled *The Bloudy Tenent Yet More Bloudy by Mr. Cottons Endeavour to Wash It White in the Bloud of the Lambe*, but Cotton passed away before he could reply. While Cotton had devoted his life to the "New England Way," a system of church power over all areas of life, Williams's strict separation of church and state would eventually triumph in the court of popular American practice.

The Congregational Way
Of all the things he is known for in the New World, John Cotton is best known for his advocacy for Congregationalism. In fact, he was the first pastor to use the term *Congregational* as descriptive of his understanding of biblical ecclesiology.[40] When giving his reasons for nonconformity, Cotton noted the issue of church power. Essentially, the question is, Who governs the church? When King Henry VIII broke from the Roman Catholic Church, he still desired to retain

---

40. Emerson, *John Cotton*, 35.

authority as the supreme leader of the Church of England. When Queen Elizabeth ascended the throne, despite all her compromises, she still desired to see the hierarchy of authority culminate at the highest levels of church leadership. However, many nonconforming Puritans believed the Scriptures to teach that Christ gave the power to govern the church to the churches themselves, not to presbyteries.

While Cotton's view of local church government existed in seed form back in England, within a year of landing in New England he took to writing a defense titled *The True Constitution of a Particular Visible Church, Proved by Scripture* (1635). The short work functioned more as a manual for church order, outlining the nature of the true church, the leadership of elders and deacons, covenanted church membership, ordinances, church discipline, and so on. This teaching became the baseline of what came to be known as the "New England Way." Cotton's teaching was seen as radical, and he answered for it in several letters to key church leaders abroad.

By the early 1640s, Cotton penned a fuller description of Congregationalism in *The Way of the Churches of Christ in New-England*, but when it was later published against his wishes, he complained that it did not fully reflect his views. As the debate over Congregationalism raged in England, three New England leaders—John Davenport, Thomas Hooker, and John Cotton—were contacted in 1642 and invited to join the upcoming Westminster Assembly in order to present and defend their ecclesiology. Knowing the support for Congregationalism would be poorly represented, all three men declined the invitation. Hooker reportedly stated it would be an insufficient call for them to go three thousand miles to agree with three men.[41] However, several leading Congregationalists sent written works to be presented to the assembly, the most important of which was John Cotton's *The Keys of the Kingdom of Heaven* (1644).

In *The Keys* Cotton presents the argument that when Jesus Christ told Peter that He would "give [them] the keys of the kingdom of

---

41. Cited in John Winthrop, *Winthrop's Journal, "History of New England," 1630–1649*, ed. James Kendall Hosmer (New York: Charles Scribner's Sons, 1908), 2:71.

heaven" (Matt. 16:19), He was giving them not only to Peter but to
all the apostles and thereby to all the church. As to the nature of "the
keys," Cotton notes, "The keys of the kingdom are the ordinances
which Christ hath instituted, to be administered in his church; as
the preaching of the word, (which is the opening and applying of
it) also the administering of the seals and censures: for by the opening and applying of these, both the gates of the church here, and of
heaven hereafter, are opened or shut to the sons of men."[42]

So persuasive was the book that some English ministers were
won over to Congregationalism, including the great John Owen.
On the writing of *The Keys*, Williston Walker remarks that it "was
looked upon on both sides of the Atlantic as the most authoritative
exposition of Congregationalism set forth by an individual writer."[43]

However, Cotton received intense backlash from *The Keys* by
those who claimed it smacked of "Brownism"—a movement of strict
separation and church democracy. But Cotton saw Congregationalism as a middle way between Presbyterianism and Brownism. In
answering key questions about his view, he then wrote *The Way of
Congregational Churches Cleared* (1648), later followed by *Of the Holi-
nesse of Church Members* (1650). However, the full systemization and
official declaration of the Congregational form of church government came in 1648 with the adopting of the Cambridge Platform.
Written in response to criticism by the Presbyterians, the platform
acted as a definitive exposition and defense of Congregationalism in
New England. While presented and endorsed by many ministers and
magistrates, Cotton was undoubtedly the architect behind "the most
important monument of early New England Congregationalism."[44]

---

42. John Cotton, *The Keys of the Kingdom of Heaven*, in *John Cotton on the Churches
of New England*, ed. Larzer Ziff (Cambridge, Mass.: Belknap Press, 1968), 88.

43. Walker, *Ten New England Leaders*, 92.

44. Williston Walker, *Creeds of Congregationalism*, cited in Emerson, *John Cotton*,
58.

His Character, Godliness, and Devotion

By all accounts, Cotton was a "devout, grace-oriented man of God."[45]
Even his opponents did not dare to bring accusations against his
character. Samuel Whiting notes, "He was of admirable candor, of
unparalleled meekness, of rare wisdom, very loving even to those
that differed in judgment from him."[46] John Flavel recounted the
story of a drunk man who confronted Mr. Cotton in the street, seeking to sport for his companions, and whispered in his ear, "Thou art
an old fool." Without missing a beat, Cotton replied, "I confess I
am so;—the Lord make both me and thee wiser than we are—even
wise unto salvation."[47] Whether before menaces, church members, or
magistrates, Cotton maintained a gentle godliness, even at the cost
of his own dignity. He writes, "Angry men have an advantage above
me; the people dare not set themselves against such men, because
they know it won't be born; but some care not what they say or do
about me, because they know I won't be angry with them again."[48]

However, his humility and kindness ingratiated himself toward
others. His ministry was ever giving and selfless. His contemporary
John Norton remarked, "He was a man of ingenuous and pious
candor, rejoicing (as opportunity served) to take notice of, and testi-
fie unto, the gifts of God in his brethren, thereby drawing the hearts
of them to him, and of others to them, both to their encouragement, and the edification of many."[49]

He was the same man at home as he was in the church. According to his grandson, Cotton Mather, he maintained a well-ordered
family. He instructed and catechized his children, offering correction
and discipline as well as prayers and singing.[50] Regarding his fatherly
dealings with his children, "In case of sin committed by child or
servant, he would call them aside privately (the matter so requiring),

---

45. Emerson, *John Cotton*, 4.
46. Young, "Life of John Cotton," 425.
47. Recorded in Norton, *Memoir*, 104.
48. Mather, *Magnalia*, 1:276.
49. Norton, *Memoir*, 69.
50. Mather, *Magnalia*, 1:277–78.

lay the Scripture before them, causing them to read that which bare witness against such offence; seldom or never correcting in anger, that the dispensation of godly discipline might not be impured, or become less effectual, through the intermixing of humane passion."[51]

Concerning hospitality toward visitors, "his heart and doors were open to receive, as all that feared God, so especially godly ministers, which he most courteously entertained, and many other strangers besides."[52] As for his personal time with the Lord, Mather notes, "He...read constantly a portion of the Scripture alone, and he prayed over what he read: prayed I say; for he was very much in prayer, a very man of prayer; he would rarely sit down to study, without prayer over it, referring to the presence of God accompanying what he did."[53]

In addition to his studies in Scripture, Cotton was a devoted reader. While he regularly engaged with the writings of William Perkins, Richard Sibbes, William Ames, and others, Cotton's primary theological influence was John Calvin. Commenting on the merit of his writings, Cotton noted, "I have read the Fathers, and the schoolmen, and Calvin too; but I find that he that has Calvin, has them all." And being asked why, in his later years, he indulged nocturnal studies more than formerly, he replied, "Because I love to sweeten my mouth with a piece of Calvin, before I sleep."[54]

Writing Contributions

John Cotton was a voracious reader and diligent student. As a result, he was also a prolific writer. Every published work had a specific purpose—to teach, instruct, defend, and encourage. Samuel Whiting notes "how useful he was...to magistrates, ministers, people, in public, in private, in preachings, counsels, dissolving hard knots and answering difficult questions, all knew that knew the grace of God

---

51. Norton, *Memoir*, 55.
52. Young, "Life of John Cotton," 427.
53. Mather, *Magnalia*, 1:278.
54. Recorded in Norton, *Memoir*, 105–6.

so evidently manifested in him."[55] Cotton ever lived and worked to edify the church of Jesus Christ.

Including his several works on Congregationalism, Cotton published more than forty titles in his lifetime. Much of Cotton's writing was born out of his preaching and polemical ministry. His early sermons at St. Botolph's Church were published into commentaries on Song of Solomon, Ecclesiastes, and 1 John. Additionally, several of his sermons from 1 John 5:12 were compiled into a book titled *Christ the Fountaine of Life* (1651), which Charles Hambrick-Stowe notes "expresses Puritanism's evangelical and pastoral impulses as plainly as any of the widely used devotional manuals published in London and Boston during the seventeenth century."[56]

As a Reformed minister devoted to the doctrines of grace, Cotton offered several theological works, such as *Gods Mercie Mixed with His Justice* (1641), *The Way of Life* (1641), *The Covenant of Gods Free Grace* (1645), *The Grounds and Ends of the Baptisme of the Children of the Faithfull* (1647), and *A Treatise of the Covenant of Grace* (1659). However, Cotton's most popular book was a catechism written for children, *Milk for Babes. Drawn Out of the Breasts of Both Testaments. Chiefly, for the Spirituall Nourishment of Boston Babes in Either England: But May Be of Like Use for Any Children* (1646). The catechism went through nine printings in the seventeenth century alone and was widely used to catechize American children for nearly one hundred and fifty years.

Death and Legacy

We are told that John Cotton was of "a clear, fair, sanguine complexion...rather low than tall, and rather fat than lean; but of a becoming mediocrity."[57] This is hardly the stuff of legend. However, Norton adds, "In his countenance, there was an inexpressible majesty, which

---

55. Young, "Life of John Cotton," 429.
56. Hambrick-Stowe, "Christ the Fountain of Life," 78.
57. Norton, *Memoir*, 107.

commanded reverence from all that approached him."[58] From his earliest years at Cambridge up to the final hours of his life, Cotton was loved and respected, cherished and admired.

In his last months, he pulled back from many of his public duties, consigning himself to his study. However, his desire to encourage young ministers compelled him to accept an invitation to preach to the students of Harvard in November 1652. While crossing the Charles River in Boston, he caught a severe cold that would eventually kill him. He struggled through his sermons from 2 Timothy, with a concluding message from John 1:14, and headed for home.

Confined to his bed for much of December, many of his friends and congregants visited him to bid farewell. His dear friend, John Wilson, prayed "unto God that he would lift up the light of his countenance upon him, and shed his love into his soul," to which Cotton "presently answered him in these words: *He hath done it already, brother.*"[59] With that, John Cotton passed into glory on December 23, 1652. He left behind his wife, Sarah, and four children; two others predeceased him. The widowed Sarah Cotton later married Richard Mather, while one of his daughters, Maria, went on to marry Increase Mather, the father of Cotton Mather.

Twice the departure of John Cotton left a gaping hole, once in England and again in New England. John Norton immortalizes him with these words: "Let it suffice to be said of Mr. *Cotton*, that he was a famous light in his generation, a glory to both *Englands*, and such an one, in whom was so much of what is desireable in man, as is rarely to be seen in one person."[60] Yet his true greatness is found in his devotion to Jesus Christ, faithfulness to the Scriptures, and love for the people of God.

---

58. Norton, *Memoir*, 107.
59. Norton, *Memoir*, 83.
60. Norton, *Memoir*, 76.

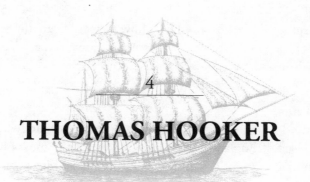

THOMAS HOOKER

Eighteen days before his death, the frail and aging Thomas Hooker preached from the pulpit of Windsor, Connecticut. He chose for his text Romans 1:18, "For the wrath of God is revealed from heaven against all ungodliness." His doctrine, as any good Puritan sermon states, was "that there be stirrings of truth in the hearts of all men naturally, and carnal men labor to beat them down." He went on to urge the congregation, "Wonder therefore at the goodness of God to man fallen, that he hath not left him wholly in darkness, without any means to help him, but hath left him some recoilings of heart to recover him. So long as a prince leaves his ambassador in another country, it is a sign he maintains peace with them, but if he call him home, they must expect war."[1]

Hooker intended God's "ambassador" here to be man's conscience as it drives him to truth. However, in other sermons, Hooker often referred to "God's ambassador" as being the preacher in his pulpit proclaiming the truth of God's Word to those unconverted.

From the moment Thomas Hooker stepped onto the gangplank in Boston in 1633, he was determined to be God's ambassador. He was an ambassador of truth to the church God would give him charge of in a new and strange world. He did not know where he

---

1. Thomas Hooker, "Notes of Mr. Hooker's Sermon. From Deacon Matthew Grant's MSS Notes," transcribed by J. Hammond Trumbull, in George Leon Walker, *History of the First Church in Hartford, 1633–1883* (Hartford, Conn., 1884), 429–30.

would settle, where he would live, how he would care for his family, or even if he would survive in this new colony, but he was assured of one thing—he was God's ambassador.

Early Life

Few would have thought the son of an overseer of landed property in the heart of England would become one of the most prominent Puritan divines of his day and one of the chief architects of the New World. Thomas Hooker was born in July 1586 into the home of a father by the same name. No records show the exact dates of his birth, baptism, or even the name of his mother. However, enough church records remain to indicate that much of his immediate and extended family were Puritan sympathizers.[2]

Marfield (possibly Markfield or Marefield), Hooker's boyhood home, was not much more than a small English village with very little day-to-day activity. The central hub of social activity was the nearby village of Tilton, with its church atop a hill that could be seen for the mile-and-a-half journey the Hooker family traveled every Lord's Day. A late nineteenth-century visitor to Tilton admired, "The picturesque old church of mottled gray on Tilton hill-top, compassed round by the dead of the different precincts of the parish; the wide prospect of alternating woodland and open fields and spire-surmounted hills toward every compass-point... and the little Marfield hamlet embowered in trees down in the valley...approached through rustic gates and stiles which the visitor opens or climbs as he descends through the sweet green fields."[3]

It is probable the Hooker children made the trip to Tilton again on Sunday evening to receive catechetical instruction by the church's rector. The same man may have also served as their first educational instructor, teaching them the English alphabet and tutoring them in other necessary lessons before they entered

---

2. George Leon Walker, *Thomas Hooker: Preacher, Founder, Democrat* (New York: Dodd, 1891), 3–4.

3. Walker, *Thomas Hooker*, 3.

a more formal educational setting.[4] A disciplined education would have been given the foremost attention, despite the many fields and glens the Hooker children would have rather explored. Thomas was instructed in penmanship with pen and ink, how to read English prose, and a rudimentary knowledge of Latin, all before entering grammar school. When thoroughly prepared, Thomas entered the Dixie Grammar School at Market Bosworth, about twenty-five miles west of his home village. Although founded in 1320, the Dixie Grammar School had been a well-known center for childhood education since it was refounded in 1601.

Thomas would have immediately been thrown into the careful tutelage of English and Latin grammars. During the seventeenth century, Latin served as a gateway to all learning and would be a close companion for the rest of Thomas's life. He would have digested the Latin classics of Cicero, Terence, Virgil, Ovid, Sallust, and Horace while also learning to speak and translate Latin with his fellow classmates.[5] His familiarity with Latin would have been so natural that even at this early intellectual stage he would have begun to develop his own style of Latin prose. Biographer Frank Shuffelton notes, "The end of all of this practice was to produce a student able to write readily and elegantly—elegance exemplified by Cicero and other select writers—and to organize his thoughts on any subject into the classical patterns."[6] In addition to being conversant in Latin, Thomas was introduced to Greek, possibly Hebrew, mathematics, and logic during his final years at Dixie. J. Howard Brown offers a vivid window into the life of a young grammar student: "School was kept six days a week, beginning at six in the morning and continuing until five or six in the afternoon; there was an hour off in the morning for breakfast and perhaps three for dinner. Discipline was maintained with a firm hand; the traditional image of the schoolmaster always showed him with his birch

4. Frank Shuffelton, *Thomas Hooker, 1586–1647* (Princeton, N.J.: Princeton University Press, 1977), 7.
5. Shuffelton, *Hooker*, 8.
6. Shuffelton, *Hooker*, 8–9.

and rod, the picture of schoolrooms of this time usually featured these implements in prominent display."[7]

In addition to being well versed in the classics of ancient Rome and Greece, grammar students were well instructed in the Christian religion, with particular emphasis on reading the New Testament and Psalms in English. Students were expected to attend Lord's Day services at Market Bosworth and were ordered to take copious notes of the sermon.

Thomas completed his educational regime at the Dixie Grammar School around the age of sixteen and was thoroughly prepared to enter university. In 1604 he matriculated at Queen's College, Cambridge, when he was almost eighteen and recorded his residence as Birstall, Leicestershire.[8] It is unknown why Thomas did not immediately enter university following the completion of grammar school. He entered Queen's College as a sizar, or an undergraduate student who receives some form of assistance such as lower fees, paid lodging, or meals during their time as a student in exchange for doing a defined job on campus. But after only a few months in Queen's College, Thomas migrated to Emmanuel College and automatically began studying rhetoric, which acted as a bridge between grammar school and university. Rhetoric, or the art of speaking well, proved invaluable to Thomas when he entered ministry and began composing public sermons. In addition to rhetoric, Thomas studied logic during his second year at Emmanuel, which shaped his mind and tongue to form arguments that would effectually convince his hearers.[9] Among others, these disciplines were essential in shaping him for a life in the pulpit.

In 1608 Thomas received his BA from Emmanuel College and in 1609 entered his graduate career at Emmanuel as a Dixie fellow. His graduate studies shifted from the classics to the discipline of theology. His participation in the fellowship of Emmanuel meant

---

7. J. Howard Brown, *Elizabethan Schooldays* (Oxford: Blackwell, 1933), 86, 108.

8. John Venn and John Archibald Venn, *Alumni Cantabrigienses*, part 1 (Cambridge: Cambridge University Press, 1922), 2:403.

9. Shuffelton, *Hooker*, 15.

that he took an active role in the religious life of the university by serving as a catechist and lecturer. After three years of theological instruction, Thomas received his MA in 1611. However, this educational achievement does not compare with the other life-altering event that took place during this same year—his conversion. This "effectual calling and implantation into Christ," as he later called it, determined his future trajectory.[10]

The doctrines that Thomas heard argued from the pulpit all of his life would have certainly been Augustinian and Calvinistic. However, it was not until his studies at Emmanuel that he began to fully grasp the meaning of these theological schools and adopt them as his own regarding the divine gift of saving grace in Jesus Christ. Once Thomas resolved to surrender his life to one of gospel ministry, the matter of his own salvation became crucial in his heart and mind. The question regarding the certainty of his salvation began to initiate a period of terrible anxiety and doubt.[11] The detailed context of Thomas's conversion to Christ are still unknown. New England divine Cotton Mather recorded, "It pleased the spirit of God very powerfully to break into the soul of this person, with a sense of his being exposed unto the just wrath of Heaven, as filled him with most unusual degrees of horror, and anguish, which broke not only his rest, but his heart also, and cause him to cry out, 'While I suffer thy terrors, O Lord, I am distracted!'"[12]

According to Mather, Thomas's conversion was accompanied by a great deal of mental and spiritual anguish and took a significant amount of time to work out in his heart. Mather notes, "He afterwards gave his account of himself, 'That in the time of his agonies, he could reason himself to the rule, and conclude that there was no way but submission to God, and lying at the foot of his mercy in Christ Jesus, and waiting humbly there, till he should please to persuade the soul of his favour: nevertheless when he came to apply

---

10. Shuffelton, *Hooker*, 21.
11. Shuffelton, *Hooker*, 21.
12. Cotton Mather, *Magnalia Christi Americana* (1702; repr., Edinburgh: Banner of Truth, 1979), 1:333.

this rule unto himself in his own condition, his reasoning would fail him, he was able to do nothing.'"[13]

His conversion experience so impacted his life and ministry that he always exercised great pastoral wisdom and sensitivity for anyone who may be experiencing the same uncertain turmoil as he had. In 1615, after great agony, Thomas reached a peaceful assurance that he had been genuinely transformed by the saving grace of Christ and could now set his focus on a fruitful pastoral career.

Pastoral Calling

Near the bustling city of London sat the rural backwater village of Esher. Surrounded by manorial estates, which prevented its further growth, this small village in County Surrey became Thomas Hooker's home in 1618.[14] A prominent resident of the Esher parish, who was also in charge of choosing the rector, was a man by the name of Francis Drake. His choice of Hooker had more to do with his concern for his wife, who was a "religious melancholic with suicidal tendencies and required a great deal of care."[15] Because of the small size of the Esher congregation, the new pastor would be able to spend much of his time and energy counseling Mrs. Drake. To inspire the pastoral care of his wife, Drake invited Hooker to live in his own household. After numerous conversations and counseling sessions, it became quite apparent to Hooker that Mrs. Drake was caught in the bonds of unbelief and should be seeking Christ with all her heart. No doubt, Hooker observed his efforts and time with Mrs. Drake as a case study for his most significant work, published in 1629, *The Poor Doubting Christian Drawn to Christ*. The essence of this work was Hooker's argument for a confident assurance of salvation. Hooker believed that, like a thief on the run, the doubting heart takes many paths and routes of escape. Drawing on Mrs. Drake's personal experience, *The Poor Doubting Christian* describes

---

13. Mather, *Magnalia*, 1:333.
14. Shuffelton, *Thomas Hooker*, 29.
15. Shuffelton, *Thomas Hooker*, 29.

the intellectual and spiritual journey the soul takes in obtaining assurance of salvation.[16]

In addition to his extensive pastoral experiences, Hooker found one other joy from his time in Esher. It was there that he met and married his wife, Susanna Garbrand, who happened to serve as personal maid to Mrs. Drake. Having a prominent position in the Drake household, Susanna's remarkable piety was widely known in local Christian circles. About three years after he first arrived in Esher, Thomas pledged his love to Susanna in a small wedding ceremony on April 3, 1621.

The Preacher

By the mid 1620s Hooker had achieved a small measure of fame among the English Puritans, although his notoriety had not yet ascended to the ecclesiastical authority. His lectures while at Emmanuel and then his pastoral success with Mrs. Drake demonstrated Hooker's gifts and pastoral acumen, which drew wide attention. It is quite possible that toward the end of his time in Esher, Hooker was occasionally preaching around the bustling city of London. Without citing authority, Cotton Mather commented that "he did more publicly and frequently preach about London; and in a little time he became famous for his ministerial abilities."[17]

Following the death of Mrs. Drake in April 1625, Hooker probably began to search for a new position. But during this period Hooker saw no need to leave the established Church of England, despite his seeming differences with the establishment regarding the organization of the church. There is some evidence that in 1626 Hooker preached in "the great church of Leicester," a shire town in his home county, as a candidate for the position of lecturer or pastor.[18]

One prominent minister who began to recognize the promise of this soon to be Separatist pastor was John Rogers (c. 1570–1636)

---

16. Shuffelton, *Thomas Hooker*, 66.
17. Mather, *Magnalia*, 1:334.
18. Shuffelton, *Thomas Hooker*, 72.

of Dedham in Essex. Earlier Hooker had formed an admiration for
the Dedham pastor and later admitted as much by writing an introduction to the second edition of his treatise *The Doctrine of Faith*,
published in 1627. About this time, Cotton Mather noted, "Mr.
Hooker grew into a most intimate acquaintance with Mr. Rogers
of Dedham; who so highly valued him for his multifarious abilitie,
that he used and gained many endeavours to get him settled at Col-
chester; whereto Hooker did very much incline, because of its being
so near to Dedham, where he might enjoy the *labours* and *lecturers*
of Mr. Rogers, whom he would sometimes call, 'The prince of all
the preachers in England.'"[19]

According to Mather, shortly afterward the church of St. Mary
at Chelmsford, Essex, "wanting one to 'break the bread of life' unto
them, and hearing the fame of Mr. Hooker's powerful ministry,
addressed him to become their lecturer," which Hooker accepted in
1626.[20] He moved his ever-expanding family to Chelmsford sometime in the following year, and his daughter Sarah was baptized
there on April 9, 1628.

It was not long before Hooker began to gain quite a reputation
among the Puritan ministers around Dedham and Chelmsford, as
he regularly preached in their assemblies and meetings. For instance,
Thomas Shepard (1605–1649) recorded the part Hooker played in
directing him to his first pulpit. Coming to Essex from Cambridge,
Shepard, who did not immediately find a call into pastoral ministry,
"enjoyed the blessing of Mr. Hooker's ministry at Chelmesford."[21]

Cotton Mather highlights that one of the preeminent reasons
Hooker's fellow pastors esteemed him highly was not only his keen
and comprehensive mind but his demonstrated effectiveness as a
godly and powerful minister. Mather wrote of his preaching, "Herby
there was a great reformation wrought, not only in the town, but

---

19. Mather, *Magnalia*, 1:334.
20. Mather, *Magnalia*, 1:334–35.
21. Thomas Shepard, "The Autobiography of Thomas Shepard," in *Publications of
the Colonial Society of Massachusetts, Transactions 1927–1930* (Boston: Colonial Society
of Massachusetts, 1932), 27:365.

in the adjacent country, from all parts whereof they came to 'hear the wisdom of the Lord Jesus Christ,' in his gospel, by this worthy man dispensed; and some of great quality among the rest, would often resort from far to his assembly; particularly the truly noble Earl of Warwick."[22]

In addition to the moral reformation implied here by Mather, Hooker's lectures and sermons at Chelmsford persuaded many to seek after what he so vehemently preached. Hooker preached to farmers and merchants and therefore never employed the use of Greek, Latin, or Hebrew in his sermons. He preached to his congregation not particularly as a whole but as individual men and women in search of God's salvation. His sermons, in keeping with Puritan doctrinal content, never lacked an emphasis on the sovereignty and immediacy of God. Mather described abundant examples of extraordinary transformations caused by his preaching. One such example makes a profound point:

> A profane person, designing therein only an ungodly diversion and merriment, said unto his companions, "Come, let us go hear what that bawling Hooker will say to us;" and thereupon, with an intention to make sport, unto Chelmsford lecture they came. The man had not been long in the church, before the *quick and powerful word* of God, in the mouth of his faithful Hooker, pierced the soul of him; he came out with an awakened and distressed soul, and by the further blessing of God upon Mr. Hooker's ministry, he arrived unto a true *conversion*; for which cause he would not afterwards leave that blessed ministry, but went a *thousand leagues* to attend it and enjoy it.[23]

Mather claims that the products of Hooker's pastoral season in Chelmsford were "those books of preparation for Christ, contrition, humiliation, vocation, union with Christ, and communion, and the rest which go under his name."[24] He is referring to a series

---

22. Mather, *Magnalia*, 1:335.
23. Mather, *Magnalia*, 1:335.
24. Mather, *Magnalia*, 1:347.

of books that appeared from Hooker's pen between 1632 and 1638 with titles such as *The Soules Exaltation, The Soules Preparation for Christ, The Soules Humiliation, The Soules Vocation, The Soules Exaltation*, and *The Soules Implantation*. These books deal directly with the process of applied redemption and were derived from sermons Hooker delivered.

Hooker's pulpit ministry at Chelmsford and beyond shaped the whole of his future ministry and caused him to gain popularity in surrounding areas. By the Spirit's blessing, he became widely known for his ability to persuade men and women of their sinful condition and their ardent need to fly to Christ to rescue them from death and destruction. A retrospective after Hooker's death reveals that his preaching "had been a high point of the English Reformation."[25]

The Netherlands

In 1622, four years after Thomas Hooker entered the pulpit at Chelmsford, King James I (1566–1625) attempted to inhibit the lecturers—who were almost all of a Puritan persuasion—by forbidding them "to preach in any popular auditory on the deep points of predestination, election, reprobation, or of the universality, efficacy, resistibility, or irresistibility of God's grace."[26] Sunday afternoon sermons, which were usually preached by the lecturer, were limited to discussion of the "Catechism, Creed, or Ten Commandments."

In June 1626 James's successor, Charles I (1600–1649), moved to bring William Laud (1573–1645) into his inner circle, electing him as the new bishop of London. By the spring of 1629, Laud was receiving intelligence on the activities of nonconformists throughout his diocese, and it became obvious that harsher restrictions on the Puritan ministers were needed. In February 1629, Parliament had presented to the king the "Heads of Articles," which protested against, among other things, "the bold and unwarrantable introducing...of sundry new ceremonies and laying of injunctions upon

---

25. Shuffelton, *Thomas Hooker*, 121.
26. Quoted in Walker, *Thomas Hooker*, 40–41.

men."[27] Charles promptly adjourned the Parliament, and Laud began suspending Puritan ministers and lecturers as quickly as possible. One of the first men to be affected was Hooker's friend and mentor, John Rogers of Dedham. By the late spring of 1629, Laud was interested in the activities of Thomas Hooker. On May 20, Samuel Collins, Vicar of Braintree, wrote to Arthur Duck, Laud's chancellor, urging the bishop to devise plans for "Mr. Hooker's departure."[28]

Hooker seems to have abstained from directly attacking the established church, but he was sharply critical of "those which are enemies to God's faithful ministers, [which] are the great adversaries that the Church or State hath."[29] Although generalized in his descriptions, Hooker attacked the persecutors of the "Ministers of Grace" from pulpits in Chelmsford and beyond.

Shortly after May 20, Hooker was summoned to appear before Bishop Laud's High Commission to answer for his oppositional preaching and nonconformity. However, by the time news reached him of the summons, he had already departed for London. Rather than forcing Hooker out of the diocese with threats to no longer preach, Laud suspended him from his lectureship and required him to post a bond that would guarantee his reappearance on demand. A Mr. Nash, tenant of the Earl of Warwick, paid Hooker's bond, at which point Hooker returned home to Essex.[30]

During this period of uncertainty, Thomas and Susanna made their family home near Chelmsford at Cuckoos Farm in Little Baddow. With three daughters and an infant son (named after his brother John) to care for, Hooker opened a grammar school after

27. Quoted in Thomas W. Davids, *Annals of Evangelical Nonconformity in the County of Essex* (London, 1863), 143.

28. All quotations from this letter are from Davids, *Annals of Evangelical Nonconformity*, 150–51. See also Shuffelton, *Thomas Hooker*, 125.

29. Thomas Hooker, *Spirituall Munition: A Funerall Sermon* (London, 1638), 31. Quoted by Sargent Bush Jr., "Four New Works by Thomas Hooker: Identity and Significance," *Resources for American Literary Study* 4 (1974): 10. This sermon was delivered in June 1626.

30. Shuffelton, *Thomas Hooker*, 128.

he was suspended from preaching. He employed John Eliot, who later achieved fame as the "Apostle to the Indians in New England." Almost as effective standing at a lectern as behind a pulpit, Hooker employed the classroom as the center of his proclamation of God's truth. In August 1629, into this peaceful interlude, Thomas and Susanna's sixteen-month-old daughter, Sarah, died.

This seemingly quiet period was interrupted when Hooker was ordered to reappear before Laud's High Commission in July 1630. Hooker chose not to appear. Cotton Mather said that Hooker "could not now attend because of an ague then upon him," but a more important reason for failing to appear was that "Mr. Hooker's friends advised him to forfeit his bonds, rather than to throw himself any further into the hands of his enemies."[31] To defy Laud's summons was to ask for exile since a man of Hooker's stature and fame could not be hidden for long by sympathizing friends. Indeed, pursuivants were becoming more zealous and efficient in tracking down nonconforming ministers.[32] Hooker, knowing he must soon depart Chelmsford, did not take lightly the abandonment of his people.

After Hooker refused to appear before Laud for this second summons, Hooker immediately became a wanted man. Now an enemy of the established church, Hooker was unable to escape aboard just any ship leaving England. In the spring of 1631, after arrangements were made for his getaway, Thomas and his family secretly took a ship for the Netherlands.[33]

The contingency of English immigrants in the Netherlands was founded in 1621 under the leadership of John Forbes (c. 1568–1634), minister to the Merchant Adventurers' church in Delft.

---

31. Mather, *Magnalia*, 1:338.

32. Shuffelton, *Thomas Hooker*, 131.

33. Alice Clare Carter transcribes the register of the Amsterdam English Church to report, "In January 1631 Mr. Thomas Hooker preacher came into these countries." *The English Reformed Church in Amsterdam in the Seventeenth Century* (Amsterdam: Scheltema and Holkema,1964), 192. Keith L. Sprunger, however, corrects this to read "in Junij 1631," "The Dutch Career of Thomas Hooker," *New England Quarterly* 46 (1973): 18. Hooker was preaching by the summer of 1631, and his invitation seems to have come after Thomas Potts's death in April.

When Thomas and his family arrived, they stayed with Hugh Peter (1598–1660), pastor of the English church in Rotterdam. Peter was a young and candid preacher who had been forced to seek refuge after a short pastoral career in England. In all likelihood, Thomas and Peter exchanged correspondence before Hooker left England, and they may have spent time together during the course of two visits Peter made to London and Essex in 1628 and 1630.

The English settlement in the Netherlands proved not to be the peaceful escape Hooker and his family no doubt desired in their flight from English persecution. For a while the Netherlands contingency sought to throw off the English yoke of organization and instead encourage men to experience Christ in their daily lives. However, the English ministers called down on themselves the very repression they had sought to escape by fleeing to Holland. In the latter part of his stay in Holland, Hooker wrote to John Cotton, complaining, "The state of these provinces to my weak eye, seems wonderfully ticklish and miserable. For the better part, heart religion, they content themselves with very forms, though much blemished; but the power of godliness, for ought I can see or hear, they know not; and if it were thoroughly pressed, I fear least it will be fiercely opposed."[34]

The result of several controversies that arose in Holland proved Hooker was right in his assessment and that the only haven in the English-speaking world for practicing the power of godliness and true religion seemed to be the settlements in New England. In addition to his general dissatisfaction with the religious situation in the Netherlands and his discontent with the numerous church quarrels in which he had been drawn into, Hooker had a more personal reason for wishing to leave Holland. He informed Cotton, "My ague yet holds me; the ways of God's providence, wherein he has walked towards me, in this long time of my sickness, and wherein I have drawn forth many wearish hours, under his Almighty hand (blessed be his name) together with pursuits and banishment, which have

---

34. Mather, *Magnalia*, 1:340.

waited upon me, as one wave follows another, have driven me to an amazement; his paths being too secret and past finding out by such an ignorant, worthless worm as myself."[35]

Numerous obstacles prevented Hooker from following his fellow Chelmsford congregants and friends to New England in 1630. No correspondence between Hooker and his "company" has survived, but one can almost imagine that Hooker was urged by his friends to immigrate to America. Sometime in the spring of 1633 Thomas Hooker left Delft for England and from there would take a ship to the New World.

Massachusetts

The *Griffin* left late in the year, and by the time she moored off the coast of America, she might well have expected to run ahead into a hurricane. Compared to other ships that sailed the tumultuous waters of the Atlantic, when the *Griffin* arrived at Boston on September 4, 1633, John Winthrop noted that they had lost only four persons, "whereof one was drowned two days before, as he was casting forth a line to take mackerel."[36] Hooker's health was apparently not endangered during the voyage. John Cotton's wife delivered their first son during the journey, "whom he called Sea-born, in the remembrance of the never-to-be-forgotten blessings which he thus enjoyed upon the seas."[37]

After making shore on the New World, Hooker journeyed to Newtown, where an offer of a pulpit had been extended to him prior to his departure from England. A meetinghouse had been constructed, with the luxury of a bell, approximately a year before Hooker's arrival. There is no record of the precise time of the church's formal gathering, but organizing a new church would have been Hooker's first concern if it had not already been accomplished. In

---

35. Mather, *Magnalia*, 1:340.
36. John Winthrop, *Winthrop Papers* (Boston: Massachusetts Historical Society, 1929–1947), 1:105.
37. Mather, *Magnalia*, 1:265.

addition, it was vital for the new settlers in this strange land to find
shelter and supplies before winter. By this time Thomas and Susanna's
growing family consisted of three daughters and two sons, and they
received a third son, Samuel, probably in the fall or winter of 1633.[38]

Upon his arrival in Newtown, Hooker found only a small, unor-
ganized community in the early beginnings of a town. Newtown was
in theory first settled in 1630, the same year as Boston, Charlestown,
Roxbury, and Watertown, but relatively few families chose to settle
there. Regardless, so many of Hooker's old friends and congregants
would have been overjoyed to see him. Mather writes, "Inexpressible
now was the joy of Mr. Hooker, to find himself surrounded with his
friends, who were come over the year before, to prepare for his recep-
tion; with open arms he embraced them, and uttered these words,
'Now I live, if you stand fast in the Lord.'"[39] Hooker came as their
pastor in a foreign wilderness, seeking to be their guide to walk "in
the ways of God, and in the truth of his worship."[40]

Hooker soon found himself at odds with John Cotton and others because, in order to vote in the new colony, a man had to be
examined for his religious beliefs. This effectively suppressed Puritans from voting if their beliefs were in opposition to the majority
religion. Therefore, in 1636 Hooker and Samuel Stone (1602–1663),
who had sailed with Hooker from England, led a group of settlers
to form Hartford in the soon to be formed Connecticut Colony.
This settlement, named after the Connecticut River, comes from

---

38. The composition of Hooker's family upon his arrival in America is uncertain.
The three daughters, Joanna, Mary, and Sarah, who grew to adulthood, and his older
son, John, were definitely there. John Winthrop reports the death by smallpox of "Mr.
Hookers younge sonne" in a letter dated December 12, 1634. *Winthrop Papers* (Boston:
Massachusetts Historical Society, 1929–1947), 3:177. It is not clear whether this son was
born in America. Also, tradition alone supports Samuel's birth in Newtown; he died on
November 6, 1697, supposedly aged sixty-four, but there is no reliable authority for his
age at death. If he were indeed sixty-four by November 6, 1697, chances are somewhat
more likely that he was born in England and came over on the *Griffin* as an infant. The
son who died in 1634 may have been born in Newtown.

39. Mather, *Magnalia*, 1:342.

40. Shuffelton, *Thomas Hooker*, 170.

the Algonquian word meaning "long tidal river." The Massachusetts General Court granted them the right to set up three towns: Windsor, Wethersfield, and Hartford.

The Hooker family and about one hundred men, women, and children followed the trail later known as the Old Bay Path across southern Massachusetts. They drove about one hundred and sixty cattle with them and took almost two weeks to make the trip. The journey seems to have been made with few major obstacles, and they arrived at their new home just after the first day of summer.

When he arrived at Suckiaug, Hooker found a dozen or more small and fairly primitive houses set up in front of the first of the hills leading west away from the river. Between this infant settlement and the river was a stretch of open bottomland called the Little Meadow, and to the south of it the Little River ran into the Connecticut. In the center of the tract of land, a large square area had been reserved for the meetinghouse yard, and presumably the first meetinghouse, a small windowless building, had been built in the corner of it. From the beginning, the settlement at Suckiaug was divided by the Little River into north side and south side plantations. By the summer of 1636, there were five plantations on the river, all separated by generous amounts of untenanted space. Hooker's message to his wilderness congregation was no different from what it had been in England—the soul's need for preparation, humiliation, and calling to Christ, and the fruit of its eventual engrafting into the life-giving stock of Christ. Hooker wrote out the notes for these sermons he delivered in America, which later became the basis for the two lengthy, posthumously published volumes titled *The Application of Redemption*.

Hooker, along with John Winthrop, believed that a New England town, regardless of its location, should be a "city upon a hill" in a political sense. That is, it should be a model for the spiritually and morally imperiled society of England, but he emphasized even more strongly the traditional image of that city as the New Jerusalem. On May 31, 1638, when the General Court of Connecticut was meeting to discuss the drawing up of formal articles for the government of the Connecticut River plantations, Hooker preached a sermon with the following doctrines:

I. That the choice of public magistrates belongs unto the people, by Gods own allowance.

II. The privilege of election, which belongs to the people, therefore must not be exercised according to their humours, but according to the blessed will and law of God.

III. They who have power to appoint officers and magistrates, it is in their power, also, to set the bounds and limitations of the power and place unto which they call them.[41]

Close consideration of Hooker's political sermons of 1638 clarifies his role in the creation of the Fundamental Orders. There is no need to presume he had a direct hand in drawing up these first laws of the new Connecticut colony. Hooker never descended from his pulpit. He reminded the magistrates of their obligation to employ the affections of the people in the commonwealth but left them to organize the mechanics of it, and he repeatedly instructed the people in their duty to comply with the laws established by their elected leaders. The social and political legacy of Hooker's religious insight in seventeenth-century Connecticut proved to be the ideal of a "union of love and concord" between people and magistrates. Hooker came to the wilderness with the ardent desire to establish a unified commonwealth among his people. His basic definition of this union was both ecclesiological and theological, but love was not to be extended to the church members alone.[42] From his extensive experience that the God of justice is also the God of mercy, Hooker continually emphasized that the liberties enjoyed by New Englanders were a gift of a loving God.

---

41. John Hooker, "Abstracts of Two Sermons by Rev. Thomas Hooker, From the Shorthand Notes of Mr. Henry Wolcott," transcribed by J. Hammond Trumbull, in *Collections of the Connecticut Historical Society* (Hartford, 1860), 1:20.

42. Shuffelton, *Thomas Hooker*, 234.

The New England Way

By the summer of 1636, it became evident that Thomas Hooker was far removed from the Old World. The distance between England and Connecticut consisted of more than just the Atlantic and a hundred miles of uncharted wilderness; it was also the distance between the social strata of London and the comparatively stark uniformity of Hartford. Hooker emphasized the necessity of individual spiritual priorities and how they should be reflected by social priorities. The small village on the Connecticut River was as close as Hooker would come to re-creating the Promised Land. Yet even in the stark wilderness Hooker was not free from the world beyond his congregation, as he was called on, like Moses, to continually face external threats to his community and new way of life.

Just a year after they arrived in this unfamiliar land, the first great danger arose when "the old Serpent according to his first malice stirred [the Pequot Indians] up against the Church of Christ" in Connecticut.[43] The Pequot War was the result of a long series of provocations, retaliations, and counterretaliations. The Hartford General Court eventually declared war on the Pequots and levied a ninety-man army under the command of Captain John Mason, a man "tall and portly, but nonetheless full of martial bravery and vigour."[44] The men were convened, and Hooker delivered a sermon for their edification and encouragement before their deployment. His text was taken from Numbers 14:9: "Only rebel ye not against the LORD, neither fear ye the people of the land; for they are bread for us; their defence is departed from them, and the LORD is with us: fear them not." This sermon and his prayers for the men constituted Hooker's personal role in the war. Hooker found his supreme joy in his pulpit and study. Time for both was afforded to him in Connecticut. His later sermons reveal an increase in theological and philosophical insight over the early years, in part because of his

---

43. John Underhill, *Newes from America* (London, 1638; repr., Underhill Society of America, 1902), 22.

44. Thomas Prince, introduction to John Mason, *A Brief History of the Pequot War* (Boston, 1736; repr., Ann Arbor, Mich.: University Microfilms, 1966), iii.

more learned audience and also because of his own maturity and greater depth of scholarship.

Even in his old age, Hooker strove for the cause of peace— peace among men and between men and God. "I confess my head grows gray and my eyes dim, and yet I am sometime in the watch-tower," he wrote to John Winthrop in 1638. Two years later he told Thomas Shepard, "I know, to begin plantations is a hard work; and I think I have seen as much difficulty, and came to such a business with as much disadvantage as almost men could do."[45]

These years in the Connecticut wilderness were probably the happiest days Hooker had experienced since his time in Esher. No dodging of bishops, no escaping the grasp of ecclesiastical authori-ties, no tumultuous sea voyages in search of a better life, and no more Indian troubles after 1637. Hooker had settled where he found sweet joy among his family and fellow parishioners. A town grateful for his years of labor among them granted Hooker large tracts of land, which were developed and overseen by his industrious wife. His children were becoming godly young men and women: Joanna was married to Thomas Shepard; John was preparing for Cambridge University; and Mary had wed Roger Newton, the pastor of Mil-ford. Sarah and Samuel were still at home having their intellectual future charted by their father. While in Hartford, Thomas and Joanna Shepard had sent their small son Samuel to live with their grandparents, and Thomas's reports of him in his letters to Shepard show us the Puritan's joy as a doting grandfather.

When a synod was convened at Cambridge in 1646 to begin consideration of an explicit, unanimous statement of church pol-ity, Hooker's infirmities hindered him from attending. Again in 1647, he was unable to consider a trip to a similar synod. When fellow laborer Samuel Stone returned to Hartford after the synod

45. Hooker to John Winthrop, *Winthrop Papers*, 4:401–2; Letter to Shepard quoted by Lucius R. Paige, *History of Cambridge, Massachusetts: 1630–1877* (Boston: H. O. Houghton and Co., 1877), 49.

adjourned early because of an "epidemicall sickness," Hooker was discovered on his deathbed.

> God refused to heare our prayes for him, but tooke him from us July 7, a little before sunne-set. Our sunne is set, our light is eclipsed, our joy is darkened, we remember now in the day of our calamitie the pleasant things, which we enjoyed in former times. His spirits and heart were so oppressed with the disease that he was not able to expresse much to us in his sicknesse, but had exprest to Mr. Goodwin before my returne, that his peace was made in heaven, and had continued 30 years without alteration, he was above Satan.... I gave thanks to my God dayly for his helpe, and no man in the world but myself knows what a friend he hath been unto me.[46]

Surrounded by family and friends, and assured of his salvation, Hooker's end was peaceful. A short time later, "a worthy spectator, then writing to Mr. Cotton a relation thereof, made this reflection, 'Truly, sir, the sight of his death will make me have more pleasant thoughts of death, than eve I yet had in my life!'"[47] Mather, noting how Hooker was unshaken to the end in his principles and his confidence about entering a state of bliss and perfection for which he had so longed, wrote, "When one that stood weeping by the bedside said unto him 'Sir, you are going to receive the reward of all your labours,' he replied, 'Brother, I am going to receive mercy.'"[48] Heaven was much more than a business transaction. It was mercy he lived for and lived by. Thomas Hooker was finally home.

Conclusion

Thomas Hooker should be remembered for more than his keen statecraft and ardent desire to bring religious freedom to his congregants in a new world. He should be remembered for more than his

---

46. Samuel Stone to Thomas Shepard, *Collections of the Massachusetts Historical Society*, 4th series (Boston, 1868), 8:544–45.
47. Mather, *Magnalia*, 1:350.
48. Mather, *Magnalia*, 1:350.

assistance in the founding of the colony of Connecticut. He should be remembered for his ability to stand behind a pulpit and proclaim the unsearchable riches of divine grace. Above all else, Hooker was a preacher, saved and called of God to assist in bringing assurance of salvation to multitudes of people. Those who made the great migration from England to the New World would have been mere wanderers in a strange land had it not been for a spiritual guide— a preacher. Hooker remained undistracted from this singular task for sixty-one years. He serves as a faithful example to all successive generations of the necessity of keeping one's eyes on the most important task—the proclamation of Jesus Christ.

5

THOMAS SHEPARD

Storm waves nearly drove the small ship carrying Thomas Shepard and his family into the shore. For two tumultuous days at sea, they contemplated the wisdom of attempting to cross the Atlantic in early winter, but no safe place remained for them to hide in England. As the wind pitched them to and fro, an emergency decision was made to chop down the mast with an ax. The decision saved their lives, and soon they were able to return to shore. But the ordeal proved too much for Shepard's infant son, who fell sick and died. The life and ministry of the young Puritan minister would be marked by affliction and death, but as Shepard later wrote, "And the Lord now showed me my weak faith, want of fear, pride, carnal content, immoderate love of creatures and of my child especially, and begot in me some desires and purposes to fear his name."[1]

Early Life and Education
On November 5, 1605, a small group of English Catholics attempted to blow up Parliament and assassinate King James I. Upon receiving an anonymous tip, authorities searched the basement of the House of Lords to discover a lone conspirator named Guy Fawkes (1570–1606) guarding thirty-six barrels of gunpowder—enough to

---

1. Thomas Shepard, *Autobiography*, in *God's Plot: Puritan Spirituality in Thomas Shepard's Cambridge*, revised and expanded edition, ed. Michael McGiffert (Amherst: University of Massachusetts Press, 1994), 63.

blast the House of Lords to smithereens. Along with Fawkes, the remaining conspirators were arrested, tried, hanged, and drawn and quartered, thus frustrating the aptly named "Gunpowder Plot." This is also the day the Lord decreed Thomas Shepard to be born.

Of the event of his birth, Shepard wrote, "Upon the fifth day of November, called the powder treason day, and that very hour of the day wherein the Parliament should have been blown up by Popish priests, I was then born, which occasioned my father to give me this name Thomas, because he said I would hardly believe that ever any such wickedness should be attempted by men against so religious and good Parliament."[2] His father, William Shepard, was "a wise, prudent man" and a "peacemaker" of strong piety.[3] His mother, Shepard writes, "did bear exceeding great love to me and made many prayers for me."[4] The Shepard family lived in Towcester, Northamptonshire, which Shepard regarded as "an English town that was a perfect Sodom and Gomorrah; a perfect sink of all sensuality and profanity; and it was his lifelong wonder and praise that he was dug out of such a ditch and was sent to Cambridge to study for the Christian ministry."[5] When he was three years old, Thomas, the youngest of nine, was sent away to his grandparents in Fossecut to avoid an epidemic sickness sweeping through Towcester. When he returned a few months later, many in his family were dead, including his mother, and his father was remarried.

At age ten, his father died and Thomas was left in the care of his stepmother, who, he wrote, "did not seem to love me."[6] After being severely neglected, Thomas was taken in by his eldest brother, John, the only survivor among his three brothers, "who showed much love unto me and unto whom I owe much, for him God made to be

---

2. Shepard, *Autobiography*, 39.

3. Thomas Werge, *Thomas Shepard* (Boston: G. K. Hall, 1987), 4.

4. Shepard, *Autobiography*, 40.

5. Alexander Whyte, *Thomas Shepard: Pilgrim Father and Founder of Harvard* (1909; repr., Grand Rapids: Reformation Heritage Books, 2007), 225.

6. Shepard, *Autobiography*, 40.

both father and mother unto me."[7] In stewarding young Thomas's education, John sent him to the Free School in Towcester under a headmaster named Mr. Rice, whom Shepard recalled as being very cruel. Upon the death of Mr. Rice, however, a new headmaster took his place who "stirred up in my heart a love and desire of the honor of learning."[8] This passion would remain kindled for his entire life.

Conversion

In 1619, Shepard was admitted to Emmanuel College in Cambridge at the age of fifteen. His first two years were relatively uneventful, as he lived the life of a busy English student. As for his spiritual life, however, he recollected his "much neglect of God."[9] By his third year, he began to fall into sinfulness and debauchery: "[I] fell from God to loose and lewd company, to lust and pride and gambling and bowling and drinking."[10] So prone to drunkenness, Shepard recalled one particular night,

> I drank so much one day that I was dead drunk, and that upon a Saturday night, and so was carried from the place I had drink at and did feast at…and I knew not where I was until I awakened late on that Sabbath and sick with my beastly carriage. And when I awakened I went…in shame and confusion, and went out into the fields and there spent that Sabbath lying hid in the cornfields where the Lord, who might justly have cut me off in the midst of my sin, did meet me with much sadness of heart and troubled my soul for this and other my sins which then I had cause and leisure to think of.[11]

His cornfield experience with God shook something loose in him, and he began to seek how he might become right with the Lord.

---

7. Shepard, *Autobiography*, 41.
8. Shepard, *Autobiography*, 41.
9. Shepard, *Autobiography*, 42.
10. Shepard, *Autobiography*, 42.
11. Shepard, *Autobiography*, 42.

At Cambridge, ministers like John Preston (1587–1628) preached soul-stirring sermons to the students. Preston's preaching on Romans 12:2 and the importance of being "renewed in the spirit of your mind" particularly resonated with Shepard.[12] The sermon so struck him that he began to realize "the hypocrisy of all my good things I thought I had in me."[13] For the next eight months, Shepard began to wrestle with God, who was berating his weary heart. "My chief meditation," he writes, "was about the evil of sin, the terror of God's wrath, day of death, beauty of Christ, the deceitfulness of the heart, etc., but principally I found this my misery: sin was not my greatest evil, did lie light upon me as yet, yet I was much afraid of death and the flames of God's wrath."[14] In his misery, he cried out to the Lord until finally he was granted repentance: "The Lord recovered me and poured out a spirit of prayer upon me for free mercy and pity, and in the conclusion of the prayer I found the Lord helping me to see my unworthiness.... Whereupon walking in the fields the Lord dropped this meditation into me: Be not discouraged therefore because thou art vile, but make this double use of it: (1) loathe thyself the more; (2) feel a greater need and put a greater price upon Jesus Christ who only can redeem thee from all sin."[15]

While Shepard obtained no true assurance of his faith as yet, he saw the sinfulness of his own heart and the absolute beauty of Christ. However, it was Dr. Preston's sermon on 1 Corinthians 1:30 that made him see that "all the redemption I had, it was from Jesus Christ, I did then begin to prize him and he became very sweet unto me."[16] Having forsaken his former life of debauchery, Shepard testified, "The Lord gave me a heart to receive Christ with a naked hand, even naked Christ, and so the Lord gave me peace."[17]

---

12. Shepard, *Autobiography*, 43.
13. Shepard, *Autobiography*, 44.
14. Shepard, *Autobiography*, 44.
15. Shepard, *Autobiography*, 45–47.
16. Shepard, *Autobiography*, 47.
17. Shepard, *Autobiography*, 47–48.

Powerful Ministry, Persecution, and Flight to New England

Shepard graduated with a bachelor of arts degree in 1624, followed later by a master of arts degree in 1627. Having left the university in 1625, he went to reside with the family of Thomas Weld in Tarling, who would prove to be a steadfast friend in the coming years of adversity. While living at the Welds' home, Shepard first met Thomas Hooker (1586–1647), who was a lecturer in Chelmsford in Essex. From there he eventually received a call to Earls Colne to serve as pastor. For three years he served the congregation faithfully and with great zeal. In fact, even years after his death, the people of Earls Colne still remembered the power and intensity of Shepard's preaching.[18]

Soon Shepard's popularity began to grow, and word of his non-conformist tendencies reached Archbishop William Laud. After three years at Earls Colne, Shepard was scheduled to take a church back in his hometown of Towcester but was intercepted by Laud. On December 30, 1630, Shepard was summoned to London to answer for his ministry in Earls Colne. Archbishop Laud, whom Shepard later referred to as "a fierce enemy of all righteousness,"[19] flew into a fit of rage, chiding and berating the young minister during the interview. At the end of the blistering interview, Laud pronounced his sentence: "I charge you that you neither preach, read, marry, bury, or exercise any ministerial function in any part of my diocese; for if you do, and I hear of it, I'll be upon your back, and follow you wherever you go, in any part of the kingdom, and so everlastingly disenable you."[20]

With Shepard now officially silenced by the Church of England, he had no means of employment or subsistence. However, many of his friends and church members determined to care for him, especially the Harlakenden family. Shepard was soon called to the home of Sir Richard Darley of Buttercrambe, Yorkshire, to serve as a chaplain. It was there that Shepard met Darley's cousin, Margaret

---

18. Werge, *Thomas Shepard*, 6–7.

19. John A. Albro, "Life of Thomas Shepard," in *The Works of Thomas Shepard* (1853; repr., New York: AMS Press, 1967), 1:lxxvii.

20. Albro, "Life of Thomas Shepard," 1:lxxvi.

Touteville, "who was a most sweet humble woman, full of Christ, and a very discerning Christian."[21] The two married on July 23, 1632.

Their newfound happiness was short-lived as the archbishop called for Shepard to appear before him again. While Shepard pleaded with Laud for leniency in allowing him to earn a living, the archbishop all but banished him to a life of academic study, never to step behind a pulpit again. Shortly thereafter Shepard's good friend Thomas Weld, who had been suspended from ministry the month prior, was formally excommunicated.

With the Great Migration under way, many of Shepard's non-conformist friends were being driven out of their churches and from England. Shepard lamented, "I saw the Lord departing from England when Mr. Hooker and Mr. Cotton were gone."[22] As time went on, the Shepards soon realized that immigration to America was the only option. "My liberty in private was daily threatened," wrote Shepard, "and I thought it wisdom to depart before the pursuivants came out, for so I might depart with more people and less trouble and danger to me and my friends."[23]

In October 1634, Shepard, Margaret, and their newborn son, Thomas, embarked for New England aboard a ship called the *Hope of Ipswich*. Their hopes were quickly dashed, however, when a fierce storm nearly drove the ship into the sandy shore. After several tumultuous days, the ship put back into harbor. However, their infant son fell sick and died two weeks later. The Shepards decided to stay with friends for the winter and try to flee again the following year. On April 5, 1635, Margaret gave birth to another son, whom they named Thomas after his deceased brother. In August, under disguise, they set sail again for New England and arrived in Boston on October 3, 1635.

---

21. Shepard, *Autobiography*, 55.
22. Shepard, *Autobiography*, 57.
23. Shepard, *Autobiography*, 58.

Ministry at Cambridge, Massachusetts

Newtown, later known as Cambridge, was fast becoming the metropolis of the Massachusetts Bay Colony. Soon after the arrival of John Cotton, Thomas Hooker, and Samuel Stone in September 1633, Hooker and Stone were ordained as ministers in the burgeoning Newtown settlement. However, by the spring of 1634 the town began to overcrowd. Many of the townspeople petitioned the General Court to allot a new piece of land for the purpose of expansion. To their dismay, the court seemed to drag its feet. Frustrated by the court's lethargy, Hooker and Stone led a group of one hundred people—nearly the entire local congregation—from Newtown through the wooded wilderness to a plot of land that would eventually become Hartford, Connecticut, in the summer of 1636.

Having arrived in Massachusetts only a few months earlier, Thomas Shepard and his young family stepped right into the midst of the land dispute. With a large group of his friends leaving, Shepard had to make a decision as to whether he would stay in Cambridge or migrate to Hartford. He chose to stay. In February 1636, after a public assembly was convened, a permanent church was founded in Cambridge, of which Shepard was installed as the pastor. The new appointment was bittersweet; on the one hand, Massachusetts now had its eleventh church under the watchful eye of the promising young Shepard, while on the other, dozens of disenfranchised families were skipping town, headed for greener pastures. The tide turned abruptly for Shepard as, only two weeks after the organization of the new church, Margaret Shepard succumbed to illness and died.

Shepard had no choice but to throw himself into his labors. Very quickly, he established himself as a faithful minister, tireless evangelist, and extraordinary preacher. Of his preaching, it was said that "Shepard's sermons were moving but not sensational, delivered in a low voice that had a strangely penetrating and compelling quality."[24] While Shepard was regarded as an average scholar by some, his

---

24. Samuel Eliot Morison, *Builders of the Bay Colony* (1930; repr., Boston: Northeastern University Press, 1981), 127.

sermons were powerful and effective. On Shepard's regular ministry, Alexander Whyte writes, "There were weeks and months and years when you could not have sat a single Sabbath under Shepard's pulpit that you would not have heard the most heart-moving and most conscience-searching sermon."[25] "So searching was his preaching," said one of his flock, "and so great a power attending, as a hypocrite could not easily bear it, and it seemed almost irresistible."[26] Unlike his contemporaries whose natural giftedness carried them along easily, Shepard had many obstacles to overcome to fulfill his ministry. He was recognized as a "'poor, weak, pale-complectioned man' of humble birth, timid by nature, no greater scholar, sweating out every sermon with moans and groans at his own vileness and inadequacy; 'his naturall parts were weake...but spent to the full.'"[27]

Beyond his preaching labors, Shepard was also known for his godliness and devotion to piety. In private, Shepard recorded his own personal battle with various sins, such as pride and faithlessness. But his fixation on the glory of Christ channeled his zeal toward soul winning and church purity. After preaching one Sunday, he writes, "I was very desirous that the Lord would make it effectual to convert some, and I saw my soul did secretly command the Lord and put him and enjoin him to a necessity to do it, because this made so much for his glory. But I saw it was my duty, as to pray for blessing, so to leave all success to God's free will and good pleasure, and so to do all the changes of my life."[28]

Shepard's earnest desire was for God to be glorified in New England, and he spent himself vigorously to that end. One of his biographers, Cotton Mather, writes, "Although Mr. Shepard were but a young man, yet there was that *majesty* and *energy* in his preaching, and that *holiness* in his life, which was not ordinary."[29]

---

25. Whyte, *Thomas Shepard*, 228.
26. Morison, *Builders of the Bay Colony*, 133.
27. Morison, *Builders of the Bay Colony*, 107.
28. Thomas Shepard, "Journal," in McGiffert, *God's Plot*, 118.
29. Cotton Mather, *Magnalia Christi Americana* (1702; repr., Edinburgh: Banner of Truth, 1979), 1:382.

No sooner had Shepard set his hand to the plow in Cambridge, however, that an insidious threat to unity and to the gospel arose in the churches.

The Antinomian Controversy

When Shepard fled persecution in England in 1635, he had no way of knowing that he would be sailing into tribulation in New England the next year. Almost immediately after his arrival, however, trouble was brewing only a few miles away in Boston. Anne Hutchinson, a member of John Cotton's congregation, had been hosting popular Bible studies in her home, which soon became a platform for her to teach her own theological views. At first no one, not even her pastor, was aware of the seriousness of her views. Highly intelligent, "a woman of masculine understanding, and of fiery zeal in religion,"[30] Mrs. Hutchinson was able to articulate with precision the theological talking points of biblical orthodoxy. Soon, however, the nuance of her position began to emerge.

At the heart of what came to be known as the Antinomian Controversy was the extreme focus on the grace of God to such an extent that it rejected any Christian obedience as an exercise in works-based legalism. Furthermore, Hutchinson taught that the indwelling of the Holy Spirit afforded believers with "immediate and special revelations" that "supercede[d] all other sources of authority"—even Scripture itself.[31] The Spirit, then, apart from any and all other evidences of saving faith, was the sole witness to salvation; no other evidences of sanctification were required. In addition, believers were to expect "immediate revelations respecting future events," which "should be received as equally authoritative and infallible with the Scripture."[32] Of course, when challenged on the content of her teaching, she passed them off as simply restatements

---

30. Albro, "Life of Thomas Shepard," 1:cxiv.
31. Werge, *Thomas Shepard*, 12.
32. Albro, "Life of Thomas Shepard," 1:cxvi.

of John Cotton's teachings, even "confirm[ing]" them "by an unfair and fraudulent use of Mr. Cotton's authority."[33]

At first Cotton did not see the threat growing inside his own church. Other ministers, however, quickly became aware of the insidious nature of antinomianism. The movement quickly grew militant, and its adherents bordered on the verge of anarchy. "They labored to destroy the reputation of all those ministers who held the commonly-received doctrines, stigmatizing them as legal preachers who were under a covenant of works, who never knew Christ themselves, and who could not be the instruments of bringing men into the light and liberty of the gospel."[34]

The spiritual movement bled into the civil and political sphere as many antinomians began to speak out against the colonies' military defenses as well as the authority of the magistrates and the General Court. "In an incredibly short time," writes John Albro, "this fanatical spirit divided not only the church of Boston, but a large number of the churches of Massachusetts and Plymouth."[35] Something had to be done.

Shortly after Hutchinson anathematized all New England ministers (except her own pastor, John Cotton, and her brother-in-law, John Wheelwright), the key leaders of the movement were summoned to appear for examination. In the seventeen months between October 1636 and March 1638, the controversy raged in the courts and pulpits of New England. In August 1637 a synod convened at Cambridge, with Shepard himself spearheading the effort. At the conclusion of the Cambridge synod, Anne Hutchinson and John Wheelwright were both banished in 1638, but not before severe damage had been done to the colonies. Shepard writes that, in the course of the controversy, "received truth came to be darkened, God's name to be blasphemed, the churches' glory diminished,

---

33. Albro, "Life of Thomas Shepard," 1:cxv.
34. Albro, "Life of Thomas Shepard," 1:cxvii.
35. Albro, "Life of Thomas Shepard," 1:cxviii.

many godly grieved, many wretches hardened, deceiving and being deceived, growing worse and worse."[36]

While the controversy was raging, Shepard labored in his own church to protect the congregation from theological error. Between 1636 and 1640 he preached forty-one sermons on the parable of the ten virgins from Matthew 25:1–13. In his expositions, he tackled issues surrounding false conversion, "easy-believism," and antinomianism. In evaluating Shepard's work, Randall Gleason writes that the parable was applied "specifically to the congregational churches of Massachusetts where the members were recognized as 'visible saints' by public profession. While a mix of 'wise and foolish virgins' was expected within the national Church of England, Shepard went on to declare than even the purest of churches contain both wise-hearted believers and foolish-hearted hypocrites. Therefore, even though the parable refers to the days immediately before the second coming of Christ (Matt. 25:1), Shepard believed its message had direct application to the 'virgin churches' prospering in New England."[37]

Shepard's sermons served their purpose, and the Cambridge church was insulated from the poisonous damage of the Antinomian Controversy. After Shepard's death, his son Thomas published the sermons in a volume titled *The Parable of the Ten Virgins* (1660).

The Founding of Harvard

Earlier in his life, Shepard had developed an appreciation for education. His headmaster at the Towcester Free School had "stirred up" in his heart "a love and desire" for learning, so much so that Shepard told his childhood friends that he was destined to become a scholar.[38] Now a seminary-trained pastor and ordained minister,

---

36. Shepard, *Autobiography*, 67.
37. Randall C. Gleason, "The Parable of the Ten Virgins by Thomas Shepard (1605–1649)," in *The Devoted Life: An Invitation to the Puritan Classics*, ed. Kelly M. Kapic and Randall C. Gleason (Downers Grove, Ill.: InterVarsity Press, 2004), 128.
38. Shepard, *Autobiography*, 41.

Shepard used his influence to create opportunities for the next generation of students in New England.

Within six years of founding the Massachusetts Bay Colony, there was already talk of establishing a college. The colonies desired to provide a high-quality liberal arts education to all serious Christian students as well as to train ministers. Mixed with their reverence for general education, they were also "dreading to leave an illiterate ministry to the churches, when [their] present ministers shall lie in the dust."[39] In 1636, the General Court voted to allot four hundred pounds toward the founding of a school. At the forefront of this effort was Thomas Shepard.

When deciding on a location for the new college, Shepard lobbied for Cambridge, his hometown. In light of the quality of Shepard's ministry, his steering the church away from the errors of the Antinomian Controversy, and his reputation for soul winning, the court agreed on Cambridge. While on his deathbed, Charlestown resident John Harvard (1607–1638) generously donated half of his estate (the sum of nearly eight hundred pounds) as well as his entire library of two hundred and sixty volumes. In March 1639 the General Court met in Boston and, in honor of their gracious benefactor, "Ordered, that the colledge agreed upon formerly to bee built at Cambridg shalbee called Harvard Colledge."[40]

The college curriculum was modeled after that of Oxford and Cambridge, especially Emmanuel College, where many first-generation New England ministers had studied. Students were trained in logic, rhetoric, ethics, metaphysics, Greek, Hebrew, Latin, Aramaic, and the natural sciences.[41] Above all, however, believing that "all truth was God's truth," the founders of Harvard College decreed, "Let every student be plainly instructed and

---

39. Cited in Leland Ryken, *Worldly Saints: The Puritans as They Really Were* (Grand Rapids: Zondervan, 1986), 160.

40. Quoted in Samuel Eliot Morison, *The Founding of Harvard College* (1935; repr., Cambridge, Mass.: Harvard University Press, 1995), 221.

41. Francis J. Bremer, *The Puritan Experiment: New England Society from Bradford to Edwards*, rev. ed. (Hanover, N.H.: University Press of New England, 1995), 119–20.

earnestly pressed to consider well the main end of his life and studies is to know God and Jesus Christ which is eternal life, John 17:3,
and therefore to lay Christ in the bottom, as the only foundation
of all sound knowledge and learning."[42] In addition to training
young Puritan students, Harvard College also served as the training
ground for John Eliot's Indian mission, an effort to bring the gospel
to the natives of Massachusetts.

Having come from meager means, Shepard recognized the great
financial burden of education on the poor. In 1644, the United Colonies gathered for their annual meeting at Hartford. At the meeting,
Shepard presented a petition to request that every family in New
England "which is able and willing…to [give] yearely but the fourth
part of a bushel of Corne, or somethinge equivalent thereunto."[43] In
essence, Shepard was requesting the colonies establish a scholarship
fund for needy students. In response, the four colonies did "cheer-
fully embrace" the idea and decree the sanctioning of "the college
corn."[44] While the school bore its fair share of struggles early on, the
dream of a Puritan college in America was realized in Harvard's early
years, in no small part due to the efforts of Thomas Shepard.

Struggles and Challenges
In addition to contending for the faith against the errors of antinomianism, Shepard also contended for what he believed to be
a biblical position on church government. In line with the other
magistrates and ministers in Massachusetts Bay, Shepard was a proponent of Independency, which would later come to be known as
Congregationalism. He saw it as "a middle way" between Presbyterianism and Brownism.[45] Along with leaders such as John Cotton,
Richard Mather, and Thomas Hooker, Shepard contributed to the

---

42. Cited in Ryken, *Worldly Saints*, 161.
43. Quoted in Morison, *Founding of Harvard College*, 315.
44. Quoted in Morison, *Founding of Harvard College*, 315.
45. The Brownists were a group of English Separatists, named after Robert Browne
(c. 1550–1633), who advocated for an extreme form of Congregationalism that bordered on the verge of pure church democracy.

Cambridge Platform (1648), "the most significant and inclusive statement of the doctrine and polity of what became known as non-separating Congregationalism or the 'New England Way.'"[46]

Shepard not only battled doctrinal skirmishes but also was plagued with extensive emotional and physical struggles. During his second year at Cambridge, he nearly died from smallpox. It would not be the last illness he would endure. In 1638, Shepard records, "I fell sick after Mr. Harlakenden's death, my most dear friend and most precious servant of Jesus Christ. And when I was very low and my blood much corrupted, the Lord revived me."[47] While sickness was never far from his own house, Shepard faced a more deadly opponent: himself.

Cotton Mather records that Shepard was "one of the *happiest* men that ever we saw; as great a *converter of souls* as has ordinarily been known in our days."[48] However, his inner life wreaked havoc on him. While he was vigorously devoted to his studies, he often lamented his own laziness and lethargy.[49] He famously said, "God will curse that man's labours, that lumbers up and down in the world all the week, and then upon Saturday in the afternoon goes to his study; when, as God knows, that time were little enough to pray in and weep in, and get his heart into a fit frame for the duties of the approaching Sabbath."[50]

---

46. Werge, *Thomas Shepard*, 11.

47. Shepard, *Autobiography*, 71.

48. Mather, *Magnalia*, 1:380.

49. On Shepard's preparation, Alexander Whyte notes, "Never did the most conscientious preacher do more than Shepard did to prepare himself every new week for a fruitful and happy Sabbath, both to his people and to himself. Shepard was a hard worker both in his pastoral visitations and in his study. He took the very greatest pains in the preparation of his sermons. He had an intellectual and a spiritual people, he respected and revered his people, and he worked hard for them. It was his rule to work hard early in the week and as a rule he had his sermons ready by two o'clock on Saturday afternoon. And then he gave up the whole of the Saturday evening and Sabbath morning to prepare his own mind and heart for his pulpit duties on the coming day." *Thomas Shepard*, 44.

50. Mather, *Magnalia*, 1:390.

However, in his diary, it becomes very clear that he, like many other Puritans, reserves the greatest judgment for himself. Despite being well loved and highly revered in ministry, he recorded in his journal in 1643,

> January 25. I saw (1) my weakness: how blind and unbelieving I was and thence unfit to teach others. (2) I saw my boldness that I had taken upon me at first a bigger and greater work than I was well able to go through with, viz., ministry and profession of Christianity, for I saw if I neglected my work in either, others would be offended; if I did anything, I could not but act without life. (3) I saw my vileness that I had polluted and blasphemed God's name by my foolish and weak and sinful walking in my place, whereby I was justly slight[ed] and God's work not carried on with success and authority. (4) I saw my misery that God, Christ, spirit, grace, mercy had forsaken me and mine to mourn and lie down and look up still to all-able and all-working mercy, and that I should be humbled by all this more than any and not lift up myself and render all my little.[51]

Despite being the recipient of accolades and honor from men, Shepard was thoroughly convinced of his own inadequacy before God and lamented it repeatedly in the pages of his private journal.

Much of his trials were mixed with joy. After the death of his first wife, Shepard married Joanna Hooker, the eldest daughter of Thomas Hooker, in October 1637. They had four children together, two of whom survived into adulthood. Just after giving birth to one of their sons, Joanna died in April 1646. In the wake of her passing, Shepard wrote, "I am the Lord's, and he may do with me what he will. He did teach me to prize a little grace gained by a cross as a sufficient recompense for all outward losses. But this loss was very great."[52] On September 8, 1647, Shepard married his third wife, Margaret Boradel, with whom he had one son. Shepard would predecease his third wife.

---

51. Shepard, "Journal," 124.
52. Shepard, *Autobiography*, 73.

Death and Legacy

In the summer of 1649, Shepard began to suffer from a sore throat, which developed into a serious infection that proved fatal. He died on August 25, 1649, at the age of forty-four. Even in his final days, he was plagued with the condition of his own soul: "O my sinful heart! O my often-crucified but never wholly mortified sinfulness! O my life-long damage and my daily shame! O my indwelling and so besetting sins, your evil dominion is over now! It is now within an hour or two of my final and everlasting release! For I am authoritatively assured that by to-morrow morning I shall have entered into my eternal rest! And then, O my ransomed soul, one hour in heaven will make me forget all my hell upon earth!"[53]

Shepard was laid to rest in Cambridge and was "universally lamented by the whole colony, in whose service he had exhausted all his powers."[54] While he did not possess the titanic intellect of John Cotton and Thomas Hooker, he was "one of the best loved men."[55]

The preaching and evangelistic ministry had spread like ripples in a pond throughout all England and New England. His biographer, John Albro, writes, "He was 'an Augustine in disputation,' as well as a Chrysostom in the pulpit; and, like a scribe well instructed, he produced several works which are of permanent value for doctrine and instruction in righteousness."[56] While he produced a handful of important smaller works during his lifetime, three distinct works stand out.

When he was still in England, one of his listeners transcribed several of his lectures on true conversion and published it in 1641 under the title *The Sincere Convert*. The book was controversial for its stark and biting tone and was criticized by some of Shepard's opponents. When confronted with the book's content, Shepard was apparently unfamiliar with it, claiming, "*That which is called the* Sincere Convert, *I have not the book, I once saw it; it was a Collection of*

---

53. Whyte, *Thomas Shepard*, 144.
54. Albro, "Life of Thomas Shepard," 1:clxxv–clxxvi.
55. Morison, *Builders of the Bay Colony*, 106.
56. Albro, "Life of Thomas Shepard," 1:clxxxii.

such Notes in a dark Town in England, *which one procuring of me, published them without my will...I scare knew what it contains*."[57] Before too long, he set out to write a more definitive work on the topic.

In 1645 Shepard published *The Sound Believer* to address the doctrine of regeneration. Scholar Thomas Werge notes, "In *The Sincere Convert*, Shepard's most powerfully tactile imagery tends to concentrate on the soul's sense of pain and eternal loss. In *The Sound Believer*, it concentrates as profoundly on the soul's conviction and assurance that Christ has come to find and to save 'that which was lost.'"[58]

Perhaps Shepard's greatest legacy lives on through his most notable work, *The Parable of the Ten Virgins*. While not directly composed with his own hand (it was compiled and published by his son in 1660), *Ten Virgins* represents the marrow of Shepard's evangelistic focus on true conversion. While admittedly difficult to read, the work presents incredible spiritual insights. Jonathan Edwards in his *Religious Affections* quotes from Shepard's *Ten Virgins* more than any other source.[59] O. R. Johnston classifies it as "a masterpiece of the thorough, sound, and practical Reformed Christianity which we associate with the names of the very greatest Puritans."[60] Furthermore, John Gerstner exhorts, "Don't read it! Study it, a few pages at a time. Decipher it. Live with it, die with it."[61]

By earth's clock, Thomas Shepard was gone too soon. Heaven only knows what more he would have offered the Puritan world had he lived another thirty years. However, Shepard was ever grateful for all the Lord had given him. In the final pages of his *Autobiography*, he rehearsed God's grace in his own life:

---

57. Giles Firmin, "To the Reader," cited in Werge, *Thomas Shepard*, 51.

58. Werge, *Thomas Shepard*, 63.

59. Joel R. Beeke and Randall J. Pederson, *Meet the Puritans* (Grand Rapids: Reformation Heritage Books, 2006), 529.

60. O. R. Johnston, "Thomas Shepard's 'Parable of the Ten Virgins,'" in *Puritan Papers: Volume 1, 1956–1959*, ed. D. Martyn Lloyd-Jones (Phillipsburg, N.J.: P&R Publishing, 2000), 126.

61. John H. Gerstner, foreword to Thomas Shepard, *The Parable of the Ten Virgins* (1852; repr., Ligonier: Soli Deo Gloria Publications, 1990), 2.

He is the God who took me up when my own mother died, who loved me, and when my stepmother cared not for me, and when lastly my father also died and forsook me, when I was young and little and could take no care for myself....

He is the God that brought me out of Egypt, that profane and wicked town where I was born and bred, under the care of one of my own brethren, and that gave me time and will to desire learning, where if I had lived I had sinned and been forever damned....

[He] is the God that convinced me of my guilt and filth of sin, especially self-seeking and love of honor of men in all I did, and humbled me under both so as to set a higher price on Christ and grace, and to loathe myself the more.... He also showed me the worth of Christ and made my soul satisfied with him and cleave to him.[62]

---

62. Shepard, *Autobiography*, 74–75.

6

ANNE BRADSTREET

In early 1629 Anne Bradstreet could not predict or even guess when she would begin the long, arduous journey across the Atlantic to the unknown world her husband and father had convinced her to live in. Anne's father and his colleagues dedicated themselves to planning every eventuality of the journey and how the new "city upon a hill" would be structured. Anne was increasingly convinced that the religious situation in England was irreversible and that to avoid becoming a victim of the growing corruption, they must escape to a land where they could worship God freely. Reluctantly, Anne parted with her worldly possessions and gave herself to this providential plan. She, along with her parents, husband, and siblings, boarded the *Arbella* and set sail to an unknown world. Her muse awaited her.

Childhood

About sixty miles northwest of London sits Northampton, a large market town and county town of Northamptonshire in the East Midlands of England. Situated on the River Nene since 1189, Northampton is the place where the story of Anne Bradstreet (1612–1672) begins. In 1612, Anne was born the second child of Thomas (1576–1653) and Dorothy (1582–1643) Dudley, who were married in 1603, the year Queen Elizabeth I died.

Anne's mother was "a gentlewoman both of good estate and extraction,"[1] and as a young man her well-educated father had been commissioned as a captain by Queen Elizabeth I to command eighty volunteers from Northampton. The volunteers joined the ranks of Henry IV (1553–1610) of France against Philip II (1527–1598) of Spain. Although never experiencing actual combat in battle, Thomas gained invaluable experience as a soldier.[2] Upon his return from France, Thomas became a clerk for a prominent judge in Northampton.[3] His position as clerk allowed Thomas the tremendous privilege of accompanying the judge to London and learning the eccentricities of the law, which greatly benefited him in his future journey across the Atlantic to the New World.

Growing Up in Sempringham

In 1620 the growing Dudley family moved from Northampton to Sempringham, the estate of Theophilus Clinton (1599–1667), the fourth Earl of Lincoln. Thomas assumed the position of steward, overseeing the financial affairs of the vast estate and the personal profits of the earl, of whom it was said conducted no "business of moment without Mr. Dudley's counsel."[4] Before their move to Sempringham, Thomas and Dorothy Dudley welcomed two more children into their home, Patience and Sarah, and another sister, Mercy, arrived within a year of the move.[5]

Growing up on the estate would have provided every possible opportunity for Anne and her siblings. The Dudley family would have been surrounded with nobility and an army of servants who oversaw the lands and household of the earl, offering them opportunities that would not have been available to them otherwise. Anne

---

1. Augustine Jones, *The Life and Work of Thomas Dudley: The Second Governor of Massachusetts* (Boston: Houghton Mifflin, 1900), 25.

2. Alexander Young, *Chronicles of the First Planters of the Colony of Massachusetts Bay, 1623–1636* (Boston: Little, Brown, 1846), 304.

3. D. B. Kellogg, *Anne Bradstreet* (Nashville, Tenn.: Thomas Nelson, 2010), 3.

4. Jones, *Thomas Dudley*, 40.

5. Patience was born in 1616, Sarah in 1620, and Mercy in 1621.

became well acquainted with the earl's mother, wife, and extended family, both those living on the estate and those who visited at regular intervals, including his sister, Lady Arbella (1597–1630). Perhaps what delighted Anne the most during this period was the access she had to the earl's immense collection of books. Her father shared her love of reading and encouraged Anne to expand her intellectual horizons with books like Sir Walter Raleigh's *History of the World*. Anne seemed taken with poetry, especially poems by the Frenchman Guillaume de Salluste du Bartas (1544–1590).[6]

Puritan Convictions

As faithful members of the Church of England, the Dudley household gradually embraced Puritanism in practice and daily disciplines. Under the tutelage of their father, the Dudley children learned to read and write and became well versed in Scripture. Anne and her family had copies of both the recently translated King James and Geneva versions of Scripture, and they often discussed their meditations on particular verses, joined together in daily prayer and psalm reading, and regularly discussed the sermons they heard in church. Anne later recalled her frequent sinful attitude toward her parents at age six or seven. She vividly remembered her ardent desire to confess all of her daily sins in prayer before God and her inability to rest until having done so. She was also "troubled at the neglect of Private Duties [meditating and praying in private]" and felt she was "too often tardy that way." However, reading Scripture gave her comfort, and the more she understood of God's truth, the more solace she found in it.[7]

In 1624, Thomas Dudley resigned his position as steward for the Earl of Lincoln and moved his family to Boston, about twenty miles northeast of Sempringham.[8] The Dudley family became acquainted with John Cotton, the pastor of St. Botolph's, where they attended

---

6. Kellogg, *Anne Bradstreet*, 4.
7. Anne Bradstreet, *The Works of Anne Bradstreet in Prose and Verse*, ed. John Harvard Ellis (Charlestown, Mass.: Abram E. Cutter, 1867), 4.
8. Kellogg, *Anne Bradstreet*, 8.

while living in Boston. Cotton, a Puritan leader, had an immense impact on the Dudley family, especially Anne, as she looked to his sermons and counsel for direction in her personal spiritual journey. Although seemingly short, their time in Boston further solidified the Puritan convictions of the Dudley family and would aid in their decision to leave their native homeland in the coming years.

The Plague of Sickness

The Dudley family returned to Sempringham by 1628, the same year Anne was stricken with smallpox and treated while living on the estate.[9] Although she praised God for recovering from this debilitating plague, Anne experienced numerous health issues the remainder of her life. Smallpox caused boils to appear on the skin, and in severe cases it could cause blindness, hemorrhaging, and even death. It had no cure. Due to sicknesses she experienced as a child, Anne's recovery was extended and gave her much time for spiritual reflection and introspection.[10] She wrote that smallpox was a sign "the Lord laid his hand sore upon me" and caused her to confess her "Pride and Vanity" to him. Later in life, recalling another childhood infirmity, she wrote,

> My burning flesh is sweat did boil,
> My aching head did break;
> From side to side for ease I toil,
> So faint I could not speak.
>
> O, heal my Soul, thou know'st I said,
> Through flesh consume to naught;
> What though in dust it shall be laid,
> To glory it shall be brought.
> Thou heard, thy rod thou did remove,
> And spared by Body frail....

---

9. Kellogg, *Anne Bradstreet*, 8.
10. Bradstreet, *Bradstreet in Prose and Verse*, 4.

O, Praises to my mighty God,
Praise to my Lord, I say,
Who hath redeemed my Soul from [the] pit.[11]

Simon Bradstreet

A young man named Simon Bradstreet (1603–1697) moved to the Earl of Lincoln's estate in 1622 after the death of his father, who had served as a nonconformist pastor at Horbling in Lincolnshire. Once Simon eventually completed a BA and MA at Emmanuel College, Cambridge, John Cotton discussed his future with Thomas Dudley, who agreed to train Simon as his assistant on the estate.[12] Simon was remembered as having a "broad, benignant forehead, clear dark eyes, and firm, well-cut nose," and a character of "strength and sweetness."[13] He was also said to possess "a sense of the keenest life and vigor, both mental and physical."[14] Under the guidance of Thomas, Simon soon became well versed in all the duties of an estate steward and stepped into the leadership role while Dudley and his family were away in Boston. When the Dudley family moved back to Sempringham, Simon transitioned to being a steward to the Countess of Warwick. Lady Warwick needed someone to manage the daily affairs of her estate while her husband was often away on business, and Simon fulfilled this role perfectly.

Simon was nineteen when he first met Anne Dudley. Because of the nine-year age difference between them, it is likely Anne looked up to Simon in the role of an elder brother. However, around the age of "fourteen or fifteen," Anne recalls, she began to experience the "vanity and follies of youth" taking hold of her as she found herself attracted to the handsome Bradstreet.[15] With time, a courtship matured between young Anne and her new beau as they shared

---

11. Bradstreet, *Bradstreet in Prose and Verse*, 12–13.
12. Isaac Greenwood, *Remarks on the Maverick Family and the Ancestry of Gov. Simon Bradstreet* (Boston: D. Clapp & Son, 1894), 1–9.
13. Helen Campbell, *Anne Bradstreet and Her Time* (Boson: D. Lothrop, 1891), 25.
14. Campbell, *Anne Bradstreet*, 26.
15. Bradstreet, *Bradstreet in Prose and Verse*, 4.

favorite books and Scripture verses, mutual likes and dislikes, and took long walks on the estate. When Simon asked for Anne's hand, Thomas Dudley agreed for his former apprentice to marry his beloved daughter. In 1628, at sixteen years old, Anne took the hand of Simon Bradstreet in marriage while she was still experiencing weakness from the smallpox that had ravaged her frail body.

To the New World
The young couple settled into their new life on the country estate of the Countess of Warwick as Simon continued his position of estate steward and Anne became familiar with running her own home. However, during this same period the Bradstreet home was bustling with an atmosphere of uncertainty as to whether Simon and Anne would join her parents and siblings in the New World. For quite some time, a group of Puritans had been making plans and preparations to sail to the American colonies. Thomas and Dorothy Dudley had made the decision to join their fellow Puritans in this unknown wilderness even before the marriage of their daughter. Simon was more uncertain than his father-in-law about taking his new bride and venturing into what was a relatively unknown future. As the English political landscape pointed toward the imminent persecution and maltreatment of the Puritans, Simon became convinced that the only alternative was to join the contingent in the Massachusetts Bay Colony.

Lincolnshire was abuzz with Calvinistic Puritan fervor.[16] From the period of the sixteenth-century Reformation, that particular part of England north of London had been inhabited by "bold, independent, thoughtful, and industrious citizens."[17] Ultimately, these faithful men and women desired not only to experience religious freedom from the tyranny of the English Crown but to plant the gospel in New England.[18] Large sums of money were invested

---

16. Jones, *Thomas Dudley*, 47.
17. Jones, *Thomas Dudley*, 47–48.
18. Young, *Chronicles of the First Planters*, 310.

in the venture. Isaac Johnson (c. 1600–1630), a wealthy landowner and husband to Lady Arbella, the sister of the Earl of Lincoln, came to be the primary investor in the venture soon to cross the turbulent seas of the Atlantic.

Among their number, John Winthrop (1588–1649) was elected to serve as governor and John Humphrey (c. 1597–1661) as deputy governor. In 1628, John Endecott (c. 1588–1665) was dispatched to Salem, Massachusetts, to make preparations for the larger regiment to arrive at a later date. Endecott's mandate was clear from the outset. He was instructed to build homes, survey the land and prepare it for planting crops, establish a house of worship, and attend to other duties that would eliminate as many hardships as possible before the Winthrop party arrived. The Dudley family, along with Simon and Anne Bradstreet, were to be among the number to depart England on the 1630 expedition.

Voyage
The lead ship was to be the *Eagle*, but it was rechristened the *Arbella* in honor of its noblest passenger, Lady Arbella.[19] Equipped to carry 350 to 400 tons, the *Arbella* was the largest and most notable ship in the fleet. The *Talbot*, *Ambrose*, and the *Jewel* joined the armada across the Atlantic in 1630. Simon and Anne joined Anne's parents, her siblings, John Winthrop, and Lady Arbella and her husband aboard the *Arbella* as they sailed from Southampton.[20] Before departing, Thomas Dudley was unexpectedly honored in being made the deputy governor, as the business affairs of John Humphrey caused him to disembark and remain in England.[21] Anne, young and uncertain about the seemingly overwhelming endeavor that lay ahead, commented in later life what she found when she

---

19. Kellogg, *Anne Bradstreet*, 20.
20. Jones, *Thomas Dudley*, 58.
21. Jones, *Thomas Dudley*, 46, 60.

arrived in New England: "I found a new world and new manners, at which my heart rose [in protest]."[22]

Salem

The *Arbella* weighed anchor in Salem Harbor on June 14, 1630. Upon disembarking in this strange new world, Simon and Anne soon discovered that the house promised prior to their departure had not been built. Along with many others aboard, they were forced to share communal living quarters. In addition to no private lodging, food was also in short supply after the harsh New England winter experienced by the envoy of John Endecott. During the winter of 1629–1630, Endecott had lost around eighty of his companions, and those remaining were so ill they were unable to build homes or plant crops for the new arrivals. Winthrop and the other leaders made the difficult decision to relocate from Salem to Charlestown, where conditions were more favorable. As the men repositioned the new colony, Anne, along with her mother and sisters, remained in Salem until living arrangements had been prepared. All manner of dwellings were constructed. From more modest dwellings for the upper echelon of the Bay Colony leaders, to mud huts with thatched roofs, to wigwams fashioned in the likeness of those of the Native Americans, to simple tents constructed of sail cloth, these new arrivals had not prepared themselves for these harsh living conditions in this new city on a hill.[23]

A Church Covenant

Never neglecting the Puritan spiritual duties of sitting under the preaching of Scripture, daily prayers, and the fellowship of believers, the colonists wrote a covenant to form a new church in Charlestown on July 30, 1630. Governor John Winthrop, Deputy Governor

---

22. Anne Bradstreet, *The Works of Anne Bradstreet*, ed. Jeannie Hensley (Cambridge, Mass.: Belknap Press, 1967), 241.

23. Samuel Eliot Morison, *Builders of the Bay Colony* (1930; repr., Boston: Northeastern University Press, 1981), 136.

Thomas and Dorothy Dudley, Simon and Anne Bradstreet, and other men and women affixed their names to the following covenant:

> In the name of our Lord Jesus Christ, and in Obedience to His holy will and Divine Ordinance,—We whose names are here-under written, being by His most wise and good Providence brought together into this part of America in the Bay of Massachusetts, and desirous to unite ourselves into one congregation or Church, under the Lord Jesus Christ our Head, in such sort as becometh all those whom He hath Redeemed and Sanctified to Himself, do hereby solemnly and religiously (as in His most holy Presence) Promise and bind ourselves to walk in all our ways according to the Rule of the Gospel, and in all sincere Conformity to His holy Ordinances, and in mutual love and respect each to other, so near as God shall give us grace.[24]

Anne later wrote that she was "convinced it was the way of God," and she "submitted to it and joined to the church."[25] The Charlestown church relocated to Boston not long after it had been established and became the First Church of Boston.

The Plague of Sickness

Sickness began to fall on the colonies like a heavy blanket, touching almost every household. In August, the friend of the Bradstreets and Dudleys, Lady Arbella, succumbed to illness and died. Within a month, her husband was also dead. Poor living conditions, inadequate diet, the intense heat of the summer months, and the tormenting mosquitoes all contributed to sickness and unending illness in the colony. By the end of 1630, more than two hundred of their English countrymen had died either on the Atlantic crossing or during their early settlement in Massachusetts.[26] While the new settlers were burying their friends, about one hundred of their other companions returned to England or Ireland.

---

24. Jones, *Thomas Dudley*, 80–81.
25. Bradstreet, *Bradstreet in Prose and Verse*, xxl, xv.
26. Young, *Chronicles of the First Planters*, 325.

As the New England winter set in, the conditions grew more challenging. Simon and Anne were still eating provisions of salty meat from their voyage.[27] Wild game, such as rabbits, ducks, deer, and other birds, was just off their doorstep, but someone had to hunt it down. The sea also teemed with creatures like fish, clams, oysters, mussels, and lobster.[28] Eventually the settlers would learn to hunt, trap, and fish. Eels were roasted, fried, boiled, or stuffed with nutmeg and cloves.[29] Venison, duck, gull, and other small game were roasted over an open hearth. The Native Americans taught the immigrants how to make succotash and hoe cakes from corn. As John Winthrop wrote to his wife on July 30, 1630, "Our fare be but coarse in respect to what we formerly had, (pease, puddings and fish being our ordinary diet) yet he [God] makes it sweet and wholesome to us, that I may truly say I desire no better.... I see no cause to repent of our coming thither."[30]

Making a Home

From the moment Anne and Simon set foot in the New World, they had no place to call home. They had boarded, along with others, in communal quarters in Boston along with Anne's parents until a home could be constructed. They had few pieces of furniture, nothing to call their own, and the living conditions were anything but ideal. Anne's father recalled how he had to write letters by the light of the fire and had "yet no table nor other room to write in."[31]

The first home Anne and Simon moved into sits on what is now known as Harvard Square, and the cow pasture next door was in what is now Harvard Yard. Anne's parents lived a few blocks away at the corner of Dunster and South Streets. Although sparsely furnished, Anne and Simon's home had a table for meals, a cupboard

---

27. Morison, *Builders of the Bay Colony*, 80.

28. Kellogg, *Anne Bradstreet*, 34.

29. Kellogg, *Anne Bradstreet*, 34.

30. Carole Chandler Waldrup, *Colonial Women: 23 Europeans Who Helped Build a Nation* (Jefferson, N.C.: McFarland & Co., 1999), 31.

31. Young, *Chronicles of the First Planters*, 305.

for tableware and other items, benches, and a bed.[32] The large stone fireplace in the central room could always be found aglow in the Bradstreet home. The hearth was cluttered with pots, pot hooks, kettles, and other cooking utensils. In the hearth corners were displayed skillets, trivets, peels, and slices, and on either side were chimney seats. Above were cluttered strings of dried apples, pumpkins, and peppers.[33] Lamps filled with fish oil and candles made of bayberry wax were found in almost every room of the house.[34]

The Newtown meetinghouse was constructed in 1633 near the home of Anne's parents. Its first pastor was Thomas Hooker, who had just arrived from Holland after hastily departing England. Until the church was established, the residents of Newtown made the journey to Boston for worship. Anne recounts that after their initial move to Newtown she was unable to attend services in Boston because of a besetting illness. In addition to her frail constitution, Anne became quite lonely as Simon was often away from home conducting business and governmental affairs. Anne writes she was tormented by a "lingering sickness like consumption" complicated by "lameness." She was convinced that she, at the young age of twenty, was facing "fatal Death." Rather than fall into depression because of her ailments, Anne was convinced God was trying to humble her and that there were great spiritual lessons to be gleaned from this experience. Her anguish is transformed into poetry:

> In anguish of my heart replete with woes,
> And wasting pains, which best by body knows,
> In tossing slumbers on my wakeful bed,
> Bedrenched with tears that flowed from mournful head,
> Till nature had exhausted all her store,
> Then eyes lay dry, disabled to weep more;
> And looking up unto his throne on high,

32. Kellogg, *Anne Bradstreet*, 40.

33. Alice Morse Earle, *Customs and Fashions in Old New England* (New York: Charles Scribner's Sons, 1893), 130.

34. Earle, *Customs and Fashions*, 127.

Who sendeth help to those in misery;
He chased away those clouds and let me see
My anchor cast i' th' vale with safety.
He eased my soul of woe, my flesh of pain,
And brought me to the shore from troubled main.[35]

By autumn of 1632, the number of residents had grown to the point that Newtown was becoming overcrowded. While Anne continued to recover from her sickness, her father and husband were out surveying new land for a possible move. They decided that Ipswich (then called Agawam) was a likely prospect about thirty miles north of Newtown as the crow flies.[36] Ipswich was on the farthest reaches of the other settled areas of the colony. The initial plans to relocate were abandoned for a short time as other concerns occupied the Bradstreet home.

Motherhood

Anne and Simon welcomed their first child, Samuel, in 1633, the year after she had feared her life was slipping. Reflecting on this monumental event later in life, Anne wrote, "It pleased God to keep me a long time without a child, which was a great grief to me, and cost me many prayers and tears before I obtained one, and after him gave me many more of whom I now take care, that as I have brought you into the world, and with great pains, weakness, cares, and fears brought you to this."[37]

Once Anne discovered she was with child, her mother and other neighboring women took much care in planning the eventual birth. Given Anne's frail state, every precaution had to be taken. In addition to every detail being attended to, the pregnancy and birth were

---

35. Anne Bradstreet, *The Poems of Mrs. Anne Bradstreet (1612–1672) together with Her Prose Remains* (n.p.: The Duodecimos, 1897), 268–69.

36. Kellogg, *Anne Bradstreet*, 45.

37. Anne Bradstreet in *The Puritans in America: A Narrative Anthology*, ed. Alan Heimert and Andrew Delbanco (Cambridge, Mass.: Harvard University Press, 1985), 139.

bathed in prayer as Anne clearly recognized, given her medical history, that this first child was a gift from God. After Samuel was born, the women continued to care for Anne for three to four weeks, at least until she could get out of bed and resume her household duties.

Anne recognized, as she and Simon eventually raised four boys and four girls, that each child possesses a differing personality and temperament. She wrote, "Diverse children have their different natures: some are like flesh which nothing but salt will keep from putrefaction, some again like tender fruits that are best preserved with sugar. Those parents are wise that can fit their nurture according to their nature."[38]

When a child was born into a Puritan home, the major responsibilities of care were given to the mother, the preeminent responsibility of which was to nourish the child from her own breast. As the head of the family, Simon was responsible for directing the children in worship, leading the household in daily prayers, devotional and Scripture readings, and catechizing. Within Puritan families, the belief that God's glory is the chief end of all things drove the philosophy of childrearing. A man who did not lead his household in these spiritual exercises was viewed by the community as a fool and a scoundrel.

Anne took Samuel to the meetinghouse as soon as she was able to do so. Children always accompanied their parents and sat in Puritan worship services. Girls usually sat with the women, and the boys were in a separate section under the ever-watchful eyes of the men. Viewing Scripture through the lens of covenant theology, the Puritans practiced infant baptism, viewing their children as part of the covenant that God establishes with believers. The baptism was reserved only for those whose parents were members of the church and was administered in the church's worship service. The baptism of children was not in any way viewed as salvific but served as a sign

---

38. Philip Greven, *The Protestant Temperament: Patterns of Child-Rearing, Religious Experience, and the Self in Early America* (Chicago: University of Chicago Press, 1977), 49.

and seal of God's promises to raise a covenant seed to serve Him even as the parents promised that they would raise their child in the "nurture and admonition of the Lord" (Eph. 6:4).

Children raised in Puritan homes did not have a dismal and dour childhood. It would have been filled with many joys and amusements as befitted the enjoyment of God's creation and fellowship with one another. As children grew, they were invited to participate in sports or recreation, such as hunting, fishing, skating, and archery.[39] Children would have enjoyed playing in the orchards, going on picnics, reading edifying literature, having sack races, ring toss, and other popular games of the day.

In 1635 Thomas and Simon, wanting to avoid the ever-growing population of Newtown, once again began to discuss relocating their families to Ipswich. Thomas had served his term as governor and was now needed in Ipswich.[40] Anne did not relish the fact of moving yet again, especially to the far-flung outreaches of the colony, but she would soon discover that her greatest writing would come to fruition in this new wilderness.

Into the Wilderness

Agawam, the Native American name for Ipswich, was founded in 1633 on the banks of the river near the ocean. Ipswich was bordered by dense wilderness to the west, marshlands to the north, and a coastline to the east, where clams were readily available. In 1635, the Massachusetts General Court ordered that no house in Ipswich was to be built more than a half mile from the meetinghouse because of the Indian threat.[41] The town meetinghouse was located on a hilltop, as most were throughout colonial towns, and behind it a stone fort was built. Native American attack was an ever-present fear for the residents of Ipswich, so much so that men would carry weapons with them to worship. If an impending attack threatened

---

39. Morison, *Builders of the Bay Colony*, 135.
40. Morison, *Builders of the Bay Colony*, 223.
41. Kellogg, *Anne Bradstreet*, 64.

the town, someone was assigned to fire three musket shots into the air to warn the residents. At night, if a cannon was fired or a beating drum was heard, an attack was at their door. If someone cried out, "Arm! Arm!" Anne knew to grab her children and run as fast as possible to the fort for safety.[42] The threat intensified in 1636 as it became apparent that the colonies of Plymouth, Massachusetts, and Connecticut must join forces to defeat the Pequot Indians. In 1638, the Treaty of Hartford (which ended the Pequot War) stated, among other restrictions on the survivors, that the Pequot name could no longer be used.[43] The tribe was no more.

A Poetic Voice

Simon, a loving husband and devoted father, was often absent from their Ipswich home while on government business. While away, he would often receive letters from Anne. Writing in poetic verse, Anne expressed her longing to have him near. In "To My Dear and Loving Husband," she writes,

> If ever two were one, then surely we.
> If ever man were lov'd by wife, then thee;
> If ever wife was happy in a man,
> Compare with me ye women if you can.
> I prize thy love more than whole Mines of gold,
> Or all the riches that the East doth hold.
> My love is such that Rivers cannot quench,
> Nor ought but love from thee, give recompense.
> Thy love is such I can no way repay,
> The heavens reward thee manifold I pray.
> Then while we live, in love lets so persevere,
> That when we live no more, we may live ever.[44]

---

42. Thomas Franklin Waters, *The Meeting House Green and a Study of Houses and Lands in That Vicinity* (Salem, Mass.: Salem Press, 1902), 5, 10. See also Kellogg, *Anne Bradstreet*, 65.

43. Kellogg, *Anne Bradstreet*, 65–66.

44. Bradstreet, *Works of Anne Bradstreet*, 225.

Anne references her desire for Simon to return from his travels in "A Letter to Her Husband, Absent upon Publick Employment," almost crying forth, "Return, return sweet *Sol* from *Capricorn*;... / Flesh of thy flesh, bone of thy bone, / I here, thou there, yet both but one."[45] In her poetic letter "Another," she implores Phoebus, the sun personified, to remind Simon of her anguish while he is absent and to implore him to return as soon as possible.[46] She writes,

> *Phoebus* make haste, the day's too long, be gone,
> The silent night's the fittest time for moan;
> But stay this once, unto my suit give ear,
> And tell my griefs in either Hemisphere:
> (And if the whirling of thy wheels don't drown'd)
> The woeful accents of my doleful sound,
> If in thy swift Carrier thou canst make stay,
> I crave this boon, this Errand by the way,
> Commend me to the man more lov'd than life,
> Shew him the sorrows of his widowed wife;
> My dumpish thoughts, my groans, my brakish tears
> My sobs, my longing hopes, my doubting fears,
> And if he love, how can he there abide?[47]

Continuing in "Another," Anne describes the images of separated pairs of deer, turtle doves, and mullets to describe the companionship she and her husband share and to depict her intense longing for him.[48] She concludes the poetic letter,

> Return my Dear, my joy, my only Love,
> Unto thy Hinde, thy Mullet and thy Dove,
> Who neither joys in pasture, house nor streams,
> The substance gone, O me, these are but dreams.

---

45. Bradstreet, *Works of Anne Bradstreet*, 226.
46. Heidi L. Nichols, *Anne Bradstreet: A Guided Tour of the Life and Thought of a Puritan Poet* (Phillipsburg, N.J.: P&R Publishing, 2006), 120.
47. Bradstreet, *Works of Anne Bradstreet*, 227.
48. Nichols, *Anne Bradstreet*, 122.

Together at one Tree, oh let us brouze,
And like two Turtles roost within one house,
And like the Mullets in one River glide,
Let's still remain but one, till death divide.[49]

Assuring him of her love regardless of where he may roam, she signs
the letter, "Thy loving Love and Dearest Dear, At home, abroad,
and every where. A.B." The love between Anne and Simon is vividly
seen in her longing to be near him, fix her eyes on him, and be in
his company. Even when separated by great distance, Anne was his
dearest companion.

One year after the Bradstreets relocated to Ipswich, the Massachusetts General Court appropriated funds to found a college
in the colonies. In 1637, John Harvard (1607–1638), a graduate
of Emmanuel College, Cambridge, was living in Charlestown. By
1638, he had died of consumption and awarded half his estate and
his personal library to the new college. It was therefore named after
him and was established in the newly named Cambridge, formerly
Newtown.[50] Anne's father, Thomas Dudley, served on the board of
overseers of Harvard College until his death. In 1638, the college
opened its doors to nine students and one instructor. They met in
a small house owned by the town in what had formerly been a cow
pasture.[51] Samuel, who was five years old when Harvard opened,
graduated from there in 1653, and his brother Simon graduated
seven years later, much to the delight of their family.[52]

As the men of the colony established its infrastructure, Anne
kept writing poetry. In "Contemplations," she observed the vast wilderness that lay beyond her home as the world of her Creator. This
is said to be one of the most carefully constructed and vividly elabo-
rate of all of Anne's poems. It alternates between almost romantic

49. Bradstreet, *Works of Anne Bradstreet*, 228.

50. Nelson Manfred Blake, *A History of American Life and Thought* (New York:
McGraw-Hill, 1963), 56.

51. Morison, *Builders of the Bay Colony*, 189.

52. Kellogg, *Anne Bradstreet*, 71–72.

visions of nature, especially the sun and streams, and stark portraits of the depraved aftermath of Adam's fall, including Cain's murder of Abel.[53] She asserts in stanzas 32 and 33 that humans look vainly on the world for pleasure and satisfaction, though eternity offers the only true security possible.[54] She muses,

> I wist not what to wish, yet sure thought I,
> If so much excellence abide below;
> How excellent is he that dwells on high?
> Whose power and beauty by his works we know.
> Sure he is goodness, wisdom, glory, light,
> That hath this under world so richly dight:
> More Heaven then Earth was here no winter &
>   no night.[55]

Anne ruminates on the vast "glistering Sun" and the ever changing "Quaternal Seasons" and then surveys the melodious song of the small creatures of the earth:

> I heard the merry grasshopper then sing,
> The black clad Cricket, bear a second part,
> They kept one tune, and plaid on the same string,
> Seeming to glory in their little Art.
> Small Creatures abject, thus their voices raise?
> And in their kind resound their makers praise:
> Whilst I as mute, can warble forth no higher layes.[56]

Referencing the casting forth of Adam and Eve from Eden and the fall of the "backsliding Race," Anne then turns her focus to the sacrifices of Cain and Abel and the pouring of Abel's blood on the "Virgin Earth," highlighting the immorality of man, no doubt having her own struggles with sickness in mind as she wrote.

---

53. Nichols, *Anne Bradstreet*, 99.
54. Nichols, *Anne Bradstreet*, 99.
55. Bradstreet, *Works of Anne Bradstreet*, 205.
56. Bradstreet, *Works of Anne Bradstreet*, 206.

Man at the best a creature frail and vain,
In knowledge ignorant, in strength but weak,
Subject to sorrows, losses, sickness, pain,
Each storm his state, his mind, his body break,
From some of these he never finds cessation,
But day or night, within, without vexation,
Troubles from foes, from friends, from dearest,
    near'st Relation.[57]

Throughout her poetry, Anne weaves together the Puritan themes of man's sinful depravity, the majesty of a sovereign God, the sweetness and loveliness of Christ, and the fleeting world with great anticipation for the world to come.

In between writing lofty verse, Anne oversaw the care of their livestock, making soap and candles, sewing bed linens and cloths for the children, and cooking laborious meals over an open hearth. Her young children would also have had chores around the house and farm—picking berries, weeding gardens, gathering vegetables, stacking firewood, and fetching water. Overseeing her children's education in the home would have also been of paramount importance to Anne. She may have even used her poetry as a teaching tool for her children as she instructed them how to read and write.[58]

Grief

In 1638, Anne's parents, Thomas and Dorothy, made their final move while in Massachusetts, transitioning a few miles southwest of Boston to Roxbury. Also in Roxbury was John Eliot, the pastor of the church there who had a thriving missionary work among the local Native Americans. This was the farthest Anne had lived away from her parents since crossing the Atlantic. However, Anne did not have much time to miss her parents as the Bradstreet home welcomed a second son in 1640 who was named after his father, Simon.

---

57. Bradstreet, *Works of Anne Bradstreet*, 212.
58. Kellogg, *Anne Bradstreet*, 88.

On December 27, 1643, Anne lost a beloved companion and role model. Her mother, Dorothy, suffered a heart attack and died after forty years of marriage to her beloved Thomas. Little is known about Dorothy Dudley except what is noted in Anne's epitaph poem to her mother after her death:

> Here lyes,
> A worthy Matron of unspotted life,
> A loving Mother and obedient wife,
> A friendly Neighbor, pitiful to poor,
> Whom oft she fed, and clothed with her store;
> To Servants wisely awful, but yet kind,
> And as they did, so they reward did find:
> A true Instructor of her Family,
> The which she ordered with dexterity.
> The publick meetings ever did frequent,
> And in her Closet constant hours she spent;
> Religious in all her words and ways,
> Preparing still for death, till end of days:
> Of all her Children, Children, liv'd to see,
> Then dying, left a blessed memory.[59]

In April of the following year, Anne's sixty-eight-year-old father, Thomas, married a widow living in Roxbury. Together they had a daughter named Deborah and two sons—Joseph, born in 1647, who would later become governor of Massachusetts, and Paul, who was born in 1650. Not long after her mother's death and her father's remarriage, Anne was faced with yet another daunting move. Simon had decided to pick up his family and move to another wilderness area in the Massachusetts Bay Colony, Andover. From this point forward, Anne's poetry lost something of its lofty voice and instead became increasingly introspective and quite personal.

---

59. Bradstreet, *Works of Anne Bradstreet*, 204.

Andover

In 1644 the Bradstreets moved to Andover, twenty miles north of Boston. Simon built a very comfortable home (some would call it a mansion) for his family. Their home included basic furniture and necessities like beds, linens, and cooking wares, and as Simon became quite successful in his various ventures in Andover, the family was able to afford silver and china to use on formal occasions for entertaining. Not long after settling into the new area, Anne welcomed a daughter in 1645, named in honor of Anne's sister, Mercy, and two more boys, Dudley in 1648 and John in 1652.

The Tenth Muse

John Woodbridge (1613–1696), who was married to Mercy, decided to take his wife and four children to England in 1647. While in England, Woodbridge served as a chaplain to the parliamentary commissioners who were trying to negotiate a treaty with the king to end the English Civil War. More importantly, concerning Anne, was the manuscript of her poetry that John took with him with the express purpose of publicly publishing her first work.

The 1650 edition of Anne's poems, published by Stephen Bowtell, filled 207 pages.[60] The title page read, *The Tenth Muse Lately Sprung Up in America, or Severall Poems, Compiled with a Great Variety of Wit and Learning, Full of Delight… by a Gentlewoman of Those Parts*. Anne's name did not appear on the title page but was included in the complimentary comments.[61] Woodbridge wrote a moving preface for the 1650 edition of Anne's poetry, dispelling any naysayers who would claim she was neglecting her family for the sake of fame.

Regardless of being published and praised, Anne felt compelled to write. Cotton Mather, in his magnificent seven-volume *Magnalia Christi Americana*, included Anne as one of the very few women mentioned. He commented that she was rightly celebrated in both England and New England for her poetic works, stating

---

60. Kellogg, *Anne Bradstreet*, 108.
61. Kellogg, *Anne Bradstreet*, 108.

that her poems, "diverse times Printed, have afforded grateful entertainment…and a monument for her memory beyond the stateliest marbles."[62]

Amid the celebration surrounding her first published book of poetry, sadness began to visit the Bradstreet household. Four years after the death of John Winthrop in 1649, Anne's beloved father, Thomas Dudley, died on July 31, 1653, at the age of seventy-seven. Dudley had faithfully served the Massachusetts Bay Colony since first setting foot in the New World in 1630. Anne remembered her father in her poem "Lamentations" as a "Father, Guide, Instructor too." She listed his merits and accomplishments as a founder of New England who spent twenty-five years of his strength for the good of the colony. He was a friend of truth, she wrote, who loved "true Religion." She affectionately imagines his homecoming into the peaceful world of heaven:

> Death as a Sickle hath him timely mown,
> And in celestial Barn hath hous'd him high,
> Where storms, nor showrs, nor ought can damnifie.
> His Generation serv'd, his labours cease;
> And to his Fathers gathered is in peace.
> Ah happy Soul, 'mongst Saints and Angels blest,
> Who after all his toyle, is now at rest:
> His horary head in righteousness was found:
> As joy in heaven on earth let praise resound.[63]

Anne took comfort that her father had lived long enough to enjoy the birth of all her children. He was buried in Roxbury in a tomb covered in white marble, leaving behind an estate of 356 acres.

For a few years after the death of her father, Anne and Simon enjoyed the company of their children in Andover. In 1654, their daughter Dorothy married Seaborn Cotton (1633–1686), son of

---

62. Cotton Mather, *Magnalia Christi Americana* (1702; repr., Edinburgh: Banner of Truth, 1979), 1:135.

63. Bradstreet, *Works of Anne Bradstreet*, 202.

John Cotton. The young couple experienced a similar love to her parents, as nineteen-year-old Seaborn journeyed the twenty miles from Boston to see Dorothy at regular intervals. As a magistrate, Simon performed the ceremony. After their marriage, Seaborn and Dorothy moved to Hampton, New Hampshire, where he served as a pastor of a local church.

Sickness and Fire

Soon after her father's death, Anne's health began to steadily decline. She had battled ailments most of her life, but this time her sickness was severely debilitating. Beginning in the summer of 1656, it rendered her almost incapacitated by the next spring. May of 1661 proved yet another weakening period of illness. She penned a poem in thanksgiving for delivery from her difficulties by June:

> Lord, whilst my fleeting time shall last,
> Thy Goodness let me Tell.
> And new Experience I have gained,
> My future Doubts repel.[64]

In addition to sickness, Anne began to experience additional grief in August 1665 at the death of her year-and-a-half-old granddaughter, Elizabeth Bradstreet, born to her son Simon and his wife Mercy. The death of children was an all too common reality in the colonies. In memory of Elizabeth, her grandmother composed a poem exploring the providence and sovereignty of God:

> Farewell dear babe, my hearts too much content,
> Farewell sweet babe, the pleasure of mine eye,
> Farewell fair flower that for a space was lent,
> Then ta'en away unto Eternity.
> Blest babe why should I once bewail thy fate,
> Or sigh thy dayes so soon were terminate;
> Sith thou art settled in an Everlasting state.[65]

---

64. Bradstreet, *Works of Anne Bradstreet*, 259.
65. Bradstreet, *Works of Anne Bradstreet*, 235.

Anne suffered the loss of two more grandchildren—Anne Bradstreet, who died June 20, 1669, and Simon Bradstreet, who died on
November 16, 1669. On September 6, 1669, Anne said goodbye to
her beloved daughter-in-law, Mercy Bradstreet, when she was only
twenty-eight years old.

Another devastating event took place the following year when
Anne and Simon lost most of their home to a damaging fire. As
usual, Anne put her quill to paper and reflected on the burning
of their home. She confessed an attachment to earthly wealth and
turned to God for solace, desiring to use this event to draw closer
to Him.[66] She concluded,

> A Prise so vast as is unknown,
> Yet, by his Gift, is made thine own.
> Ther's wealth enough, I need no more
> Farewell my Pelf, farewell my Store.
> The world no longer let me Love,
> My hope and Treasure lyes Above.[67]

A new home was constructed on the same site for the Bradstreet family, but Anne suffered emotionally for the remainder of her life from
the trauma of losing three grandchildren and her daughter-in-law.

Final Days

In 1671 Anne experienced uncontrollable fevers and fainting spells
as she became desperately weak. She became convinced that this
world is nothing more than a "vale of sorrow" and that her thoughts
should rest entirely in heaven.[68] At fifty-nine years old, Anne had
begun to suffer from consumption, which literally caused her to
waste away. Consumption, or severe weight loss, was the result of
tuberculosis, which sets up in the lungs and causes a chronic cough,

---

66. Nichols, *Anne Bradstreet*, 142.
67. Bradstreet, *Works of Anne Bradstreet*, 260.
68. Charlotte Gordon, *Mistress Bradstreet: The Untold Life of America's First Poet*
(New York: Little, Brown, 2005), 280.

fever, and excessive night sweats. Her arm was swollen due to an extremely large ulcer that did not heal, likely caused by the tuberculosis. No one could ease her pain, and she prayed unceasingly for release from this life, while her children, friends, and family, and indeed most of the colony, awaited news of her demise.[69] On September 16, 1672, at the age of sixty, Anne Bradstreet closed her eyes in Andover with her treasured husband at her side and opened them in eternal glory.

She was buried the following Wednesday in an unknown plot. There is no record of her funeral services or elegies written upon her death. The only memorial in her remembrance is from her son Simon. Writing in his journal, he longed "to walk in her steps… so wee might one day have a happy & glorious greeting."[70] Beyond Simon's words, Anne left behind her own elegy—numerous poems describing her life in the new colony, her hardships in the wilderness, her musings about her heavenly Father, her severe debilitating sickness, and her darling husband.

Simon waited four years after Anne's death before he remarried. He was elected deputy governor and governor of Massachusetts from 1679 to 1686. After sixty years of public service, Simon died at age ninety-four, being one of the final survivors who sailed from England in 1630. He was entombed in Salem, Massachusetts.

Conclusion

The young couple, Simon and Anne Bradstreet, who sailed from England aboard the *Arbella* in 1630 arrived in the New World with little intention of making such ineradicable marks. Simon, a faithful husband and doting father, left his mark in government on the Massachusetts Bay Colony. Anne left her legacy from her pen in the copious poems she composed about life and her God. The Bradstreets remain a reminder that life in the new wilderness was difficult and costly and that freely serving God comes with the

---

69. Gordon, *Mistress Bradstreet*, 280.
70. Quoted in Gordon, *Mistress Bradstreet*, 282.

abandonment of all the comforts of this life, with a keen eye fixed on the next. A fitting word at the conclusion of this brief account of Anne Bradstreet's remarkable life flows once again from her pen. Written on August 31, 1669, she conveys her desperate tiredness and how ready she was to join her heavenly Bridegroom:

> As weary pilgrim, now at rest,
> Hugs with delight his silent nest...
>   His dangers past, and travails done...
> A pilgrim I, on earth, perplexed
>   with sins, with cares and sorrows vexed
> By age and pains brought to decay
>   and my Clay house mouldering away....
> No fainting fits shall me assail
>   nor grinding pains my body frail....
> A corrupt Carcass down it lies
>   a glorious body it shall rise....
> Lord make me ready for that day
>   then Come, dear bridegroom, Come away.[71]

---

71. Bradstreet, *Works of Anne Bradstreet*, 294.

7

JOHN ELIOT

"I am but a shrub in the wilderness" John Eliot (1604–1690) wrote in 1664.[1] By this date, Eliot had lived and ministered in the New England wilderness for thirty-two years and would live another twenty-six years longer.[2] He continued to reflect on his life, "My doings! Alas! They have been poor and small and lean doings and I'll be the man who shall throw the first stone at them all." Surveying his life and ministry among the people of the Massachusetts Bay Colony and outlying areas amid the Native American tribes of the New World, John Eliot was a man of the seventeenth century. A man of tireless efforts and resolved diligence to see the gospel spread like a brushfire throughout the colonies and the native peoples, Eliot viewed himself, like so many who had previously traveled the gospel way, as a debtor to grace whose desire was to see Christ exalted long after his bones had turned to dust. This "shrub in the wilderness" has long passed from living memory, but his zeal resides in all those who desire the gospel to spread from sea to shining sea.

---

1. John Eliot to Robert Boyle, August 26, 1664, in *The Correspondence of Robert Boyle*, ed. Michael Hunter, Antonio Clericuzio, and Lawrence M. Principe (Burlington, Vt.: Pickering and Chatto, 2001), 2:305–6.

2. Ola Elizabeth Winslow, *John Eliot: "Apostle to the Indians"* (Boston: Houghton Mifflin, 1968), 188.

Boyhood

While many English families boasted of the Eliot name—tracing their ancestors to a notable knight who immigrated to England with William the Conqueror in 1066, or the Eliots of East Coker, Somersetshire—John Eliot was unable to take pride in any notable forebears or progeny among the English social upper class.[3] Owning more land than his social standing demanded, John's father, Bennett Eliot, called himself a simple "yeoman."

Little is known about the Eliot family in Hertfordshire and Essex or even of John's childhood. The local parish church of St. John the Baptist in Widford, an obscure village about twenty-five miles from London on the river Lea, records the baptism of John on August 5, 1604. Given that baptism ordinarily took place less than a week after the birth of a child, it is quite probable that John's cry was heard in the Eliot household in the early days of August 1604. He was the third child of Bennett and Lettese Aggar. John's siblings, Sarah, Philip, and Jacob, were also baptized and recorded in the registry at St. John's.

In 1610, just across the border from Hertfordshire, the Eliot family appears in the church registry of Nazeing in Essex.[4] In the forthcoming years, Lydia, Francis, and Mary, the youngest of the Eliot children, were all born and baptized in Nazeing. John's mother, Lettese, lived only five days after the baptism of his youngest sister, Mary, and was buried in Nazeing on March 16, 1620. John's father,

---

3. On the life and work of John Eliot, see *John Eliot and the Indians, Being Letters Addressed to the Rev. Jonathan Hanmer of Barnstable* (New York: Adams and Grace Press, 1915); *John Eliot's Indian Dialogues* (Westport, Conn.: Greenwood Press, 1980); and Richard Baxter, *Some Unpublished Correspondence of the Reverend Richard Baxter and the Reverend John Eliot, the Apostle of the American Indians* (Manchester: Manchester University Press, 1931). See also Henry W. Bowden and James P. Ronda, *John Eliot's Indian Dialogues, a Study in Cultural Interaction* (Westport, Conn.: Greenwood Press, 1980); Alden T. Vaughn, *The New England Frontier: Puritans and Indians, 1620–1675* (Boston: Little, Brown, 1965); Williston Walker, *Ten New England Leaders* (New York: Silver, Burdett, and Co., 1901); and Ola Elizabeth Winslow, *John Eliot: "Apostle to the Indians"* (Boston: Houghton Mifflin, 1968).

4. Winslow, *John Eliot*, 8.

devastated by the death of his wife and the overwhelming task of caring for his prodigious family, succumbed to illness and was buried on November 21, 1621, only a year and a half after his dear wife was laid to rest. Reflecting on the passionate and committed religious piety of his parents, John recalled, "I do see that it was a great labour of God unto me, to season my first times with the fear of God, the word, and prayer."[5]

Grammar School

Prior to their deaths, John's parents had instructed their children in the areas of reading and writing, adequately preparing them to enter the local grammar school. John's grammar school career seems to have advanced smoothly, as he matriculated in Jesus College, Cambridge, in 1618, several months before his fourteenth birthday. His seven years attending grammar school trained him in the rigors of Latin, both spoken and read; probably some Greek and Hebrew; acquaintance with the Bible, both textual and historical; the beginning of logic; and training in public speaking.[6] In choosing Cambridge over Oxford, John had positioned himself within a particular religious influence that would be the impetus for his transition to the New World.

Jesus College

In 1618 Cambridge boasted of nearly three thousand students and would have been overwhelming to a boy acquainted with only a small, rural English village. Jesus College, one of the smallest of the Cambridge colleges, was far removed from town and surrounded by open fields and plentiful groves. A huge walnut tree standing in the open court towered over the college and had become famous for its ancient branches. Jesus College proved to have an indelible impact on John for many years to come.

---

5. Cotton Mather, "The Life of the Renowned John Eliot," in *Magnalia Christi Americana* (1702; repr., Edinburgh: Banner of Truth, 1979), 1:529.

6. Winslow, *John Eliot*, 14.

During the years of 1618–1622, John's education and training were as medieval as the architecture of the stately campus buildings. When he took his BA degree in 1622, he was well versed in Latin, the classics, logic, rhetoric, and public speaking. Beyond the aforementioned tribute to his parents, nothing exists that indicates Eliot's boyhood religious experience or his calling into pastoral ministry after graduating from Cambridge.

Little Baddow

The next significant place John is found is at the school of Little Baddow in Chelmsford, serving briefly alongside Thomas Hooker before Hooker's escape to Holland in July 1630. The school at Little Baddow served as a temporary refuge for Hooker during a time of increasing political and religious persecution of the Puritans. The school, according to Cotton Mather, was established within the home of the Hooker family, where John Eliot was also reported to be living during this period. With great fondness, Eliot recalled, "To this place was I called through the infinite riches of God's mercy in Christ Jesus to my poor soul, for here the Lord said to my dead soul, live! live! And through the grace of God I do live and shall live forever! When I came to this blessed family I then saw as never before, the power of godliness in its lovely vigor and efficacy."[7]

Thomas Hooker's flight to Holland in 1630 forced the school to close when John was twenty-six years old. Having experienced much joy at Little Baddow and the mentorship of Hooker, it appears that John's formal training for ministry had been completed. Circumstances looked quite dire for John as the allowance he received from his father's estate had been paid in full. Additionally, he had met a young woman whom he hoped to soon marry, which forced him to consider how he would establish a proper home for his soon to be growing family. While it would have been easy to find a position in

---

7. Cotton Mather in his life of Thomas Hooker, *Magnalia Christi Americana* (1:336), says he possessed an account of this school in John Eliot's own hand. Early writers on Eliot quote it, but apparently no one else has seen the original sheet.

another school, apparently he decided the schoolroom was not the place God desired him to be for the remainder of his life. Having been greatly influenced and mentored for a short time by Hooker, Eliot was convinced that he belonged in a pulpit. However, non-conformist ministers were finding it increasingly difficult to secure a pulpit in England outside the grip of Archbishop William Laud.

The immediate decision for Eliot to secure passage aboard a vessel sailing for the shores of New England is not recorded. However, when Captain William Pierce (1591–1641) weighed anchor in the late summer months of 1631 and turned the *Lyon* out of the English Channel into the vast horizon of the Atlantic Ocean, John Eliot was on board. Apparently, he was the first of the Nazeing emigrants to embark for the New World, and he did so with the great anticipation that his family and friends would soon follow. He sailed to the Massachusetts Bay Colony while it was still in its infancy. Until this time in his young life, nothing could have quite prepared him for the first time his eyes beheld the new village of Boston, nestled against the distant mountains just beyond the swamp marshes of the coastline.

The New World

On November 2, 1631, after a ten-week voyage, Captain Pierce steered the *Lyon* into Nantasket. "The wind being contrary," John Winthrop wrote, "the Ship stayed at Long Island for the night," but the next morning, "the wind coming fair, she came to an anchor before Boston."[8] The entire colony and many residing in neighboring towns had come to greet the sixty passengers from their English homeland. A curious interest and hospitality attended the welcome for the wife of the governor, Margaret Winthrop, who was aboard with two of her own children and the children of John Winthrop's former marriage. She had spent a year selling their estate and settling their affairs in England while her husband had sailed in 1630

8. Entries for November 2 and 3, John Winthrop, *The Journal of John Winthrop, 1630–1649*, ed. Richard S. Dunn and Laetitia Yeandle (Cambridge, Mass.: Belknap Press, 1996), 42.

aboard the *Arbella*. As this little contingency of tired and sea-weary passengers stepped on the new land, volleys of shots were fired into the air and an armed guard advanced as escort. To welcome Mrs. Winthrop and her fellow passengers, the colonists brought out a "great store of provisions, as fat hogs, kids, venison, poultry, geese, partridges, etc., so as the like joy and manifestation of love, had never been seen in New England." It was a great marvel, John Winthrop continued, "that so many people and such store of provisions could be gathered together at so few hours warning."[9] In response to Governor Winthrop's plea for supplies, Captain Pierce and the crewman aboard began immediately unloading the two hundred tons of provisions that accompanied them on the journey across the sea. Many of the Boston residents were dying of scurvy, and many more had been grievously ill. The *Lyon* arrived in time for its cargo to save many lives.

In his journal report of the passengers aboard the *Lyon*, John Winthrop spoke in the third person, mentioning Margaret Winthrop as "the governor's wife" but calling his infant daughter who had died on the voyage by her name, Anne. Among the other passengers, he mentioned by name only "Mr. John Eliot, a minister." It is doubtful that these two men were close acquaintances; rather, they more than likely had at least met one another during the numerous planning meetings held before the governor's departure with his fleet of twelve ships during the preceding spring.

Upon disembarking, John Eliot took up residence in Boston. On the Boston church book, his name appears on page 3, with Margaret Winthrop's name following. John's arrival in the colony was a sign of God's providence since the Boston church required a minister until the residing pastor, John Wilson (c. 1588–1667), returned from his journey to England. John's labor in the pulpit pleased the people, and on May 26, 1632, when John Wilson returned to his congregation, they invited Eliot to remain as "teacher," thereby

---

9. John Winthrop, *The History of New England* (Boston, 1825), 1:36–37 (commonly called Winthrop's journal).

completing the pastoral office as early New England had organized it. He declined the offer, not because of unhappiness among them but because during his six-month interim the first company of people from Nazeing, including his family and numerous friends, had arrived and settled in Roxbury, just two miles across the narrow neck of land from Boston. Before his departure from England, Eliot had promised his friends that if they immigrated, he would joyfully serve as their pastor. Winthrop's account of what happened in the Boston-Roxbury situation was that "although Boston labored all they could, both with the congregation at Roxbury and with Mr. Eliot himself," he could not be "diverted from accepting the new call."[10]

Pastor at Roxbury

The Roxbury settlers welcomed John Eliot with abundant joy. The congregation there had gathered in late 1631 or early 1632 and immediately set about building a meetinghouse in which they could worship. As in most early settlements, the central meetinghouse was positioned on high ground to retain a station of prominence in the village and among trees to supply lumber for its construction. The name given to the location was "Meeting House Hill." Measuring only twenty by thirty feet and built of squared logs, the original structure was strikingly modest and insignificant compared to the soaring cathedrals in England. The roof was thatched and the walls remained unplastered. It had no gallery, no pews, no spire, and, for a long time, no floor. Worshipers sat on long rough wooden benches without backs, with men and women assembling on opposite sides of the church. This first meetinghouse served Eliot's congregation for forty years. It was the heart of the town and served as a place of prayer, a refuge in times of danger, and the center for all civil business transactions. John had left everything of ostentation and comfort in England and now fully embraced a new call in the New World.

---

10. Winthrop, *History of New England*, 1:93.

Eliot's Family

In 1632 John's older sister, Sarah, arrived with her husband and four of her children. Sarah's oldest son had sailed with John the year before. Along with Sarah was Mary, another of the Eliot siblings, and their brother Philip. Upon their arrival, brothers Francis and Jacob joined the church in Boston. John experienced the joy of having family and friends whom he had known for many years living within close proximity of Roxbury, a comfort and encouragement that many in the new settlements were never privileged to experience.

For the new pastor, the happiness of his transition from Boston to Roxbury increased with the arrival of his intended bride, Hanna Mumford (1604–1687), who was aboard the same ship carrying his sisters. Their wedding took place in October 1632 and was recorded as the first wedding in the town. Besides being an important and acclaimed community event, the Eliot wedding would have been a truly festive occasion. During this period in New England, weddings were civil ceremonies, not religious ones. However, on the first Sunday thereafter, the bride, adorned in her wedding dress, would have been escorted to her seat in the meetinghouse, which she would occupy for fifty-five years.

While little is known about Hanna Mumford Eliot, tradition insists that she graced her home with a spirit of hospitality for her numerous guests and travelers. She also served as a dutiful mother of the six children born into the Eliot home over the next fourteen years. Trained in nursing, Hanna would have answered innumerable urgent calls. She was self-sufficient, a hard worker, and a diligent overseer of the abundant acreage of the Eliot family. Built down the hill from the meetinghouse, the Eliot home, village, and surrounding area would not have drastically contrasted with John's boyhood home. Beyond the little cluster of village homes were sloping fields, pastures, the river, and deep woods in the distance. In this new settlement and new world, John was now living among familiar people and had a home, a new wife, and work to do. Eliot includes himself and his wife in the Roxbury membership roll along with the baptisms of their six children, Hannah, John, Joseph, Samuel, Aaron, and Benjamin.

Roxbury Grammar School
During these early years, Eliot began to take interest in the local affairs of the town, none more notable than his share in the founding of the Roxbury grammar school. Eliot's name is second on the 1645 agreement for the founding of the school, which is often referred to as the oldest grammar school in America (although such boasting is challenged by the grammar school founded in Boston). The Massachusetts Education Law, passed in 1642, emphatically stated that it was the duty of every parent to take responsibility for the education of every child under their roof and that every apprentice under his roof must be taught to read and write. Eliot's faith in education was absolute, and his unending efforts to found numerous schools speak to his ardent desire for disseminating knowledge among all the inhabitants of New England. During his future ministry among the Indians, he often founded schools for their education. In his later years, too infirm to walk up Meeting House Hill on the Sabbath, he was known for collecting the Indian and black children of his neighborhood in order to teach them how to read and write. Cotton Mather remembered his prayer at a synod meeting in Cambridge and recorded it in his tribute to Eliot in these words: "Lord, for schools every where among us! That our schools may flourish! That every member of this assembly may go home and procure a good school to be encouraged in the town where he lives! That before we die, we may be so happy as to see a good school encouraged in every plantation of the country!"[11]

The Preacher
Eliot was known as a preeminent preacher, a task to which he had dedicated his life. Regrettably, none of his sermons appear to have survived either in print or manuscript. Cotton Mather, young

---

11. Mather, *Magnalia*, 1:551.

enough to be Eliot's son, offers a brief glimpse of the Roxbury pulpit ministry. From Mather's description, it appears that Eliot's sermons were very simple and not ostentatious in any way. Calvinistic doctrine demanded something of the mind, but apparently Eliot could interpret the doctrines of Scripture in such a way that the "lambs of the flock" could follow him with relative ease. In response to the questions asked by his Indian hearers, Eliot often used concrete analogies to explain the eternal truths of the Bible. This was also a feature he employed in his pulpit in Roxbury. His primary textbook was the Bible—always the Bible—and although this was generally true of contemporary preachers of the day, Eliot excelled among them in having the gift of instantly using Scripture to speak to any life situation. It appears that Eliot often spoke extemporaneously, sometimes without any pulpit notes at all. His delivery was lovingly graceful and warm, with occasional crescendos of vigor if sin were being rebuked and "God's trumpets of wrath against all vice" needed to be sounded.[12] During the fifty-eight years of ministry among the people of Roxbury, there is no indication that the congregants would have wished for anyone but Eliot to grace the pulpit Sunday after Sunday.

Eliot: The Man

In addition to his recognized faithfulness as a pastor and orator, Eliot was recognized as a man of deep piety and simplicity of life, refusing rich foods and strong drink. During visits with friends, meetings with ministers, and gatherings in the churches, one could always anticipate his inducement to adjourn the meeting with prayer. To a family he knew well he said, "Come, let us not have a visit without prayer; let us pray down the blessing of Heaven on your family before we go."[13] Mather comments, "He was one who lived in heaven while he was on earth."[14] To feed his own soul, he often attended weekly religious lectures and sermons in Boston,

12. Mather, *Magnalia*, 1:548.
13. Mather, *Magnalia*, 1:532.
14. Mather, *Magnalia*, 1:534.

Charlestown, Cambridge, and Dorchester. The only guide he could consider worthy for life was Scripture: "It is to be confessed that the written word of God is to be regarded as the perfect and only rule for our lives; that in all the articles of religion, if men 'speak not according to this word, there is no light in them.'"[15]

Eliot not only performed various pastoral duties at Roxbury, nearly to his final days, but also served on discipline committees, petitioned for repeal of a law requiring that civil laws and penalties be read in the churches, urged the establishment of schools in all New England communities, and supported the holding of synods for matters of mutual concern among the churches. In 1636 or 1637 he wrote a justification for Roger Williams's banishment, and in 1637 he served as one of Anne Hutchinson's interrogators during her examinations before the General Court at the Boston church. In 1640, Eliot participated in translating the metrical Psalter the *Bay-Psalm Book*, which was the first book printed in British North America. The breadth of Eliot's ministry and civic participation was prodigious, but perhaps nothing was more significant than the indelible impact he had on the Native Americans of New England.

"Apostle to the Indians"

John Eliot's mission to the Indians began fifteen years after he arrived in the Massachusetts Bay Colony. There is no indication that he came to the region for the sole purpose of missionary endeavors, as there are only a few allusions to Native Americans prior to the start of his ministry among them. In 1633, in a lengthy letter to Sir Simonds d'Ewes (1602–1650), an English politician and member of the Long Parliament, Eliot remarked, "I trust, in God's time, they shall learn of Christ."[16] A second mention of the Indians was Eliot's reference in the church records to the Narragansett-Mohegan War of 1645, more commonly known as the Pequot War.

---

15. Mather, *Magnalia*, 1:544.

16. John Eliot in Everett Emerson, ed., *Letters from New England: The Massachusetts Bay Colony, 1629–1638* (Amherst: University of Massachusetts Press, 1976), 106.

The Indian Mission

The first time Eliot attempted to preach to the Indians, led by Cutshamekin (d. 1654), in 1646 at Dorchester Mills, he failed miserably to properly communicate in their native tongue. Cutshamekin was a Native American leader (a sachem of the Massachusett tribe based along the Neponset River and Great Blue Hill) and became the first Massachusett Indian converted to Christianity in 1646. The second time Eliot preached to the Indians was at the wigwam of Waban near Watertown Mill, which was later called Nonantum.

Frustrated with the failure of his sermons and his lack of knowledge of the Massachusett language, Eliot immediately began language training shortly after his sermon at Nonantum. His language teacher, who also served as his interpreter in the early years of his ministry, was residing with fur trader and land investor Richard Callicott (1604–1686) of Dorchester. The Indian's legal status at the time is unclear; while Eliot calls him a servant, he is referred to at other times as a slave.[17] The young Indian, Cockenoe (c. 1630–c. 1687), was captured during the Pequot War, which took place between 1636 and 1638 in New England between the Pequot tribe and an alliance of the colonists of the Massachusetts Bay, Plymouth, and Saybrook Colonies and their allies from the Narragansett and Mohegan tribes. The war concluded with a decisive defeat of the Pequots. At its bloody end, about seven hundred Pequots had been killed or taken into captivity. Hundreds of prisoners were sold into slavery in the West Indies and the colonies, of which Cockenoe was one.

Language Study

Cockenoe was not able to write (which Eliot soon remedied) but was well versed in both the Massachusett and English languages. In addition, Cockenoe had been educated in Christian theology and was a candidate for full church membership in Dorchester

---

17. The teacher is not named in the Massachusetts sources. William Tooker is almost certainly correct in surmising that he was an Indian named Cockenoe, who lived on Long Island from 1649 until his death in 1690. *John Eliot's First Indian Teacher and Interpreter* (New York: F. P. Harper, 1896).

in February 1649. With his help, Eliot was able to translate the Ten Commandments, the Lord's Prayer, and other scriptures and prayers. The dialects of the Wampanoag language were formerly spoken by several peoples of southern New England, including all the coastal and insular areas of eastern Massachusetts as well as southeastern New Hampshire, the southernmost tip of Maine, and eastern Rhode Island. By July 1649, Eliot was evidently able to instruct the Indians without any assistance from his interpreter.

Eliot recounted very little about the arduous task of learning the Massachusett language, a language Cotton Mather considered so difficult that demons who understood Hebrew, Greek, and Latin were unable to fathom it. This highly inflected Algonquian dialect lacked Indo-European grammatical conventions like prepositions, "be"-verbs, comparative and superlative forms, and the future tense.[18] In 1666, in his only discussion of the matter, Eliot briefly explained that he first transcribed Massachusett phonemes into roman characters and eventually had to create a non-roman character to represent an additional vowel. After learning the phonology of the language, he turned to its morphology and discovered its many "new ways of grammar." He said, "I diligently marked the difference of their grammar from ours, [and] when I found the way of them, I would pursue a word, a noun, a verb, through all variations I could think of. And thus I came at it."[19]

Praying Indians

In 1646, the Massachusetts General Court passed the Act for the Propagation of the Gospel amongst the Indians. This act, along with

---

18. Richard W. Cogley, *John Eliot's Mission to the Indians before King Philip's War* (Cambridge, Mass.: Harvard University Press, 1999), 50.

19. Cotton Mather, *The Triumphs of the Reformed Religion, in America* (Boston: Harris, Allen, and Brunning, 1691), 86; and John Eliot, *The Indian Grammar Begun* (Cambridge: Marmaduke Johnson, 1666), 312. For the details about the Massachusett language, see Stephen A. Guice, "The Linguistic Work of John Eliot" (PhD diss., Michigan State University, 1990), 128, 132–33, 145, 149; and Ives Goddard and Kathleen J. Bragdon, *Native Writings in Massachusett* (Philadelphia: American Philosophical Society, 1998), 492–93.

the success of Eliot's and other missionary endeavors among the Indians, raised interest in England. In 1649 the Long Parliament passed an ordination forming the Corporation for the Promoting and Propagating the Gospel of Jesus Christ in New England, which raised approximately £12,000 to invest in the cause. There was a general agreement that the gospel of Christ must be taken to the Indian tribes on the doorstep of the new colonies. Eliot, among others, took this injunction seriously, and having no doubt been involved in Indian affairs during his time in Roxbury, he now began a ministry that would span the remainder of his life.

In 1650, Eliot and several Indian converts began searching for suitable acreage for a settlement of Christian Indians. Such towns became known as "praying towns." By October of that same year, they had selected Natick, along the Charles River, which was part of the two-hundred-square-mile land grant given by the General Court to the town of Dedham. The residents of Dedham objected to Eliot's selection and implored him to select a site outside of their town grant. In October the following year, the General Court assigned Natick two thousand acres just north of the river. The Nonantum Indians were delighted with the location of their new town. Eliot immediately set about instructing the converted Indians how to establish a Christian community at Natick.

Eliot's Bible
Having fully established his mission among the Indians, Eliot initiated a seemingly insurmountable task: translating the Bible into the Massachusett language. Rather than instructing the Indian tribes in the English language, Eliot was convinced that they needed a Bible in their own language. He translated the entire sixty-six books of the English Bible in just over fourteen years, publishing it in 1663 as *Mamusse Wunneetupanatamwe Up-Biblum God*. To achieve this overwhelming realization, Eliot became a lexicographer and grammarian in the Algonquian language. This required him to first devise an Algonquian book of grammar and dictionary, which were eventually published in 1666 under the title *The Indian Grammar*

Begun. Eliot used a few local Massachusett Indians to assist in this project, including John Sassamon (c. 1620–1675), Job Nesuton (d. 1675), James Printer (1640–1707), and his previous Algonquian instructor, Cockenoe.

In 1653, Eliot assembled a one-volume primer catechism into the Massachusett language. Over the course of 1655–1656, he then began translating and printing the Gospel of Matthew, Genesis, and Psalms into the Massachusett language. A sample run was printed and shipped to a London corporation to demonstrate what a completely finished Algonquian Bible would look like. In 1658, Eliot penned a letter to the treasurer of the Society for the Propagation of the Gospel in New England:

> I shall not trouble you with anything at present save this one business of moment, touching the printing of the bible in the Indian language…that yourselves might be moved to hire some honest young man, who hath skill to compose, (and the more skill in other parts of the work, the better) send him over as your servant, pay him there to his content, or engage payment, let him serve you here in New-England at the press in Harvard College, and work under the College printer, in impressing the Bible in the Indian language, and with him send a convenient stock of paper to begin withal.[20]

The corporation recognized the task that lay before Eliot and, after wholeheartedly approving his sample, sent Marmaduke Johnson (d. 1674), a professional printer, to the Massachusetts Bay Colony to assist in the printing of the whole Bible. In 1660 Johnson, along with one hundred reams of paper and eighty pounds of new type for the printer, arrived to the aid of Eliot and his assistants. Johnson was under a three-year contract to assist in printing Eliot's Algonquian Bible. The following year, at Harvard College, with the aid of Johnson and a Nipmuc Indian named James Printer, Samuel Green (c. 1614–1702) rolled off his printing press 1,500 copies of

---

20. George Emery Littlefield, *The Early Massachusetts Press, 1638–1711* (Boston: The Club of Odd Volumes, 1907), 209.

the New Testament. In 1663, one thousand copies of all sixty-six books of the complete Bible were printed in a 1,180-page volume.

The toilsome task of translating the English Bible into the Algonquian language had John Eliot's blood, sweat, and tears on every page. To demonstrate the difficulty of the Algonquian language used in Eliot's Indian Bible, Cotton Mather offered an example of the Algonquian word *Nummatchekodtantamoonganunnonash* (thirty-two characters), which means "our lusts." Eliot translated this copy of God's Word from an unwritten Native American language into a written alphabet the Indians could read and properly understand. In the course of a thousand years since Ulfilas (c. 311–383) constructed the Gothic alphabet, Eliot was the only missionary to devise a new alphabet from an unwritten language for the purpose of teaching and preaching the Scriptures.

More Praying Towns

After the establishment of Natick as the first settlement of praying Indians, many towns followed its example and model. Eliot established Pakenit, or Punkapoag, as the next organized village after Natick. Within eight thousand acres situated fourteen miles south of Boston, twelve families gathered from Neponset Mill, one of Eliot's first preaching posts. In addition to tending cattle and pigs, the Punkapoag Indians made clapboards and shingles from a cedar swamp on their border. This industry created a thriving and successful town. The residents of Punkapoag received regular spiritual instruction under the leadership of Eliot's son, John Eliot Jr., who preached among them until his death in 1688 just prior to King Philip's War. After his death, Eliot's son-in-law from Boston, Habakkuk Glover, took up the mantle and preached through an interpreter until a church could be established following the war.

Hassanamesit, meaning a "place of small stones," was established thirty-eight miles from Boston. Also encompassing eight thousand acres and inhabited by approximately sixty Indians, Hassanamesit was a thriving village that experienced greater success than any other praying town. The Indians of Hassanamesit were well versed in husbandry and also planted fields of orchards, harvesting plentiful crops of apples. Additionally, this was the home of James Printer, who had proved invaluable to Eliot during his production of the Algonquian Bible. The church was established in 1671, and the town's pastor was trained at Natick. Hassanamesit and Natick were the only founded churches within praying towns prior to King Philip's War.

Okommakamesit was settled with ten families thirty miles west of Boston on six thousand acres of land that, for them, proved to be too close to the English town of Marlborough. Neither the Indians nor the English were pleased with the proximity of their settlements, which created continual friction and restlessness. Eliot wrote that the Okommakamesit Indians "do not much rejoice under the Englishmen's shadow, who do so overtop them in their number of people, stocks of cattle, etc."[21] Eliot tried to solve the dispute between the two towns by petitioning the General Court to grant land elsewhere for the Indians. Despite the court agreeing to do so, the Indians remained at Okommakamesit.

Another settlement was instituted ten miles to the southeast of Boston and became home for Pawtucket Indians known as Nashobah. Being on the roadway of the Mohawk Indian hunting grounds caused many of the Pawtucket Indians to flee in fear owing to a feud that existed between the Mohawks and several New England Indian groups. The town's resettlement began in 1670.[22] By the dawn of King Philip's War, ten Indian families called Nashobah's eight thousand acres home.

Located between Natick and Hassanamesit, the settlement of Magunkog was created at Eliot's request in October 1669. The following year, the General Court enlarged the town because the original grant had been "grievous to the poor Indians" and had "disappointed…their hopes." In 1674 the town was three thousand

---

21. John Eliot, *A Brief Narrative of the Progress of the Gospel amongst the Indians in New England* (London: John Allen, 1671), 6.
22. Cogley, *John Eliot's Mission*, 145.

acres in size and its residents were being taught in 1669 and 1670 by Wohwohquoshadt and Simon, two natives about whom nothing else is known.[23]

These five praying towns within twenty-five miles of Natick were visited by Eliot during intervening weeks when he was not in Natick. His schedule is unknown, but it is likely that he visited Punkapoag and Magunkog more frequently than Hassanamesit, Okommakamesit, and Nashobah because the former two towns were closer to his home in Roxbury.[24] After the initial settlement of these praying towns, Eliot petitioned the General Court to also create the towns of Wamesit and Pantucket. Wamesit, the smallest of the older towns, boasted fifteen families who took up residence on 2,500 acres in 1674, on the eve of King Philip's War. Pantucket was never awarded land and remained a "pagan enclave" until the early 1670s.[25] Eliot's vision for all the praying towns was that others would be drawn to the influence of Christianity springing up among them. From schools, churches, and commerce with the English, these Indians were being incorporated into civilized society and becoming part of the day-to-day culture of the early colonies.

King Philip's War
New England colonists and their Indian allies fought against other native inhabitants from 1675 to 1678. The armed conflict was named for Metacom (c. 1638–1676), a chief of the Wampanoag people who adopted the name Philip because of the mutual relations between the Mayflower Pilgrims and his father, Massasoit (c. 1581–1661). After Massasoit's death in 1661, Metacom became tribal chief but would not share his father's relations with the colonists after three Wampanoags were hanged for murder in the Plymouth Colony in 1675. Over the next six months, Indian raiding parties and colonial militia spread across Massachusetts, Rhode Island, Connecticut,

---

23. Cogley, *John Eliot's Mission*, 145.

24. Cogley, *John Eliot's Mission*, 145.

25. Cogley, *John Eliot's Mission*, 145.

and Maine. The largest colonial army, consisting of 1,000 militia-men and 150 Indian allies attacked the Narragansetts, allies of the Wampanoags, in November 1675. An estimated 150 Narragansetts were killed, many of whom were women and children. The colonial militia overwhelmed their Indian opponents, and the Wampanoags and the Narragansett were almost completely destroyed. Metacom retreated to Mount Hope, where he was finally killed. King Philip's War was the deadliest bloodbath to occur in seventeenth-century New England, and it is often considered to be the most important war in the history of American colonization. In the space of a year, twelve of the region's towns were destroyed, more than half of New England's towns were attacked by Indian invaders, and the economies of Plymouth and Rhode Island were in ruins.

The war also devastated John Eliot's praying towns, destroying all fourteen that had previously been settled. Over the coming months, some straggling and demoralized Indians filtered back to their towns, but it would never again resemble the height of Eliot's ministry among them. Natick was one of the towns to be rebuilt, but it was under close supervision by the colony immediately following the war.

Eliot's labors were relatively unknown in the postwar years. The war had so demolished his mission that to start over was the only option. His first task was to reorganize the schools, employing the teachers who had returned from the throes of war and immediately training others. Supplies of food, clothing, farming tools, and seed had to be acquired before another winter engulfed them. Eliot's visits to the praying towns were brief, but his heart for advancing the gospel among the Indian peoples never waned, even in the face of insurmountable odds.

Final Years
Riddled with age and infirmity, John Eliot was preparing for the survival and success of the Indian missionary work after his death. In 1683 he persuaded the Natick Indians to ordain their own pastor, Daniel Tokkohwompait. Eliot's frailties caused great grief among the

Indians to which he had brought the saving message of Christ. "You are now grown aged," Tokkohwompait wrote in a letter to the English in March 1684. In it he expresses gratitude to Eliot: "God hath made you to us and our nation a spiritual father, we are inexpressibly engaged to you for your faithful constant indefatigable labors, and love, to us and for us, and you have always manifested the same to us as well in our adversity as prosperity, for about forty years making known to us the glad tidings of salvation of Jesus Christ."[26]

Over the course of many years, Eliot had protected newly converted Indian Christians from the other natives and his own people, learned the Massachusett language and translated the Bible into their own tongue, appealed the General Court to found praying towns for the Christian Indians, established schools for the training of Indian children, trained and ordained men into gospel ministry, and delivered the "glad tidings of salvation of Jesus Christ" to every person who would listen.

In his final years, when he had assigned others to take over much of the Indian work, his concern turned to the black slaves on the English plantations. As an institution, slavery was still accepted during this time. It had existed among the peoples of Africa and had been introduced into the New World during the early decades of Spanish colonization and exploration.[27] During the mid-seventeenth century, the number of African slaves in New England remained small but was a reality nonetheless. New England slaves were not segregated into separate quarters and were generally working side by side with the other members of the workforce that also included members of the family. During this period slaves were educated, many learned to read, and others were reported to have joined the Puritan faith. He desired to teach and train them as he had done the

---

26. John W. Ford, ed., *Some Correspondence between the Governors and Treasurers of the New England Company in London and the Commissioners of the United Colonies in America, the Missionaries of the Company and Others between the Years 1657 and 1712 to Which Are Added the Journals of the Rev. Experience Mayhew in 1713 and 1714* (New York: Burt Franklin, 1970), 74–76.

27. Bremer, *John Winthrop*, 51.

Indians, but he met with little success in securing permission from their masters to catechize those men and women who were enslaved within two or three miles of him. Cotton Mather commented,

> He had long lamented it, with a bleeding and burning passion, that the English used their *negroes* but as their *horses* or their *oxen*, and that so little care was taken about their immortal souls; he looked upon it as a prodigy that any wearing the *name* of *Christians*, should so much have the *heart* of *devils* in them, as to prevent and hinder the instruction of the poor black-amores, and confine the souls of their miserable slaves to a destroying ignorance, merely for fear of thereby losing the benefit of their vassalage.[28]

During Eliot's final years, much grief visited the pastoral parsonage of Roxbury. In 1687, his dear wife, Hanna, a woman loved and honored by the whole community, died. Every household in Roxbury and the surrounding area was well acquainted with the hospitality of Hanna Eliot. Remembering his wife, John wrote these words in the church registry: "In year my ancient dearly beloved wife died, I was sick to death, but the Lord was pleased to delay me and keep in my service which was but pure poor and week." Two entries later, he wrote, "My son Benjamin was buried." Benjamin, who had lived with his parents since his graduation from Harvard, had served as a ministerial assistant to his father in the pulpit of Roxbury.

Only a few scant details surround the final days of John Eliot. His earthly labors came to an end on May 20, 1690, after he spoke two final words: "Welcome joy!" The "Apostle to the Indians" was buried in the parish tomb of Roxbury Burial Ground. The inscription reads:

Here lies the remains of
John Eliot
Apostle to the Indians
Ordained over the First Church, Nov. 5, 1632
Died May 20, 1690, Aged LXXXVI.

---

28. Mather, *Magnalia*, 1:576.

Conclusion

John Eliot was a colonial pastor who possessed an ardent call to go
to his neighbors and share the gospel of Jesus Christ. He was not a
great statesman or intellectual. He was a very simple man: simple
in his acceptance of Scripture as the Word of God, simple in his
trust that God saves all who call on the name of Christ, simple in
his endeavors to establish a Christian society among the Indians,
and simple in his belief that all men and women are in need of the
saving gospel message. From his voyage to the New World to his
first sermon around Waban's wigwam in 1646, Eliot remained at the
helm of all missionary endeavors thereafter, and he serves as a preeminent example of the power of the gospel in the lives of ordinary
and seemingly insignificant people.

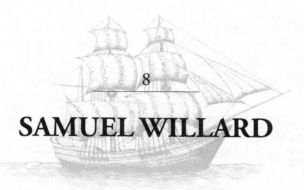

8

SAMUEL WILLARD

By the end of the seventeenth century, Puritanism in America was on the decline. What began in Plymouth as an escape, and in Massachusetts Bay as an experiment, soon became a tyranny that engulfed all of New England. As the early founders began dying off, their children did not possess their zeal or conviction for Puritanism, and the successive waves of diverse migrants had their own ideas about what the New World should be. What was good and righteous in the Puritan movement was often clouded by fanaticism. As the eighteenth century approached, it was fast becoming clear that the earnest Christian movement that had arrived on ships from England was being carried off by adverse winds. However, even in the midst of decline, Puritanism still had its stalwarts. Of all of the second-generation ministers, no one typified strong Reformed orthodoxy and sincere Christian piety more than Samuel Willard.

Birth and Early Life
In the middle of the Great Migration, Simon Willard made his way across the Atlantic Ocean with his family and settled in Massachusetts Colony. Having become thoroughly convinced of the Puritan cause while in England, Willard had witnessed the persecutions by Archbishop Laud and knew that his days were numbered. The Willard name was honorable and the ancestral ties were deep, but twenty-nine-year-old Simon and twenty-one-year-old Mary

Willard would give up nearly everything when they boarded the ship headed for the New World in April 1634.

But the Willards were not alone. Thousands of other Puritans had fled during the 1630s. Upon his arrival in the colony, the distinguished minister Peter Bulkeley (1583–1659) set out with Simon Willard in September 1635 to establish the town of Concord, where approximately fourteen families would settle.[1] While in Concord, Simon Willard fathered nine sons and eight daughters—by his first wife, formerly Mary Sharpe; by his second wife, Elizabeth Dunster; and by his third wife, Mary Dunster. Willard's second son, Samuel Willard, was born on January 31, 1640.

Growing up in a prominent home would have had its blessings as well as its challenges. Samuel's father was a respected military officer in the Concord militia, served as a delegate to the General Court for fifteen years,[2] and was elected to the Massachusetts Bay supreme judiciary in 1654, holding the position for twenty-two years.[3] While young Samuel would have had many watchful eyes on him, his childhood would have afforded him the benefits of witnessing the inner workings of Puritan government and politics.

However, Samuel received a first-class religious education from his local pastor, Peter Bulkeley. A graduate of Cambridge University at the age of sixteen, Bulkeley had been silenced by Archbishop Laud for his nonconformity, which drove him out of England in 1635. Once settled in Massachusetts, he became the minister in Concord, where he served until his death in 1659. Bulkeley was a respected scholar, preacher, and writer as well as a leading proponent of covenant theology. His most notable work, *The Gospel Covenant* (1641), expounded the theology and was regarded as "one of those massive, exhaustive, ponderous treatises into which the Puritan theologians put their enormous learning, their acumen, their industry, fervor,

---

1. Seymour Van Dyken, *Samuel Willard, 1640–1707: Preacher of Orthodoxy in an Era of Change* (Grand Rapids: Eerdmans, 1972), 13.

2. George William Dollar, "The Life and Works of the Reverend Samuel Willard (1640–1707)" (PhD diss., Boston University, 1960), 2.

3. Van Dyken, *Samuel Willard*, 15.

pathos, and consecration of their lives."[4] Week after week, the young Samuel sat under Bulkeley's teaching and was trained up solidly in the Reformed tradition.

At age fifteen, Samuel entered Harvard College on July 17, 1655. The requirements for entrance were rigorous. Prior to admission, potential students were expected to "read and understand Tully Vergill or any such ordinary Classicall Authors, and…speak or write true Latin in prose…. Competently grounded in the Greek Language; so as to be able to Construe and Grammatically to resolve ordinary Greeke, as in the Greeke Testament, Isocrates, and the minor poets, or such like."[5] It is believed that Willard would have learned Latin privately from Peter Bulkeley, which would have served him well as it would have been spoken colloquially on the Harvard campus.

In 1659 Willard graduated from Harvard with honors. Having devoted himself strictly to his studies, young Samuel was trained up in all the rudimentary elements required for theological excellence and pastoral ministry. After earning his degree, Willard continued his studies and pursued the master of arts, which he later obtained. Having immersed himself in the professional study of theology, Willard would have become conversant with such theological works as John Calvin's *Institutes of the Christian Religion* (1559), Johannes Wollebius's *Christianae Theologiae Compendium* (1626), and William Ames's *Medulla Theolgiae* (*Marrow of Sacred Divinity*, 1656). Willard's education laid the foundation for his becoming "a *Great Man*, a profound *Divine*, a very considerable *Scholar*, and an Heavenly *Divine*."[6]

---

4. Samuel Eliot Morison, *An Intellectual Life of Colonial New England* (New York: New York University Press, 1956), 161; cited in Dollar, "Life and Works of the Reverend Samuel Willard," 3.

5. Cited in Van Dyken, *Samuel Willard*, 19.

6. Ebenezer Pemberton, "The Author's Character," in Samuel Willard, *A Compleat Body of Divinity in Two Hundred and Fifty Lectures on the Assembly's Shorter Catechism* (Boston, 1726), 1.

Ministry in Groton

Thirty-five miles northwest of Boston, along the Nashua River, was the town of Groton. A relatively small settlement, it was "on the outermost fringe of civilization."[7] It was there, to "a flock in a more obscure part of this Wilderness,"[8] that twenty-three-year-old Samuel Willard began to preach. Like many frontier towns of the day, the people were in desperate need of a good minister, and upon the death of the Reverend John Miller in 1663, the Groton church called Willard to be their minister "as long as he lives."[9] After a year of preaching regularly, he was ordained on July 13, 1664.

A month after his ordination, Willard married Abigail Sherman, daughter of the Reverend John Sherman of Watertown, near Cambridge. The following year the town voted to build a church meetinghouse as well as a home for their minister. It was there that Samuel and Abigail began to raise "a Puritan-sized family"—the two would have six children together.[10] In 1670 he became a freeman, which conferred on him all the status and privileges of citizenship in Massachusetts Bay.

As Willard labored among the eager saints at Groton, he came into his own as a minister. As a preacher, he made use of the "plain style," in line with most Puritan ministers. "He was a *Judicious Textuary*," said Ebenezer Pemberton. "Like *Apollos* a Man mighty in the Scripture."[11] Fully convinced of the infallibility and sufficiency of the Word of God, Willard made ready use of it and applied it generously to the spiritual condition of his congregants. Commenting on the sufficiency of Scripture, Willard asserts "*the* SCRIPTURES *of the Old and New Testament*...contain in them all that is needful to be known, to guide and direct fallen man to the attainment of

---

7. Van Dyken, *Samuel Willard*, 26.
8. Van Dyken, *Samuel Willard*, 26.
9. Van Dyken, *Samuel Willard*, 27.
10. Van Dyken, *Samuel Willard*, 28.
11. Pemberton, "Author's Character," 1.

his chief end."[12] More than relying on his own spiritual wisdom or theological acumen, Willard placed a tangible trust on the Word of God to minister practically to his people.

In 1671 a sixteen-year-old girl named Elizabeth Knapp was taken with a bout of awful seizures. Immediately Willard began to minister to the girl and her family. Soon word got out that she had been breaking out in hysterical fits, excessive weeping, roaring, barking like a dog, cursing her parents, and the like. As the fits progressed, the girl confessed to making a deal with the devil, who instructed her to kill her parents and drown herself in the well.[13] The citizens of Groton naturally assumed it to be witchcraft and feared a demonic outbreak in the town. Willard, exercising caution and discernment, labored for many weeks and finally concluded that the girl was indeed being demonically afflicted. Through the ministry of Scripture and prayer, the thirty-one-year-old minister began to wear down Elizabeth to the point that she finally began to acknowledge her own sinfulness and ask God for forgiveness. The fits eventually came to an end, and Willard was able to stave off a town-wide witch hysteria. However, some members in town began to suspect that the Lord was bringing judgment to Groton.

On March 13, 1676, nearly four hundred Indians attacked the town, setting much of it on fire. What came to be known as King Philip's War had begun the previous year, and now all of New England was engulfed in the ordeal. Groton had been attacked a few times earlier, but this last raid would lay waste to what remained. One of the first buildings destroyed was *"The House of God,"* wrote Increase Mather, "they scoffed and blasphemed, and came to *Mr. Willard*...his house...and tauntingly, said, *What will you do for a house to pray in now we have burnt your Meeting-house?*"[14] After torching most of the buildings and killing several townspeople, the

---

12. Samuel Willard, *A Compleat Body of Divinity in Two Hundred and Fifty Lectures on the Assembly's Shorter Catechism* (Boston, 1726), 16.

13. Dollar, "Life and Works of the Reverend Samuel Willard," 9.

14. Increase Mather, *A Briefe History of the Warr with the Indians in New-England,* cited in Van Dyken, *Samuel Willard,* 33.

war party moved on. One of the casualties of the Groton attack was Samuel's own father, Simon Willard. Having lost nearly everything, including the father he loved, Samuel Willard had no choice but to abandon the town of Groton and move his family to Boston.

Removal to the Third Church in Boston

By 1678 there were four churches in Boston. Even though a Baptist church had been formed in 1665, it was not officially recognized by the New England establishment; thus, what was referred to as "South Church" was officially known as the Third Church of Boston.[15] Earlier in 1650 the explosion of the Boston population necessitated the formulation of the Second Church, of which the famed Increase Mather (1639–1723) was the pastor. However, Third Church was born not out of expansion but dissension.

The Synod of 1662 had adopted the Half-Way Covenant—the practice of baptizing the infants of churchgoers who could not provide a credible confession of faith though they lived upright lives and promised to raise their children morally so that they might transmit the privileges of membership to them. However, when John Davenport (1597–1670) was called as pastor of the First Church in 1667, he opposed the Half-Way Covenant, insisting that every recognized church member be able to give a credible profession of faith. When this occurred, twenty-eight members withdrew and founded the Third Church in 1669, calling Thomas Thatcher (1620–1678) as their pastor. Within a few years of the founding of Third Church, Samuel Willard, newly arrived from Groton, became the assistant to Reverend Thatcher. Two years later he became the associate pastor. When Thatcher fell sick and died six months later, Willard was called to be their senior pastor.

When Abigail Willard died in early 1679, Samuel remarried Eunice Tyng, daughter of Edward Tyng, a prominent member of the colony. Fourteen children were born to Samuel and Eunice, and in an effort to help support the growing family, Third Church

---

15. Dollar, "Life and Works of the Reverend Samuel Willard," 12–13.

increased his salary substantially.[16] The investment was well worth it for them, as 605 members would be added to the church during Willard's thirty years as pastor.[17]

Although clouded with the tensions between First and Third Churches, the ministry of Samuel Willard was fruitful. Third Church maintained a healthy membership consisting of many prominent Bostonians such as John Hull, treasurer of the colony; Samuel Sewall, a businessman; John Alden, eldest son of John and Priscilla Alden of Plymouth; Edward Rawson, secretary of the colony; and Thomas Brattle, one of the wealthiest merchants in Massachusetts. In addition to the doctrinal positions of the church, the people were drawn to Willard's preaching and teaching. Very quickly, Willard was gaining a reputation for being "altogether the greatest minister of the church throughout the colonial period…an acknowledged leader throughout New England…a preacher, lecturer, administrator, and in every function an uncommon man."[18] Ebenezer Pemberton mused,

> At *first* in his younger Years, his Master committed to his Pastoral Care a Flock in a more obscure part of this Wilderness: But so great a Light was soon observed thro' the whole Land: And his Lord did not deign to bury him in obscurity, but to place him in a more eminent Station, which he was qualifyed for. The Providence that occasioned his Removal to this Place was an *Awful Judgment* upon the whole Land; yet was Eventually a *Mercy* in this respect, that it made way for the Translation of this bright Star to a more Conspicuous Orb; where his Influence was more Extensive and Beneficial; and in this it was a great *Blessing* to this *Congregation*, to this *Town*, nay, to all *New-England*.[19]

---

16. Van Dyken, *Samuel Willard*, 38.

17. Dollar, "Life and Works of the Reverend Samuel Willard," 21.

18. George A. Gordon, *250th Anniversary of the Founding of Old South*, in Dollar, "Life and Works of the Reverend Samuel Willard," 19.

19. Pemberton, "Author's Character," 2.

Dealing with Decline

The success of Puritanism in England effectively put a stop to the Great Migration around 1640. However, after the restoration of the monarchy, the ejection of nearly two thousand Puritan ministers under the Act of Uniformity in 1662 dealt a difficult blow to the movement. In America, Puritanism began to experience decline in the second half of the seventeenth century. Everett Emerson cites four main causes for the decline of Puritan influence in New England. First, Puritan ministers began losing their exclusive status as leaders in Massachusetts and Connecticut. This was primarily caused by the second reason, the rise of competing denominations such as the Baptists and the Anglicans. Third, Puritanism began losing out to the rising spirit of secularism as New England became more culturally and politically diverse. Fourth, the rise of new philosophies and sciences slowly pushed Puritanism from prominence. Even the battle over competing doctrines shook loose the moorings of Puritanism, as "Calvinism was gradually to give way to Arminianism and eventually to Unitarianism."[20] In response to the increasing decline, a large number of second-generation ministers took a stand.

In Boston, key leaders called the Reforming Synod in 1679 for the purpose of confronting "worldly prosperity, the growth of secular views in religious life, the relaxation of moral and theological sternness in the Colony, and their fear that these conditions would bring inevitable judgment and serious retribution upon the people.[21] The synod was made up of Urian Oakes, president of Harvard; Increase Mather of Second Church; and John Hull, Thomas Savage, Edward Raynsford, Peter Thatcher, and Samuel Willard of Third Church, among others. In the course of their discussions of the New England climate, it became clear that they did not need *new* recommendations but older ones. In addition to adopting the Savoy Declaration, a Congregationalist confession derived from the

---

20. Everett Emerson, *Puritanism in America, 1620–1750* (Boston: G. K. Hall, 1977), 135.

21. Williston Walker, *A History of the Congregational Churches in the United States*, in Dollar, "Life and Works of the Reverend Samuel Willard," 22.

Westminster Confession, they also recommended more attention be given to family worship, church discipline, prayer, and caution in admitting people to the Lord's Table.[22] Willard was chosen to present their recommendations to the General Court in 1680.

However, there was much doubt as to how effective the synod's recommendations were in producing the desired results. Despite the apparent momentary failure of the Reforming Synod, Willard still preached for reform, warning against the dangers of rejecting God's covenant with His people. As the first settlers had believed that God had blessed them for their covenant obedience, the second generation was risking it all by turning away from Him. In a sermon to Increase Mather's church in March 1680, Willard contended, "It is not enough for men to return by an outward profession, to make vows, and enter into promises and engagements. There may be a great deal of formality, and a shew of much solemnity in such things, but if the heart be not true in it, all is in vain."[23] Three months later he preached again, and to Willard's joy, the people responded faithfully, pledging to renew their commitment to the Lord's covenant. At a time when New England was falling into cultural decline, the people of God were recommitting themselves under the watchful eye of His faithful shepherds.

The Witchcraft Ordeal

By early 1692 it was discovered that the daughter and niece of the Reverend Samuel Parris of Salem were experimenting with the occult. The practice of witchcraft had been a popular phenomenon in both England and New England prior to the 1690s, but when it broke out in Salem, the people feared the worst. When pressed for more information, the two girls, who were claiming to be sick and afflicted, accused Parris's slave Tituba and two other women of

---

22. Dollar, "Life and Works of the Reverend Samuel Willard," 23.

23. Samuel Willard, "The Necessity of Sincerity in Renewing Covenant," in Samuel Willard with chapters by C. Matthew McMahon, *God's Covenant and Our Duty*, ed. Therese B. McMahon (Coconut Creek, Fla.: Puritan Publications, 2015), 217.

being witches. Almost immediately the matter was brought before the local magistrates. During the interrogations, the two girls flew into a terrible frenzy, which caused a panic among the onlookers.

Within a short time, the magistrates and townspeople began to believe that the devil had been unleashed in Salem and that God's judgment had come. Hysteria took over. The two girls began accusing other members of the community of witchcraft. News traveled throughout New England, and Governor William Phips (1651–1695) appointed a special court to investigate the matter, led by Lieutenant Governor William Stoughton (1631–1701). Soon the accusations were flying, and the pace of the hearings picked up. It was not long before the executions began. Reputable members of Salem, such as John Proctor and Rebecca Nurse, were put to death. By the end of the summer, the accusations went further than Salem and into other parts of the colonies. Prominent citizens such as Captain John Alden, Dudley Bradstreet, and Samuel Willard were named in the accusations. Even the governor's own wife was accused of witchcraft.

At first Willard did not speak up, in order to allow the magistrates to do their jobs. Yet after the first few hangings, the court petitioned the ministers of Boston, asking for advice—after all, this was no doubt a spiritual matter. Fourteen ministers, including Willard, signed an address to be made to the court. While they unanimously agreed that the proceedings should continue in order to determine the spiritual threat to New England, they stressed that caution should be taken and that "clear evidence must determine a case" and not by "that which refers to something vulgarly called *Spectre Evidence*."[24]

However, the court all but disregarded the counsel of the ministers and proceeded in their trials and executions. By the time Governor Phips visited Salem to end the trials, nineteen people had been hanged, one crushed by stones, four died in prison, and more than one hundred others were jailed and awaited trial. While

---

24. Cotton Mather, *The Wonders of the Invisible World* (London: John Russel Smith, 1862), 223.

the shameful proceedings, no doubt the zealous work of William Stoughton, were a black mark on New England history, ministers such as Willard were seen as faithful at the time. Ebenezer Pemberton believed that Willard had "exercised unusual reasonableness." Harvard president Josiah Quincy remarked, "Amid the agitation of Salem witchcraft, the conduct of Mr. Willard was marked by prudence, firmness, and courage. He neither yielded to the current, nor feared to cast the weight of his opinion publicly in opposition to the prevailing delusion...and the circumspection and boldness of Willard was remembered and honored."[25]

Perhaps Willard was able to draw from his experience with the Elizabeth Knapp case or simply from his nearly three decades of wisdom in ministry at the time. Despite the ugliness of the ordeal, Willard's reputation remained intact for being sound in his doctrine and upright in his conduct.

The Battle for Brattle Street

When religious dissenters began to arrive in New England in the mid-1600s, the magistrates reacted swiftly and severely. In the beginning, the reaction was out of fear of incurring God's judgment by allowing apostasy, but as the years progressed and the first generation died off, religious zealotry began to take over. The Baptists and the Quakers, for example, were treated so poorly that letters of protest began arriving from England. In the matter of religious tolerance, however, there existed a broad spectrum among Puritan leaders.

Increase Mather was cut from an older cloth. While loved and respected by his people, he was seen by others as rigid and dogmatic. In the late 1670s Mather had opposed the formation of the Third Church, in many ways regarding it as nothing more than a faction that split unnecessarily from the First Church. Furthermore, Mather was a stalwart of New England Puritanism—Reformed in doctrine, Congregational in polity—and had very little toleration for those

---

25. Josiah Quincy, *History of Harvard University*, in Dollar, "Life and Works of the Reverend Samuel Willard," 42.

outside that tradition. However, in many ways, the die had already been cast thirty years earlier with the acceptance of the Half-Way Covenant, a loophole that would allow the children of unconverted parents to be baptized in the church. But the tide was turning in New England, and the churches were flooded with Christians who held to varying degrees of orthodoxy.

In the last decade of the seventeenth century, a group of young ministers and laymen from Harvard began to advocate for more progressive positions. The "party of progress," as it has been called, consisted of men like John Leverett (1662–1724), Ebenezer Pemberton (1671–1717), Thomas Brattle (1658–1713), and the Reverend William Brattle (1662–1717). While they held vigorously to Reformed orthodoxy and subscribed to the Westminster Confession, the group was eager to modify many of the accepted church practices and make room for new additions, such as the "elimination of public 'relations' of spiritual experience by applicants for communicant membership, reading of the Scriptures without comment at Sunday services, use of the Lord's Prayer, baptism for children of all professing Christians who promised to nurture them in the faith, and selection of ministers by all supporting baptized male adults."[26]

While Increase Mather staunchly opposed the proposed changes, calling the leaders of the progressive movement "profane mockers and scornful neuters overgrown with thorns and nettles...so that the glory of the Lord gradually has departed,"[27] Samuel Willard was sympathetic to the movement. After all, the religious culture of New England was changing, and he was not about to get in the way of genuine Christian believers worshiping together despite minor differences in church practice.

In 1698 the Leveretts and the Brattles joined forces with a group of Boston merchants to organize a new church. On land donated by Thomas Brattle, the Brattle Street Church was born. For their first pastor, they chose Benjamin Colman (1673–1747). A Bostonian by

---

26. Van Dyken, *Samuel Willard*, 82.
27. Cited in Dollar, "Life and Works of the Reverend Samuel Willard," 46.

birth, he studied with Cotton Mather at the renowned school of Ezekiel Cheever. He was admitted to Harvard in 1688, received a bachelor of arts degree in theology, and traveled abroad in London before returning to Boston a few years later. By all rights, Colman was a good choice, and he remained in ministry at Brattle Street for forty-seven years, but Willard's endorsement of the new church did nothing to ingratiate himself to the Mathers. A protracted written exchange ensued between the more conservative contingency of Increase Mather, James Allen of First Church, and John Higgison and Nicholas Noyes of Salem, and the "liberal" party of Brattle Street. Finally, on January 31, 1700, all the Boston ministers joined together for a special Fast Day service in the new church. Samuel Sewall observed, "Mr. Willard pray'd to pardon all the frailties and follies of Ministers and people; and that they might give that Respect to the other churches that was due to them though were not of their Constitution, and Mr. Cotton Mather in [his] prayer to the same purpose. Mr. Willard and C. Mather pray'd excellently and pathetically for Mr. Colman and his Flock."[28]

While the representatives from all the Boston churches were able to preserve the peace, the event would not mark the end of tensions between Increase Mather and Samuel Willard.

The Harvard Situation

When the Massachusetts Bay Colony lost its charter in 1684, and after the 1689 insurrection that removed Sir Edmund Andros, the royally appointed governor, Increase Mather was sent to England to negotiate the terms of a new charter. While the new charter was not as widely accepted by New Englanders as the old one, he was nonetheless successful. At the same time, Samuel Willard was tasked with securing a charter for Harvard College, thus protecting their Puritan interest, which he accomplished in 1700.

---

28. Samuel Sewall, *Diary of Samuel Sewall*, cited in Van Dyken, *Samuel Willard*, 83.

At that time, Increase Mather had served Harvard College for nearly twenty years as president, but because of complications with the charter, he did not always retain the title. He was officially recognized as president in 1685. However, by 1698, the college was in disarray. Many viewed the poor condition of the school as a result of Mather's latent leadership. For his entire presidency, Mather remained in Boston, serving the Second Church. In the terms of the new charter, it was mandated that the president would need to reside in Cambridge in order to oversee the operations of the college. But Mather was unwilling to move.

In March 1701 it was decided by the General Court that "as the Constitution requires the President to reside at Cambridge…it is therefore ordered…in the case of Mr. Mather's refusal, absence, sickness, or death, that Mr. Samuel Willard nominated to be Vice President."[29] While Mather did not doubt Willard's leadership abilities, the two disagreed on many of the procedures of the college, which served to elevate the tension.

However, when Willard refused to move to Cambridge to serve as vice president, the court decreed that the residency mandate applied only to the president, not to the vice president. With no other plans to appoint another president, Willard would now function as acting president without an official title. So now, on a technicality, Willard was in and Mather was forced out. Mather was furious. He later wrote, "The Colledge was through the malice of mr Cooke and Byfield put into the hands of mr Willard as vicepresident, who readily accepted the offer without so much as once consulting with me about it."[30] Despite the deceptive nature of the move, it was readily acknowledged that Willard was "far more generally acceptable than Mather…being equally learned and sound in the articles of the faith…. He was quite retiring while fundamental, phlegmatic and unpretendful of his public services…and devoted to his professional

---

29. Samuel Eliot Morison, *Harvard College in the Seventeenth Century*, in Dollar, "Life and Works of the Reverend Samuel Willard," 57.

30. Cited in Van Dyken, *Samuel Willard*, 86.

research and pastoral studies. His study was the scene of his private labors and his church the theater of his public action."[31]

Willard took the post seriously and devoted himself wholeheartedly, serving in the unrecognized lead position until his death in 1707.

The Westminster Catechism Lectures

Along with nearly all the New England Puritans, Samuel Willard fought numerous doctrinal battles. Perhaps the most dire of all of these was against Arminianism. John Cotton had opposed it in the mid-1610s and 20s, Thomas Shepard in the 1630s and 40s, and the Mathers all throughout the second half of the seventeenth century. Named after Dutch theologian Jacobus Arminius (1560–1609), the system of theology known as Arminianism emphasized the free will of mankind in salvation over and against the sovereignty of God. The Puritans on both sides of the Atlantic regarded Arminianism as a serious error that smacked of the semi-Pelagianism of Rome, and they viewed its opposition as a nonnegotiable tenet of orthodoxy. Along with the majority of English Puritans, Willard was a stalwart of Reformed theology, an ardent Calvinist who never shied from preaching the doctrines of grace. Robert Godfrey notes, however, "that Calvinism has never summarized itself in five points. Calvinism is summarized in full confessional statements such as the Heidelberg Catechism, the Belgic Confession, and the Westminster Confession of Faith. To be very accurate, Calvinism does not have—and never has had—five points. Rather, it has five answers to the five errors of Arminianism."[32]

Willard embodied the truth of the fact that Reformed—or Calvinist—theology extends far beyond what was contended for at the Synod of Dort. While Willard was ever ready to debate an opponent

---

31. Quincy, *History of Harvard*, 60.

32. W. Robert Godfrey, *Saving the Reformation: The Pastoral Theology of the Canons of Dort* (Sanford, Fla.: Reformation Trust, 2019), 13.

point by point, his master plan was to train his church thoroughly, immersing them in the Westminster Catechism.

On January 31, 1687, Samuel Willard began his systematic exposition of the Westminster Shorter Catechism. He delivered his lectures "monthly on the Tuesdays in the afternoon, in his public congregation."[33] So "universally and justly admired" were these lectures, they "drew many of the most knowing and judicious persons both from town and college."[34] Working methodically through each question of the catechism, expounding line by line, doctrine by doctrine, Willard continued his lectures for two hundred and twenty months, until he fell sick and died in 1707.

After his death, however, two of his former students, Joseph Sewall and Thomas Prince, underwent the task of gathering up his lectures and preparing them for publication. There was just one problem—Willard never finished his lectures. To their joy, they discovered that he had "most diligently redeemed his time and prepared about 26 others, even to the end of the 100th *Question*."[35] The remaining four lectures were compiled from notes kept by his family and students. In 1726, Willard's 250 expositions of the Westminster Catechism were published under the title *A Compleat Body of Divinity*. The task of publishing the enormous volume—roughly one and half times the size of Calvin's *Institutes*—was so immense that the Boston presses had to pool their resources in order to print the nearly one thousand double-columned folio pages.[36] At the time, the single-volume work was the largest book ever printed in America.

Willard's *Compleat Body* stands as a tour de force of seventeenth-century Reformed theology. In many ways dwarfing even the works of William Ames and Thomas Watson, Willard's volume

---

33. Joseph Sewall and Thomas Prince, preface to Samuel Willard, *A Compleat Body of Divinity in Two Hundred and Fifty Lectures on the Assembly's Shorter Catechism* (Boston, 1726), 1.

34. Sewall and Prince, preface, 1.

35. Sewall and Prince, preface, 2.

36. Ernest Benson Lowrie, *The Shape of the Puritan Mind: The Thought of Samuel Willard* (New Haven, Conn.: Yale University Press, 1974), 3.

traces the robust thread of God's sovereignty and goodness throughout the whole of Christian theology: the Scriptures, the knowledge
of God, the sinfulness of mankind, God's covenants, the doctrines
of salvation, the person and work of Jesus Christ, the law of God,
and Christian living. For more than a hundred years in New England, the Westminster Confession (and catechism) was regarded
as "*orthodoxy*," and "no American ever expounded the ancient
creed more thoroughly than that 'Teacher of a Church in Boston,'
Samuel Willard."[37]

Death and Legacy

The spring of 1707 was merciless to Mr. Willard's health. A series of
sicknesses plagued him, and by fall he had suffered an illness from
which he would never recover. One of his good friends, Samuel
Sewall, came to visit him on his deathbed. When he arrived, Ebenezer Pemberton was already at the home, along with several other
church members. Sewall records, "After prayer many went out, I
[stayed] and sat down: and in a few minutes saw my dear pastor
expire: it was a little after Two, just about two hours after his being
taken. It was very surprising. The Doctors were in another room
Consulting what to do.... Tis thought cutting his finger might
bring on this tumultuous passion that carried him away."[38]

But Willard was gone, having passed on to glory that day,
September 12, 1707. Willard's assistant at Third Church, Ebenezer Pemberton, conducted the funeral. Increase Mather, Cotton
Mather, Benjamin Colman, James Allen, and Thomas Bridge—
otherwise theological opponents yet united in love for their dear
brother—were pallbearers. His body was finally laid to rest across
from Boston's Park Street Church in Granary Burying Ground.

Willard was remembered as "a person of excellent accomplishments naturally acquired...an ardent student, a powerful preacher

---

37. Lowrie, *Shape of the Puritan Mind*, 8.
38. Samuel Sewall, *Diary of Samuel Sewall*, cited in Dollar, "Life and Works of the
Reverend Samuel Willard," 110.

of the Word of God, an exemplary Christian and a mirror of all that is good."[39] In his funeral sermon, Pemberton noted, "He had a sanctified heart as well as a well-regulated logical head; and was a scholar of great proficiency in the school of Christ."[40] As a pastor, "he expressed a true love and zeal for Christ, and tender compassion to immortal souls...[h]is affection & tenderness to this his own flock was singular. He might have said with the Apostle, that he could have imparted with the gospel his own soul to them."[41] His theological output was stellar; Perry Miller calls *A Compleat Body* "a landmark in American publishing and a magnificent summation of the Puritan intellect."[42] More than this, however, Samuel Willard was a watchman on the wall, a guardian of Reformed orthodoxy. Not a more fitting remark can be made than this: "Willard's whole ministry jealously guarded the honor of sovereign grace."[43]

---

39. Charles F. Adams, *Three Episodes in Massachusetts History*, in Dollar, "Life and Works of the Reverend Samuel Willard," 111.

40. Pemberton, "Author's Character," 2.

41. Pemberton, "Author's Character," 2–3.

42. Cited in Lowrie, *Shape of the Puritan Mind*, vii.

43. Attributed to Ebenezer Pemberton in Van Dyken, *Samuel Willard*, 121.

9

COTTON MATHER

New England winters are known for being bitterly cold, and the February of 1728 would have been no different. After suffering from a long sickness, Cotton Mather—the "American Elijah"—died. A sea of people flooded into Boston to mourn the loss of the beloved pastor. Four funeral sermons were preached, a rare occurrence. And when it was time to return his body to the dust, Mather was followed by a long procession to Copp's Hill. At the time of his death, his enemies were few, but in time they would multiply and suffocate his blessed legacy.

The Mather Dynasty

Cotton Mather was born on February 12, 1663, into a distinguished family dynasty. His grandfather, Richard Mather (1596–1669), was born in Lancashire, England, where he was eventually ordained to the ministry. By 1633 Mather was suspended from ministry because of his nonconformity, which led him to flee to New England in 1635. The following year he participated in founding the church in Dorchester, Massachusetts, where he ministered until his death at age seventy-three. Along with leaders like John Cotton, Thomas Hooker, Thomas Shepard, and John Davenport, Richard Mather contributed mightily to what became known as "the New England Way." His grandson, Cotton, remembered him fondly as a man who was "calm, sedate, studious, ever busy, devout, yet pleasant withal, he was an embodiment of the best form of godliness."[1] Richard's first wife, Katherine Holt, gave birth to six sons, of which four were ministers. When Katherine died in 1655, he married Sarah Hankredge, the widow of Boston minister John Cotton.

Richard's youngest son, Increase Mather, was born on June 21, 1639, in Dorchester, Massachusetts. As a boy he studied under John Norton before entering Harvard College, where he graduated with a bachelor of arts degree in 1656. After studying abroad at Trinity College, Dublin, he returned to Boston in 1661. In March 1662, Increase married Maria Cotton, the daughter of John Cotton. The two had seven daughters and three sons that survived into adulthood, two of whom became ministers. In 1664 Increase was called to pastor the Second Church in Boston (also known as "Old North Church"), where he served for nearly six decades until his death in 1723. Regarded as "the foremost American Puritan,"[2] Increase was a serious-minded minister and devout Puritan, widely respected in every corner of New England. However, no one revered him higher than his eldest son, Cotton, who would spend his entire life working to fill both his father's and grandfather's shoes.

Early Life and Education

At an early age, Cotton Mather was drawn to learning. A bright young boy with a prodigious mind, he very quickly learned Hebrew, Greek, and Latin, with the latter being his favorite. In fact, he was so proficient in it that he could listen to a sermon delivered in English and take notes on it in Latin.[3] Furthermore, Cotton had a broad attention span and a long memory. He would often listen in church to his father and write out all that he remembered upon returning

---

1. Abijah P. Marvin, *The Life and Times of Cotton Mather* (Boston: Congregational Sunday-School and Publishing Society, 1892), 1.

2. Everett Emerson, *Puritanism in America, 1620–1750* (Boston: Twayne Publishers, 1977), 139.

3. Robert Middlekauff, *The Mathers: Three Generations of Puritan Intellectuals, 1596–1728* (Berkeley: University of California Press, 1999), 195.

home.[4] His appetite for Scripture was so insatiable that he made a practice of reading upward of fifteen chapters each day, in three courses of five at a time.[5] His family enrolled him at Ezekiel Cheever's excellent school, but it quickly became apparent that Cotton was excelling beyond his peers.

In 1675, at age eleven, after a rigorous examination, Cotton Mather was admitted to Harvard College—the youngest student to have been enrolled there. Mather thrived at Harvard and maintained a strong affinity for the school throughout his life. As a student, he devoured many of the numerous volumes in the library, making "ingenuous remarks upon them in his diary."[6] He quickly obtained a reputation for his great "capacity for learning" and "modest inquisitiveness" among the students and faculty.[7] He earned a bachelor of arts degree in 1678 and a master of arts degree in 1681. On the momentous day of Mather's graduation, Harvard president Urian Oakes offered up a glowing tribute: "Mather is named Cotton Mather. What a name! My hearers, I mistake; I ought to have said what names! I shall not speak of his father, for I dare not praise him to his face. But should he resemble his venerable grandfathers, John Cotton and Richard Mather, in piety, learning, splendor of intellect, solidity of judgment, prudence, and wisdom, he will indeed bear the palm. And I have confidence that in this young man Cotton and Mather will be united and flourish again."[8]

He had all the giftedness and promise of a world-class pastor-theologian, but Cotton Mather would have his own share of obstacles to overcome.

---

4. Kenneth Silverman, *The Life and Times of Cotton Mather* (New York: Welcome Rain Publishers, 1984), 13.

5. Marvin, *Life and Times of Cotton Mather*, 6.

6. Marvin, *Life and Times of Cotton Mather*, 7.

7. Marvin, *Life and Times of Cotton Mather*, 8.

8. Marvin, *Life and Times of Cotton Mather*, 8.

Conversion to Christ

A few months prior to graduating from Harvard, Cotton began recalling his experiences with *"a Closure with the Lord Jesus Christ."*[9] He had begun keeping a diary in 1681 at the age of eighteen, but it is apparent that he wrestled his entire life with the realities of his own spiritual condition. Having been raised in a Christian home—the home of a minister!—Cotton was keenly aware of his own sinfulness, often rehearsing things like, "I have plunged my Soul down into an *horrible Pitt* of Sin and wo[e] .... *Salvation*, I must, I must bee made Partaker of. And what shall I do? I am utterly unable to save myself."[10] Lamenting his own condition constantly, Cotton was wracked with guilt and shame. "I am convinced," he writes, "of the utter Insufficiency in my own *Righteousness* to procure my *Salvation*. I See the *Nothingness* of my own *Righteousness* in Point of Acceptance with God. I See indeed a wo[e]ful *Hypocrisy* hath acted me, and *Sluggishness* and *Selfishness* hath attended me in the very best of all my Services."[11]

However, at age sixteen, Cotton recalled, "I perceive now no other way for my *Salvation*, but only by ye Lord JESUS CHRIST; *Refuge* fails elsewhere on Every hand."[12] In fact, the constant refrain on nearly every page of his diary is the beauty and all-sufficiency of Jesus Christ. "I behold a *Fulness* and a *Bounty* in ye Lord JESUS CHRIST. He is worth Loving, worth Prizing, worth Following Hard after Him."[13] Often overlooking his Christ-focused posture of faith (Mather noted, "My Life is almost a continual Conversation with Heaven"[14]), history often seizes on the painful honesty of Mather's personal confessions. Putting it into perspective, Richard Lovelace

---

9. Cotton Mather, *The Diary of Cotton Mather*, vol. 1, *1681–1709* (New York: Frederick Ungar, 1911), 1.

10. Mather, *Diary*, 1:33.

11. Cotton Mather, *Paterna: The Autobiography of Cotton Mather*, ed. Ronald A. Bosco (New York: Scholars' Facsimiles & Reprints, 1976), 12.

12. Mather, *Paterna*, 12.

13. Mather, *Paterna*, 12.

14. Cotton Mather, *The Diary of Cotton Mather*, vol. 2, *1709–1724* (New York: Frederick Ungar, 1911), 267.

notes, "It is true that Mather was a complex personality; though he was probably no more so than any other human being, few other human beings have revealed themselves to us as fully as he did."[15]

While struggles with sin and spiritual torment would haunt Mather for the rest of his life, he was also plagued with physical maladies. One such hindrance nearly prevented him from answering the call to the highest office in the land.

Called to Boston

While his heart and mind were set on pastoral ministry, Cotton was plagued with a terrible stutter. So inhibitive was the stammer that he had all but given up hope of public speaking. However, one of his teachers had encouraged him to devote himself to singing, noting that "by prolonging your pronunciation you will get an habit of speaking without hesitation."[16] So Cotton worked hard at his enunciation and was eventually able to train himself to speak with diction and eloquence.

As he started preaching publicly, he began to receive several pastoral invitations. Even the prestigious church of New Haven, Connecticut—once the home of John Davenport—called him to be their minister. The call was "a striking proof of the reputation of the youthful preacher,"[17] but Cotton turned it down in favor of pursuing ministry in his father's church in Boston. On February 23, 1681, Cotton was invited to assist his father in ministry, which he was honored to accept. While overjoyed at the thought of laboring alongside his father, Cotton was also struck with the weightiness of ministry, writing in his diary, "*Lord, help me to serve thee, love thee, and glorify thy Name. Fill mee with thy Spirit. It will bee so! Oh! Who am I, that I should bee filled with the Spirit of the Holy God! But it will bee so! The Lord hath caused His Servant to trust in His Word.* Isa. 44. 3.

---

15. Richard F. Lovelace, *The American Pietism of Cotton Mather: Origins of American Evangelicalism* (Grand Rapids: Christian University Press, 1979), 2.

16. Marvin, *Life and Times of Cotton Mather*, 14.

17. Marvin, *Life and Times of Cotton Mather*, 28.

This Day in the Assurance, the glorious and ravishing Assurance, of the Divine Love, my Joyes were almost insupportable!"[18]

Cotton was so devoted to his work and well-loved by the church that they soon called him to the role of pastor-preacher, with his father remaining in the position of teacher. At first he demurred out of timidity. He records that the prospect of serving in such a high calling caused an "earthquake in him" to read the words from Hebrews 13:17: "They watch for your souls, as they that must give account."[19] However, in early 1685 he finally accepted his church's pastoral call. He was ordained on May 13, 1685; his father preached the sermon, John Allen of First Church and Samuel Willard of Third Church laid hands on him, and eighty-one-year-old John Eliot gave him the right hand of fellowship.

Cotton took immediately to his new duties, often working sixteen hours per day.[20] He engaged in discipleship and counseling, the catechizing of children, Bible studies, door-to-door evangelism, and mercy ministry. As for his preaching, he writes that he labored to preach "as excellent and well studied Sermons as ever I can and contrive all my public Exercises in the most edifying manner that I am able."[21] Cotton's reputation as a powerful preacher grew very quickly, but not just because of his gifted oratory; he set a precedent for being an orthodox and Christ-centered preacher. Robert Middlekauff notes, "Christ provided the center in all these pulpit efforts. Mather was dazzled by the splendor of Christ's sacrifice and humble before it. If Mather's listeners heard anything he said they must have received the impression that they too should worship the miracle of Christ's incarnation."[22]

As Cotton progressed in his ministry, the congregation grew to love him. Kenneth Silverman notes, "They often commented in their diaries or to others on his soul-saving power and warmth,

---

18. Mather, *Diary*, 1:6.
19. Cited in Marvin, *Life and Times of Cotton Mather*, 31.
20. Middlekauff, *Mathers*, 192.
21. Silverman, *Life and Times of Cotton Mather*, 194.
22. Middlekauff, *Mathers*, 254.

appreciatively left him small bequests in their wills, or wrote to him commending his 'Compassionate Regard for the Good of Souls' and asking for his help."[23] There was no question that the congregants at Second Church revered their teacher, Increase Mather, but they deeply adored his son.

Challenges with the Charter

For five decades Massachusetts Bay Colony had functioned under its own charter, which granted the colonists the privilege of self-government, property rights, and religious liberty. However, as the colony became more and more profitable, England began to tighten its grip. Loyalists like Edward Randolph (1632–1703) lobbied for strict royal control over Massachusetts, and over the course of ten years he made five trips to America. In 1683 King Charles II demanded that Massachusetts surrender their charter, but they refused. On May 14, 1686, Randolph arrived for the fifth time and delivered the news that the Massachusetts charter had officially been revoked and the king had commissioned a new provisional government. Seven months later, Sir Edmund Andros (1637–1714) arrived to assume control over New England.

The already growing resistance movement sprang into action, with Increase and Cotton Mather at the forefront. With the arrival of Andros came a wave of sweeping changes, both political and religious. Within months, Andros insisted that the Boston churches allow their buildings to be used by the Church of England. By March 1687 he began issuing new revenue laws and additional taxes. Also, he sought to restrict town meetings and began regulating land ownership. But Andros was no fool; he knew that if he were to succeed in New England he would have to temper his opponents, which meant silencing the Mathers. Almost prophetically, on the same day that King Charles II died on February 6, 1685, Increase Mather had delivered an address in which he cried,

23. Silverman, *Life and Times of Cotton Mather*, 196–97.

"God will deliver New England!"[24] Now with the charter gone and the newly minted governor Andros on American soil, the wave of protest was only increasing.

As New Englanders were preparing to launch their political countermeasures, Increase Mather, disguised in a wig and white cloak, escaped aboard a ship destined for England on March 30, 1688. With Increase gone to England to renegotiate for the charter, Andros turned his attention on Cotton, of whom Abijah Marvin says, "No young man in the colony was more alive than Cotton Mather to all that concerned its growth and prosperity. He was a true son of the soil."[25] On April 18, 1689, Boston took up arms against Andros's government, Cotton Mather being one of the "chief designers" of the revolt.[26] At noon, a great crowd of Bostonians surrounded the Town House as Cotton read aloud a document he penned outlining the reasons for their revolt, titled *Declaration of the Gentlemen, Merchants, and Inhabitants of Boston and the Country Adjacent*. By two o'clock, an armed militia stormed Fort Hill, where Governor Andros had been hiding since hearing the news of a revolt. When he realized that he was outnumbered, he surrendered and was taken to the Town House, where he was deposed. Before too long, Andros was on a ship headed back to England, his administration thwarted "without the least *Bloodshed* or *Plunder*, and with as much *Order* as ever attended any *Tumult*…in the world."[27]

Increase Mather returned from England on May 14, 1692, with a new charter. It had been granted by Queen Mary in November 1691, although not to the colony's full satisfaction. But it did allow them to operate their own government and retain their religious liberty. While many complained that Increase Mather had not done more to further the interests of New England, it was far better than English despotism. However, the hometown hero of America's version of the Glorious Revolution was no doubt Cotton Mather.

---

24. Silverman, *Life and Times of Cotton Mather*, 64.
25. Marvin, *Life and Times of Cotton Mather*, 44–45.
26. Silverman, *Life and Times of Cotton Mather*, 69.
27. Cotton Mather cited in Silverman, *Life and Times of Cotton Mather*, 72.

Biographer David Levin notes, "In the spring of 1689, then, Cotton Mather had reached the highest popular recognition and public usefulness of his young life, and he was probably happier in these weeks than he would ever be again."[28]

Salem Witch Trials

By the time the news of witchcraft in Salem arrived at Cotton's doorstep, it was already a growing controversy. For years New England ministers had been warning the people about God's coming judgment, hoping to steer them away from spiritual laziness, and the apparent outbreak of evil seemed only to confirm their greatest fears. The belief in witchcraft and demonic possession was widespread in Europe and America, with several eminent biblical scholars such as Matthew Poole, Matthew Henry, Simon Patrick, and Richard Baxter having written extensively about it.[29] Cotton had prior personal dealings with the demonic realm in 1688 when the Goodwin family brought their afflicted children to be ministered to. Cotton's treatment consisted of bringing one of the daughters into his own home so that he and his wife could regulate her diet and sleep, all the while ministering to her spiritually. In the end, the Goodwin children recovered, and their father, John Goodwin, publicly thanked Cotton for his pastoral care.[30]

However, once Betty Parris and Abigail Williams began accusing various persons of witchcraft in Salem, the magistrates quickly got involved and examinations began. At first, Cotton recommended the kind of healing program that he had employed with the Goodwin children, having their lives regulated with the aid of long sessions of prayer. Rick Kennedy surmises, "If Cotton's advice had been followed, it is safe to assume that matters in Salem would

---

28. David Levin, *Cotton Mather: The Young Life of the Lord's Remembrancer, 1663–1703* (Cambridge, Mass.: Harvard University Press, 1978), 172.

29. Paul Wise, "Cotton Mather and the Invisible World," in *Cotton Mather and Biblia Americana—America's First Bible Commentary: Essays in Reappraisal*, ed. Reiner Smolinski and Jan Stievermann (Grand Rapids: Baker Academic, 2010), 243.

30. Silverman, *Life and Times of Cotton Mather*, 86.

have turned out better."[31] But the twenty-nine-year-old minister was ignored, and the trials ensued.

Once the court in Salem, led by Lieutenant Governor William Stoughton, began executing convicted witches, the Boston ministers were called on to further advise them. Despite being appalled by the manner of the proceedings, all of the ministers were unanimous in their support of further examinations, but they insisted on the utmost caution before putting anyone else to death. Further, they advised that genuine confessions of wrongdoing be obtained, and not the use of "spectral evidence," to condemn them. Cotton himself believed that the surest test of witchcraft was a credible confession. Kenneth Silverman notes that he followed English Puritan William Perkins in his view, who argued, *"Among the sufficient means of Conviction, the first is, the free and voluntary Confession of the Crime, made by the party suspected and accused, after Examination."*[32] Yet the court seemed determined to proceed based on the flimsy testimony of the two girls.

As the witchcraft ordeal continued, very few ministers made visits to Salem—Cotton Mather never visited Salem during the trials, nor did he have any authority over the proceedings.[33] He was, however, active in his writing about it. Earlier in 1689 he had published *Memorable Providences, Relating to Witchcraft and Possessions*, but it was the 1693 publishing of his book *The Wonders of the Invisible World* that has been regarded as his tacit endorsement of the trials.[34] However, Puritan scholar Perry Miller contends that Cotton had been pressured by Governor William Phips and Lieutenant Governor William Stoughton to write the damning account. Miller writes, "If ever there was a false book produced by a man whose heart was

31. Rick Kennedy, *The First American Evangelical: A Short Life of Cotton Mather* (Grand Rapids: Eerdmans, 2015), 63.

32. Silverman, *Life and Times of Cotton Mather*, 95, emphasis original.

33. Kennedy, *First American Evangelical*, 64.

34. David Levin notes that *The Wonders* is "the book that enabled Robert Calef to tie on the name of Cotton Mather a tin can that has rattled through nearly three centuries." *Cotton Mather*, 120.

not in it, it is *The Wonders*."[35] Most modern historians concur with Miller's assessment that Cotton was "insecure, frightened, [and] sick at heart" over the whole situation.[36] In fact, almost prophetically, Cotton had warned the court that if they continued to execute the accused citizens on the basis of spectral evidence, "a door may be thereby opened for the devils to obtain from the courts in the invisible world a license to proceed unto the most hideous desolations upon the repute and repose" of those who were otherwise innocent.[37]

Increase Mather returned from England in 1692 and journeyed to Salem with Governor William Phips, who had been away on other business. When they arrived, twenty townspeople were dead and nearly a hundred others were in jail. Under Increase's advisement, the remaining prisoners were immediately set free, and Lieutenant Governor Stoughton resigned. Five years later, the magistrates issued a formal apology. While Cotton had grown progressively disenchanted with the court (namely, with William Stoughton), he had tried vigorously to distance himself from the wrongdoings. Critics of the Mathers would later use the witch trials to implicate them, but according to the Mathers' biographer, Robert Middlekauff, "There is no evidence that they contributed to the venomous atmosphere that swirled around Salem Village when witchcraft appeared there in 1692."[38] In fact, he concludes, "The most admirable act, of course, was the advice given to the Governor.... Increase, more than anyone else, had stopped the whole grisly business."[39] But not everyone was convinced of the Mathers' virtue.

Enemies at Home, Friends Abroad

The most vicious and relentless critic of Cotton Mather was a local merchant named Robert Calef (1648–1719). While a respected man

---

35. Perry Miller, *The New England Mind: From Colony to Province* (Cambridge, Mass.: Harvard University Press, 1953), 201.

36. Miller, *New England Mind*, 201.

37. Cited in Levin, *Cotton Mather*, 205.

38. Middlekauff, *Mathers*, 148.

39. Middlekauff, *Mathers*, 154.

in his own right, he believed that Cotton was exploiting the witchcraft trials for his own notoriety. Furthermore, Calef was skeptical
of the existence of the supernatural realities written about by the
Mathers. As early as June 1698, Cotton was made aware that Calef
was writing a full-length book against him. In preparation for its
release, Cotton prayed against it:

> There is a sort of *Saducee* in this Town; a man, who makes little
> Conscience of lying; and one whom no Reason will divert
> from his malicious Purposes. This man, out of Enmity to mee,
> for my public Asserting of such Truths, as the Scripture has
> taught us, about the Existence and Influence of the *Invisible
> World*, hath often abused mee, with venemous *Reproaches*, and
> most palpable *Injuries*.... Wherefore, in my Supplications, I
> first of all declared unto the Lord, that I freely *Forgave* this
> miserable Man, all the Wrongs which hee did unto mee, and I
> pray'd the Lord also to *forgive* him, and to do him good even
> as to my own Soul.[40]

Despite Cotton's prayers, Robert Calef published *More Wonders
of the Invisible World* in 1700. While several of the Boston ministers
named in the book simply ignored the outlandish claims, Cotton
took it personally, and for good reason. Calef claimed that, during
their treatment of a bewitched girl named Margaret Rule, Increase
and Cotton both sexually assaulted her. Despite dozens of witnesses
present during the alleged misconduct, Calef maintained his uncor-
roborated story. According to David Levin, "Calef at best distorted
the facts and at worst lied about them."[41] Calef was arrested on
charges of libel but was released due to the fact that no one in
Boston believed his account. However, following Cotton's death his
enemies seized on Calef's account to tarnish his name. With regard
to Calef, Rick Kennedy concurs with modern scholars who "dis-
count as thoroughly untrustworthy" his writings.[42] In time, Calef

---

40. Mather, *Diary*, 1:264–65.
41. Levin, *Cotton Mather*, 242.
42. Kennedy, *First American Evangelical*, 147.

himself gave up on his attempts to ruin Cotton Mather. However, the incredulous narrative had circulated through Europe and the Americas and tarnished his reputation for the next three centuries.

Despite his troubling relationships at home, Cotton excelled at making friends throughout New England and Europe. Prone to letter writing, Cotton engaged in prolonged correspondence with university scholars, historians, scientists, and churchmen. For example, Scottish church historian Robert Wodrow (1679–1734) treasured his letters from Cotton, calling the exchanges "one of the greatest satisfactions kind Providence has allowed me."[43] Mather kept active correspondence with such persons as German scholar August Hermann Francke (1663–1727), novelist Daniel Defoe (1660–1731), hymn writer Isaac Watts (1674–1748), and Sir Isaac Newton (1643–1727). According to biographer Kenneth Silverman, Cotton sent more than five thousand letters worldwide to countries like Germany, Holland, France, India, Scotland, and England; his six hundred surviving letters comprise the largest extant correspondence of any American Puritan.[44]

In addition to sending personal letters, Mather sent manuscripts for books he longed to publish as well as collected data of scientific experiments he had performed. In 1710 the University of Glasgow awarded Mather a doctor of divinity degree, an honor he cherished deeply. In 1713 the Royal Society in England, to which Mather had contributed over the course of many years a "valuable Collection of many Curiosities,"[45] conferred on him the title of fellow. In 1715 he sent them a manuscript titled *The Christian Philosopher*—the first American scientific textbook—which was later published in 1721. His research in the fields of astronomy, botany, geology, meteorology, and zoology did nothing short of solidify him as a respected scholar on the world stage. However, it was his ecumenical aspirations that represented his most ambitious pursuits.

43. Silverman, *Life and Times of Cotton Mather*, 223.
44. Silverman, *Life and Times of Cotton Mather*, 199.
45. Silverman, *Life and Times of Cotton Mather*, 243.

Seeking Unity

By the end of the seventeenth century, visible Christianity in Europe and America appeared to be on the decline. Recognizing this problem, several key leaders such as Increase Mather, Matthew Meade, and John Howe worked to form an interdenominational, intercontinental alliance known as the United Brethren. Increase labored to secure the alliance during his 1688 trip to England, while Cotton tarried at home, penning his treatise *Blessed Unions* (1692), in which he advocated for ecumenical dialogue and charity between Congregationalists and Presbyterians, adding "the EPISCOPAL too when Piety is otherwise visible...and I may add, the Name of, ANTIPEDOBAPTIST."[46] Invitations to the "ecumenical" union did not go out to members of the Roman Catholic Church, which Mather noted is "entirely possessed by *Satan* [and] is resolved upon the Extermination of all the Christians upon the Earth, who come not into a Combination with her, in her *Detestable Idolatries.*"[47]

In 1690 the United Brethren was formed between the Congregationalists and Presbyterians. However, the adherents agreed that for there to be genuine Christian fellowship and unity there must also be unity in doctrine. Throughout the course of his life, Cotton developed a series of unifying credos called the "maxims of piety"— essential truths he believed every Christian was required to affirm in order to maintain an orthodox faith. Even though he would have had substantial doctrinal and ecclesiastical differences with various non-Congregationalist denominations, Mather believed that true unity was possible for those who affirmed the maxims of piety—namely, "a fear of God...a full acceptance of the righteousness of Christ as justifying men, and the love of one's fellow man as a way of honoring God."[48] While not diminishing the importance of doctrinal distinctives—the Mathers were notorious for towing the Calvinist and Congregationalist line—Cotton still upheld the blessedness of

---

46. Cited in Lovelace, *American Pietism of Cotton Mather*, 262.

47. Cotton Mather, *Suspiria Vinctorum*, cited in Lovelace, *American Pietism of Cotton Mather*, 259.

48. Middlekauff, *Mathers*, 227.

the core of Christianity, declaring, "A Soul Sanctified with the *Love* of GOD, and of CHRIST, and of our Neighbor, is altogether to be preferred before all the *Extraordinary Gifts* of the Holy SPIRIT."[49]

Within a few short years the integrity of the union became compromised. Very quickly European rationalists, in seeing the moral and social value of such an alliance, began to capitalize on it for their own pietistic and altruistic purposes. Upon hearing about the incursion of rationalism in England, Mather blasted those who focused on "the strange care taken to fabricate a *Christian Religion* without a *Christ*, or the most Vital parts of *Christianity*." Further, he attacked "a nation full of Preachers, that will contrive to make Harangues upon Moral Vertues, but banish Christ."[50] Yet there were even bigger problems on the horizon.

Within the ranks of like-minded Reformed brethren, questions began to arise about the basis of the gospel—namely, the doctrine of justification. While the New England churches uniformly upheld the Reformed teaching of justification by faith alone, Richard Baxter's view bordered on the position of Rome. In July and August 1699, Cotton delivered two addresses at his church in Boston expounding the doctrine of justification. So germane to his own understanding of Christianity, Lovelace writes, "There are innumerable treatments of this doctrine in Mather's work. It is alluded to in every application section that deals with regeneration, and that means virtually every sermon Mather preached."[51] His sermons were heralded in New England and published together under the title *The Everlasting Gospel* in 1700, which he dedicated to the United Brethren.

By the first decade of the 1700s the Christian union had failed. In many cases, the differences were too great, and maintaining orthodoxy amid a growing number of rationalistic Pietists was proving to be impossible. In his love for unity, Cotton kept an ecumenical spirit. In an unprecedented move, he participated in the ordination

---

49. Cited in Lovelace, *American Pietism of Cotton Mather*, 185.
50. Lovelace, *American Pietism of Cotton Mather*, 42.
51. Lovelace, *American Pietism of Cotton Mather*, 51.

of a Baptist minister, Elisha Callender, in 1718. In his address to Callender's congregation, Mather apologized for any "unbrotherly treatment" they may have received from fellow Bostonians, citing that "*Liberty of Conscience* is the Native Right of Mankind."[52] His actions would have been unthinkable to his grandfathers' generation, but Cotton was consistently pushing the envelope through his prayers, his preaching, and his pen.

A Busy Pen

From the moment he could hold a pen, Cotton Mather was writing. Being an avid reader, he amassed a large library and gorged himself on every kind of book he could get his hands on. He notes, "Seldome any *new Book* of Consequence finds the way from beyond-Sea, to these Parts of *America*, but I bestow the Perusal upon it. And, still, as I read, I note Curiosities in my blank Books, which I entitle, *Quotidiana*."[53] Along with his insatiable appetite to read, he threw himself headlong into the regular discipline of writing. In addition to his public works, Cotton also kept his diary from 1681 to 1724, which is now reprinted in two large volumes.

Beyond his personal thoughts and meditations on miscellany, Cotton also amassed hundreds of pages of notes on the Bible. Beginning in 1693, he threw himself into what he regarded to be the most important project of his career—the *Biblia Americana*.[54] Every day for the next thirty years, Cotton studied the Scriptures and made assiduous notations on the text. Once completed, the massive Bible commentary weighed in at 4,500 double-spaced folio pages in six volumes. However, unable to secure a publisher for the work, the manuscript sat untouched in a family chest for years. Not until the twenty-first century has the *Biblia Americana* seen publication.[55]

---

52. Cotton Mather, *Brethren Dwelling Together in Unity*, in Silverman, *Life and Times of Cotton Mather*, 302.

53. Mather, *Diary*, 1:548.

54. Jan Stievermann, "Cotton Mather and 'Biblia Americana,'" in Smolinski and Stievermann, *Cotton Mather and* Biblia Americana, 3.

55. Cotton Mather, *Biblia Americana: America's First Bible Commentary*, 10 vols.,

As for the works published in his lifetime, Cotton Mather wrote an estimated 469 published works in the areas of biblical studies, theology, church history, eschatology, biography, science, and philosophy.[56] Some of his more famous works include *The Call of the Gospel* (1686); *Memorable Providences* (1689); *The Life of John Eliot* (1690); *The Wonders of the Invisible World* (1692); *Eleutheria* (1698), a work about the continuation of the Reformation in America; *A Family Well-Ordered* (1699); *The Everlasting Gospel* (1699), a treatise on the doctrine of justification; *Magnalia Christi Americana* (1702), his magisterial work of early American church history; *The Christian Philosopher* (1721), a science textbook; *Parentator* (1723), Cotton's biographical memoir of his father, Increase; *The Angel of Bethesda* (1724), a complete medical guide; *Ratio Disciplinae Fratrum Nov-Anglorum* (1726), a manual on Congregational church polity; *Manuductio ad Ministerium* (1726), a manual for ministerial candidates; and *Triparadisus* (1727), the largest colonial work on the millennium.

Adventures in Doing Good

Mather's most famous work, however, was undoubtedly his 1710 work *Bonifacius, or Essays to Do Good*. Not only was his book popular abroad—it became an anthem of sorts for philanthropists—it reflects Cotton's own commitment to personal sanctification. So devoted was he to deeds of righteousness, Mather even scheduled regular daily activity to be done for his church, his family, relatives, his country, society in general, and for his "own heart and life."[57] However, Mather does not advocate for a vague sense of moralism or good for its own sake. Lovelace notes, "Mather rarely mentions goodness without qualifying the term theologically and spiritually.

---

ed. Reiner Smolinkski and Jan Stievermann (Grand Rapids: Baker Academic and Tübingen: Mohr Siebeck, 2010–).

56. Joel R. Beeke and Randall J. Pederson, *Meet the Puritans* (Grand Rapids: Reformation Heritage Books, 2006), 422.

57. Mather, *Diary*, 2:24–28, cited in Lovelace, *American Pietism of Cotton Mather*, 164.

Believers are to do good in order that 'the Great GOD and His CHRIST may be more Known and Serv'd in the World.'"[58]

Mather's concern for the poor and underprivileged was palpable. He personally gave money, collected wood for their fires in winter, provided clothes, and raised money for education.[59] He founded schools for poor and orphaned children as well as a school for teaching and catechizing African American children, which he paid for out of his pocket for a number of years.[60] Cotton frequently boxed up collections of books and sent them to poor or young ministers serving on the frontier. At one point, Cotton calculated that he was giving away nearly six hundred books a year for free.[61] He was committed to evangelistic mission to the Indians and other unreached peoples. In 1721 Cotton introduced a smallpox vaccination, which was successful in Africa according to his slave Onesimus and European medical journals. "Cotton's humanitarian zeal," writes Kennedy, "often comes off in print as an obsession."[62]

Committed to deeds of righteousness, he challenged himself in every corner of his life. On Mather's daily discipline of "doing good," Rick Kennedy notes,

> As was normal for him, he focused first on his neighborhood and worked outward. Out and about walking almost every day, always taking care for personal exercise, he took every opportunity to chat with North Enders. In these chats he would admonish the rich, give money to needy widows, and make sure every boat tied up at the wharf had a Bible on board. He carried small trinkets in his pockets to give away to the children playing in the streets—each gift came with friendly encouragement to pursue holiness. Many evenings and afternoons were spent with the private [philanthropic] societies he

---

58. Lovelace, *American Pietism of Cotton Mather*, 167.

59. Middlekauff, *Mathers*, 273.

60. Michael A. G. Haykin, introduction to Cotton Mather, *Christianity to the Life: A Call to Imitate Christ*, ed. Garnetta Sweeney Smith (Peterborough, Ontario: H&E Publishing, 2019), xvii.

61. Kennedy, *First American Evangelical*, 123.

62. Kennedy, *First American Evangelical*, 125.

belonged to and had usually organized himself—at one point he noted that he was a member of twenty such societies.[63]

Despite Cotton's penchant for generosity and service, he was plagued with sorrows, not only as a result of his own sinful human condition but due in part to his experiences of great heartbreak and loss.

Family Trials and Losses

While Cotton experienced all the normal joys of life—marriage, children, friendships, and so on—he also suffered tremendous loss. In 1686 Cotton married Abigail Phillips of Charlestown. Together they had nine children: Abigail, Catherine, Mary, Joseph, Abigail, Mehetabel, Hannah, Increase ("Cressy"), and Samuel, five of whom did not survive early childhood. As a parent, Cotton was "notably mild and amiable,"[64] seeking to train and correct his children lovingly. To his great sadness, Abigail died of breast cancer on December 5, 1702.[65]

Cotton married his second wife, the widow Elizabeth Clark Hubbard, on August 18, 1703. She bore him six children: Elizabeth, Samuel, Nathaniel, Jerusha, and twins Martha and Eleazer. However, the measles epidemic of 1713 brought terrible calamity on the Mather family. While several in his family caught the illness, his wife Elizabeth—his "dear, dear, dear Friend"—died on November 9, ten days after giving birth. A few days later, one of Mather's maidservants died, followed by the infant twins, and then his daughter Jerusha. Having lost so many people inside of one month, Cotton was devastated. At one point he scribbled down the names of his children on the back of one of his books, dividing the list by a line

---

63. Kennedy, *First American Evangelical*, 123.

64. Silverman, *Life and Times of Cotton Mather*, 267.

65. The precise date of Abigail's death is not entirely clear. Some biographers note December 5, while others note December 1. This inconsistency is likely due to the use of Old Style versus New Style.

between those still living and those he had lost to date; at the bottom he wrote, "Of 15, Dead, 9."[66]

In 1715 Cotton married his third wife, Lydia Lee George. Whereas his first two marriages were joyful and loving, his marriage to Lydia was contentious and difficult, as she struggled with severe bouts of depression and insanity. Additionally, Lydia came from a wealthy family, but after their marriage she grew bitter toward Cotton and shunned him and his surviving children. At one point Cotton began selling off possessions, even large numbers of books, to sustain himself financially. And while Cotton and Lydia did have short seasons of happiness, their thirteen-year marriage was marked by tumult.

In honor of his own father, Cotton Mather had a son whom he named Increase, or "Cressy" for short, born in 1699. Both Increase Sr. and Cotton had high hopes for the young man, hoping that he would lead the fourth generation of New England Mathers,[67] but he turned out to be nothing but a disappointment. He was uncouth and ungentlemanly, his Christian faith itself was questionable, and in 1717 he was charged with a paternity suit after fathering a child out of wedlock. Cotton's own sadness and shame over his son was only intensified when, on August 23, 1723, his beloved father died from a stroke at the age of eighty-four. Cotton mourned the loss of his father deeply, having served alongside him for four decades and greatly respected him in all ways paternal, intellectual, and pastoral. His wounds of sadness were opened again the next year when Cressy, his twelfth child to die, drowned at sea. After the death of his daughter Elizabeth in 1726, only two of his children, Hannah and Samuel, would outlive him.

Despite suffering so much loss, Cotton had grown acquainted with grief but labored to subject his heart to the sovereign purposes of God. Writing in his diary in August 1724, Cotton confessed,

> My SAVIOUR yett affords me this Light in my Darkness, that He enables me, to offer up all the Sacrifices He calls me

---

66. Silverman, *Life and Times of Cotton Mather*, 274.
67. Kennedy, *First American Evangelical*, 135.

to! And as for the continual Dropping which I suffer in my Family, I freely submitt and consent unto it, that the Glorious Lord should continue the Sorrows of it upon me all the few remaining Days of my Pilgrimage, and never give me any release until I dy; only lett me obtain this one Thing of Him; a Soul full of a CHRIST! A mind, not only assured of His being my SAVIOUR, but also sensible of His gracious and quickening Influences, and continually irradiated with the precious Thoughts of Him.[68]

Death and Legacy

Throughout 1724 and 1725 Cotton began suffering long bouts of sickness. Sensing his end, his thoughts became transfixed on the Lord. After a long winter sickness, he uttered these words: "Now I have nothing more to do here; my will is entirely swallowed up in the will of the Lord."[69] On February 13, 1728, Cotton Mather died peacefully in his home at the age of sixty-five. On his deathbed, he said, "Is this dying? Is this all? Is this all that I feared, when I prayed against a hard death? O! I can bear this! I can bear it! I can bear it!" His wife, Lydia, wiped his eyes, to which he replied, "I am going where all tears will be wiped from my eyes."[70] Of his passing, his son Samuel writes, "God was graciously pleased to favor him with an easy dismission out of life, and with a sweet composure of mind to the very last; blessings which he had often and earnestly prayed for."[71]

Mather's body lay awaiting burial for nearly a week, according to custom. Mourners lined the streets as all of Boston came out for the funeral. A nearly unprecedented four funeral sermons were preached by Benjamin Colman, Thomas Prince, Joshua Gee, and Samuel Mather. On the significance of the four sermons, William Van Arragon notes that "the use of these biographical parallels

---

68. Mather, *Diary*, 2:754.
69. Marvin, *Life and Times of Cotton Mather*, 570.
70. Marvin, *Life and Times of Cotton Mather*, 570–71.
71. Samuel Mather, *The Life of Dr. Cotton Mather* (1729; repr., Minneapolis: Curiosmith, 2012), 82.

was certainly justified by the saintliness of Mather's life and death, and the terms seem also to be expressive of genuine, widely-held respect and admiration from many friends and admirers."[72] After the funeral, Mather's body was escorted through the streets of Boston to Copp's Hill in a long procession. Hailed as an "American Elijah,"[73] the Boston newspapers revered him as "perhaps the *principal Ornament* of this Countrey, & the *greatest Scholar* that was ever bred in it."[74] Even after his death, the funeral sermons, as well as Samuel Mather's biography, were printed and sold. In addition, a mezzotint print of Cotton Mather's portrait was mass-produced and sold, and scores of people displayed his image in their homes. On both sides of the Atlantic, Mather was well loved, cherished, and hailed as a spiritual father.

However, by the early 1800s Unitarianism was spreading like wildfire through the Congregational churches of New England. What has been called the "Unitarian take-over" advanced by way of undermining both the traditional Calvinist theology of the Puritans and their strongly elder-led brand of Congregationalism.[75] To do this, they went on the attack against the most prominent Puritan hero of New England—in this case, Cotton Mather. According to E. Brooks Holifield, the primary task of religious liberals in New England was "to subvert Mather's reputation as an authority on church government."[76] In undermining church authority, new leadership could be sought, and the course of New England Christianity could be altered.

By the 1850s, it was open season on Mather, and everyone from Nathaniel Hawthorne to Washington Irving joined in dancing on

---

72. William Van Arragon, "The Glorious Translation of an American Elijah: Mourning Cotton Mather in 1728," in Smolinski and Stievermann, *Cotton Mather and Biblia Americana*, 71.

73. Van Arragon, "Glorious Translation of an American Elijah," 63.

74. Van Arragon, "Glorious Translation of an American Elijah," 65.

75. Jan Stievermann, "Cotton Mather and 'Biblia Americana,'" in Smolinski and Stievermann, *Cotton Mather and* Biblia Americana, 15.

76. E. Brooks Holifield, "The Abridging of Cotton Mather," in Smolinski and Stievermann, *Cotton Mather and* Biblia Americana, 84.

the grave of the once-beloved Boston minister. What was their ammunition? Holifield explains,

> The chief weapon in the Unitarian subversion of Mather's authority was the unceasing accusation that he had been the dark figure in the background of the 1692 witchcraft trials. The flogging of Cotton Mather for mismanaging the witchcraft episode had begun during his own lifetime when the Boston merchant Robert Calef published *More Wonders of the Invisible World* (1700) to ridicule him as the man whose recklessness and folly resulted in a fatal debacle. By the late eighteenth century, New England liberals had latched on to the witchcraft episode.... Even after the battle about associations faded away, Mather remained the Unitarian example of orthodoxy's latent dangers and the chief exhibit for the prosecution was Salem.[77]

However, the true legacy of Cotton Mather is one of an adoring husband, a gentle father, a loving pastor, a passionate preacher, a prolific writer, a generous philanthropist, a political figure, a soul-winning evangelist, a helpless sinner, and a sincere Christian.

---

77. Holifield, "Abridging of Cotton Mather," 96–97.

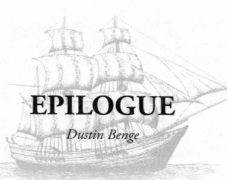

EPILOGUE

Dustin Benge

On July 7, 2019, while visiting with Nate and his dear family in their hometown of Gilmanton, New Hampshire, after morning worship service at Harvest Bible Church, Nate exclaimed that he wanted to show me a local historic site. Not far from the Pickowicz home, the Smith Meeting House, built around 1840, currently stands on the site of the former eighteenth-century meetinghouse that housed local Gilmanton worshipers for decades. Situated on a small knoll, the meetinghouse is a white clapboard framed structure with a gabled roof and granite foundation. Unadorned in simple architecture, reminiscent of many Puritan meetinghouses that dot the New England landscape, the land on which it stood was about to reveal something, or should I say someone, that neither Nate nor I knew anything about.

Adjoining the property of the Smith Meeting House is the Smith Meeting House Cemetery. Naturally, as historians do, we began meandering through the granite stones etched with hundreds of years of Gilmanton history. Not long after entering the cemetery, we noticed an aboveground tomb with a large charcoal slate covering etched with "Isaac Smith, Pastor of the congregational church and Society in Gilmanton who died March 25, 1817, aged 72, and in the 43 year of his ministry." The long epitaph following his name outlined his ministry in Gilmanton, his indefatigable exertions in pastoral ministry, his commitment to the doctrines of grace, and his exemplified zeal for truth and the gospel of Christ. Here was the memorial of a man who had continued the work first envisioned by Thomas Hooker, William Bradford, John Cotton, John Eliot, and untold scores of men and women who departed their native homeland of England to settle in a new country for the purpose of advancing the kingdom of Christ. Isaac Smith was a third-generation pastor who had been a product of the influence of Jonathan Edwards, who had been impacted by the first Puritan settlers in America. Standing side by side in this historic cemetery were two preachers who are products of the zeal, passion, and gospel commitment of these same seventeenth-century men and women. Nate and I stood in silence, with an occasional tear, as we surveyed the goodness and providence of God, who has promised to build His church.

The Spirit of Puritanism
By the eighteenth century, the golden era of Puritanism had essentially concluded. There are varying opinions as to when this era ended. Some historians point to the Act of Uniformity in 1662, which stated that all ministers and churches must adhere to a prescribed form of public prayers, administration of sacraments, and other rites of the established Church of England. One immediate result of this act of Parliament was more than two thousand clergymen refused to take the oath and were therefore ejected from the church in a period known as the Great Ejection of 1662. Other historians, who allow the continuance of Puritanism after 1660, highlight the 1689 Act of Toleration as the official conclusion of the movement. This legislation, passed on May 24, 1689, was an act granting freedom of worship to nonconformists (i.e., dissenting Protestants such as Baptists and Congregationalists).

Although Puritanism ended as an official movement around the dawning of the eighteenth century, the "spirit of Puritanism" did not. Two generations after those first Pilgrims emerged, men like Jonathan Edwards (1703–1758), David Brainerd (1718–1747), and George Whitefield (1714–1770) took up the Puritan torch.[1]

---

1. Some Puritan scholars consider Edwards to be the last Puritan, as one born out of due time.

Although not officially considered Puritans, these men, and count-less others, continued church reform, preaching and teaching the Scriptures, evangelizing the lost, and desiring to live holy lives.

Jonathan Edwards has perhaps one of the more interesting ancestries in colonial New England. His maternal grandfather was Solomon Stoddard (1643–1729). His forebears included Winthrops and Mathers and, on his mother's side, Thomas Hooker.[2] Born in 1703 to the Reverend Timothy Edwards and Esther (Stoddard), Edwards grew up in East Windsor, Connecticut. After a brief pas-torate in New York and receiving his degree at Yale College, Edwards succeeded his grandfather as pastor of the church in Northampton in 1729. Edwards stood at the helm of the Great Awakening of 1740–1742 and published multiple treatises, including *The Distin-guishing Marks of a Work of the Spirit of God* (1741), *Some Thoughts concerning the Present Revival of Religion in New England* (1742), *A Treatise concerning Religious Affections* (1746), and *Freedom of the Will* (1754). Due to his opposition to the Half-Way Covenant[3] instituted by his grandfather, Edwards was dismissed from his Northampton church and preached his farewell sermon on July 1, 1750. In 1751 Edwards became pastor of the frontier church at Stockbridge, Mas-sachusetts, and missionary to the Indians in the surrounding areas. Edwards accepted the presidency of the College of New Jersey (later Princeton University) in late 1757. After an inoculation for smallpox, Edwards died in 1758, leaving behind voluminous works, treatises, and disciples. Edwards assumes the position of what we often refer to when defining the American Puritans. However, Edwards, who lived outside of official Puritanism, is the product of the writings,

---

2. Francis J. Bremer, *The Puritan Experiment: New England Society from Bradford to Edwards*, rev. ed. (Hanover, N.H.: University Press of New England, 1995), 228.

3. In the Half-Way Covenant, baptized but unconverted children of believers might have their own children baptized by "owning the covenant." Stoddard had instituted the subsequently widespread practice of admitting to the Eucharist all who were thus "in the covenant," even if they knew themselves to be unconverted. Edwards gradually came to believe that the profession required for admission to full communion should be under-stood to imply genuine faith, not merely doctrinal knowledge and good moral behavior.

pastorates, missionary endeavors, poetry, and influence you have read about in this work.

Onward!

The resurgence of interest in the English and American Puritans attests to the fact that the "spirit of Puritanism" is alive and well almost four hundred years since the first Puritans set foot in the New World. According to Peter Lewis in his book *The Genius of Puritanism*, Puritanism grew out of three needs: (1) the need for biblical preaching and the teaching of sound Reformed doctrine; (2) the need for biblical, personal piety that stressed the work of the Holy Spirit in the faith and life of the believer; and (3) the need to restore biblical simplicity in liturgy and church government so that a well-ordered church life would promote the worship of the triune God as prescribed in His Word.[4] If Puritanism was birthed from these three needs, then it could be argued that maintaining those needs continues the spirit of Puritanism, even to the present day. In our current climate of pragmatism and cultural relevancy, the church must once again take up the torch of Scripture-based preaching, gospel-centered evangelism, Christ-embracing church service, and God-glorifying lives. We may be called on to stand against the swelling tide of political correctness, as the Puritans against the English Crown, for the sake of the gospel. Etch in your memories these stories, for their story is our story.

As Nate and I stood in the Smith Meeting House Cemetery considering our spiritual forebears, it became evident that our priority in writing this book was to awaken a new generation not only to the lives of the men and women who blazed the trail of faith before us but principally to the God and Christ they so passionately pointed. It is our sincere hope that this work will introduce you to names and stories you have never heard—stories that will be passed down to our posterity so that they may never forget the cost of being able to worship God freely, according to the Scriptures, from sea to shining sea.

---

4. Peter Lewis, *The Genius of Puritanism* (Grand Rapids: Soli Deo Gloria, 2012), 11.